ON THE MIDDLE EAST

Part 2: An Introduction To The Middle East

Maitland Hyslop

Reiver Marketing Limited

ISBN-13: 9798536848098

*This book is dedicated to all those who made my
stay in the Middle East 2014 - 2019 so enjoyable,
interesting and challenging.*

CONTENTS

Preface

I lived and worked in the Middle East for much of the period 2015 – 2020 CE. To begin with I chaired a number of organisations In Saudi and UAE, worked as the CEO of a worldwide oilfield service company based in Dubai; later as the CEO of my own consultancy company based in Dubai, Bahrain, and Kuwait; as the COO of the African Eye Project for a period; and as a contracted trainer to Bahrain Oasis Training WLL in which role I trained many very senior and middle management corporate personnel across the GCC.

Consequently, I have worked and met everyone from rulers and royalty to the taxi drivers and street cleaners. I have worked with or for some of the biggest companies in the Middle East, both state and private. I have worked with or for universities. I have travelled extensively for both work and pleasure.

I have a master's degree in Middle Eastern and African Studies from the University of Durham in the UK; and my MA thesis concerned freshwater conflict in the Middle East. In 2016 – 2018 I was the Bahraini representative for the then Middle East Association.

This book follows up 'On The Middle East Part 1: An Expatriate Journal 2014 – 2019'[1], published, as this is, by Reiver through Amazon. Part 1 was a summary of my subjective, interesting, and amusing, personal experiences in the Middle East, and elsewhere, over a five-year period. This book is a more formal, objective, approach and addresses the key issues in the Middle East as of 2021. However, I have kept it reasonably short. It should be viewed as an introduction to the region.

It is not a hagiography, but it is the case that some of the more outlandish criticisms of the Middle East by liberal western observers, I count myself as a liberal western observer, are challenged. Many Middle East leaders can be crass, just as western leaders can be. Many, however, display, sometimes at the same time as crassness, an ability to understand the personal difficulties of those within their care to a degree unparalleled in the west, and act accordingly. Their history is fascinating.

This book is not for academics, although many may find it interesting; nor is it a *vox pop.* It is a compendium/anthology of interesting pointers to the Middle East that all students, visitors, businessmen, politicians etc. may find helps them along the way.

The book is in two sections: Section 1 deals with what one might call the more traditional, objective, overview of the Middle East. Section 2 is a more subjective interpretation: what each country looks like in a variety of contexts, anecdotes regarding each country and a personal view on the Middle East. This book has no maps or figures because this suits the Amazon printing process better.

The endnotes are acknowledgements to those others who have assisted this book, references, and bibliographies.

I thank all those who gave me permission to use their resource for Section 1.

Section 1

The Middle East: Physical and Human Geography

CHAPTER 1:
INTRODUCTION

What is the Middle East? In this book the definition of the Middle East is as stated by W.B. Fisher in *The Middle East* [2].The Middle East therefore consists of: Libya, Egypt, Sudan (now less South Sudan), Yemen, Saudi Arabia, Oman, UAE, Qatar, Bahrain, Kuwait, Iran, Iraq, Jordan, Syria, Lebanon, Israel, Palestine, Cyprus, Turkey. It is remarkable, given everything that has occurred in the Middle East since 1971 CE (and the original definition by Fisher in 1951 CE) that the countries are still there. Boundaries in Europe have changed as much, if not more, in the period. It is true that some states are more secure than others today in both regions.

Few regions of the world provoke more interest, controversy, or international crises than the Middle East. However, outside of Europe, and some parts of Asia, the region has only come to the fore, internationally, in more recent times, especially after World War Two. This is because the region has become a great world source of oil, gas, and mineral wealth; regained a role as an international crossroads in a modern world (at least pre-COVID); is identified as the source of global, regional and national Islamic development and terrorist inspired strife; and contains a huge, unfulfilled, young adult, population – ten times what it was in 1960.

Humans are not born with an awareness of cultural difference; exposure to difference is necessary to gain that awareness.

Often the exposure to places outside of immediate experience is filtered by historical representations that focus on what early explorers, usually western, thought was significant, or which governments used as propaganda, or which marketers used to entice the public, etc. Clarifying the following misconceptions will hopefully dispel these notions and provide a better basis on which to build knowledge.

The most pervasive misconception that can obscure objective thinking about the Middle East is the idea that throughout history certain civilizations 'progressed', and others lagged or regressed. This 'evolutionary' historical construct[3] frames history in terms of progress from primitive to advanced. It forms the basis of the perception that many communities were only significant in the past, and tends to represent such communities as primitive, or as though they are still living in the past. The Middle East is often framed in terms of a glorious past, often relegated to the study of ancient history. Intentionally, or unintentionally, many of the sources of information one encounters tend to negate the present reality because of this.

In addition to the way this region is often portrayed as trapped in antiquity, repeated images of violence, exotic others and stereotypes have deeply infiltrated the way it is seen. The Western knowledge base contains biases which hark back to historical power struggles between the Egyptians and Hittites, the Greeks and the Persians, the Eastern Romans (Byzantines) and the Persians, and later the Austro-Hungarians and the Ottomans after Constantinople fell in 1453 CE. These give us a historical sense of the 'East vs. West' divide.

This divide was intensified and accelerated during the era of European global colonization. Despite this perceived 'us vs. them' difference, however, people in the West share many of the same cultural roots as the Middle East. These communities overlapped a great deal. Greek culture, which is considered a cultural foundation for Europe, was spread by Alexander the Great as far as what is now Afghanistan and Pakistan, for example. Furthermore, Persian civilizations and Turkic communities had a deep and lasting impact on the literatures, philosophies, and sciences of Western civilizations.

Civilizations worldwide have adopted, and continue to adopt, many scientific developments from the region. From the pre-industrial era, all the way back to antiquity, in the times of the Sumerians, Greeks, Persians, Romans and Ancient Egyptians. Some examples from the past include innovations in writing, astronomy, optics, hydraulics, textiles, decorative arts, crop rotation, urban planning, irrigation, geometry, mathematics, organized libraries and universities, means of financial exchange, theological and philosophical achievements. Other developments from the region have had a significant impact on Europe and the world. Today, Middle Eastern countries are contributing to scientific breakthroughs, such as the growing of liver cells, participating in the research at CERN, soil desalinization, sending a spacecraft to Mars and many others.

Out of the 49 Muslim-majority countries today, only four were never fully colonized: Iran, Afghanistan, Turkey, and Saudi Arabia. That said European power struggles and European institutions have encroached into all economies[4].

The geography, history and religion of the Middle East is defined by:

- Geography.

- Climate.

- Water.

- The Monotheistic Religions: Islam, Judaism, Christianity, and latterly Hindu.

- Language.

- Tribe.

7

- Persian Empire.
- Greek Empire
- Roman Empire.
- The Caliphates.
- Mongols and Tatars.
- The Ottoman Empire.
- The British Empire.
- The Sykes - Picot Agreement.
- The American Hegemony.
- The Six-Day War of 1967.
- Palestine.
- The War on Terror.
- The Arab Spring.
- ISIS.
- The Abraham Accords.
- The Chinese Expansion.
- Sovereign Wealth Funds.

These critical areas of understanding are explored in the next few chapters, before moving on to look at each country individually, to deliver an anecdotal view, and finally to look to the future.

CHAPTER 2: GEOGRAPHY

Geography

The Middle East is a large and diverse geographical area located in southwest Asia and northeast Africa. It extends over 3 000 km from the Black Sea in the north to the Arabian Sea in the south, and about 3 000 km from Libya in the west to the mountains of Iran.

One term sometimes applied to part of this area is '*The Fertile Crescent*', which was coined by James Henry Breasted in 1914 CE[5] to refer to the arc of fertile agricultural zones that formed the basis for early civilizations, in what is now Iraq, Syria, Lebanon, and Israel. Scholars studying the ancient past tend to use the term 'Near East' for this area.

Mountains and deserts divide the Middle East into seven zones[6] that are both geographically distinct and have influenced the development and maintenance of cultural traditions through much of the history of the region.

The first of these zones is the arid area to the west of the Nile south of the Mediterranean and north of the Sahara. This area was once a fertile producer of wheat for the civilisations both pre- and post-Romans. Climate change is not a new phenomenon.

In the second of these zones, the Nile River flows northward through the Sahara Desert from Khartoum in Sudan (where its

two major tributaries join), through Egypt, and to the Mediterranean Sea. As a source of water, food, and fertile soil deposited
in annual floods as well as a transportation route, it was the
ecological basis for ancient Nubian and Egyptian civilization.
In the southern part of this region, the broad alluvial plain is
broken by six 'cataracts'; areas in which the narrow river valley,
strong current, islands, and rapids make navigation difficult.
The rich mineral resources of the deserts around the Nile, particularly gold, have historically been important to economic
development in this area.

East of the Nile Valley, across the Eastern Desert and the Sinai
Peninsula, is the eastern Mediterranean coastal plain, which
has historically related to the mountains and river valleys
that run parallel to it. Comprising the modern countries of
Israel, Lebanon, and western Syria, as well as parts of Jordan
and Turkey, this region is sometimes called the Levant (after
the French term for *'rising'*, here referring to the rising sun).
Located in the Mediterranean climatic zone with rich agricultural land and relatively abundant rainfall, and having easy
access to land and sea routes, the Levant has always been a cultural crossroads and has frequently been conquered. Among
the first areas to develop agriculture (as far back as 11 000
BCE), ancient cultures that developed in this region include Ca-
naanite, Amorite, Israelite, and Phoenician.

The Levant is bordered on the north by the Taurus Mountains
reaching up to 4 000 m in elevation, which separate the Levant
from the Anatolian plateau in modern Turkey. The Anatolian
plateau is a relatively isolated but fertile agricultural zone, and
the Taurus Mountains are rich in metals and minerals; they
were known as the *'silver mountain'* in some ancient texts, but
copper was even more abundantly available. The western coast
of Turkey had closer contact with cultures of Greece and the
Aegean Sea than with the rest of the Middle East through much
of its early history. Ancient cultures in Anatolia included the
Hittite empire and a Hurrian-speaking population.

Southeast of the Levant is the Arabian Peninsula with its extensive deserts, oases, and coastal regions along the Red Sea, Arabian Sea, and Persian Gulf that were more often suited to permanent settlement. Today, this area includes the countries of Bahrain, Kuwait, Oman, Qatar, Saudi Arabia, the United Arab Emirates, and Yemen. Distinctive ancient cultures of this area include the South Arabian kingdoms in what is now Yemen that traded incense to the Levant and communities in Oman that were rich in copper and hard stone. Arab culture first appears in the historical record after the introduction of the camel in about 1200 BCE, which allowed more extensive use of arid zones of Saudi Arabia.

East of the Levant and south of the Taurus Mountains is the area defined by the Euphrates and Tigris Rivers that has sometimes been called Mesopotamia (the "land between the rivers"), now encompassing eastern Syria, Iraq, and a small area of southwestern Iran. In many ways, what we call Mesopotamian civilization is a series of diverse languages and cultures bound together by a common script and written tradition. Ancient languages in the area included Sumerian, Akkadian, Amorite, Babylonian, Assyrian, and Aramaic.

Mesopotamia is a particularly fertile agricultural zone with vast areas available for cultivation. Northern Mesopotamia receives enough rainfall to grow grain crops, while southern Mesopotamia receives virtually no rain, so agriculture there depended on extensive networks of irrigation canals. At the southern end of the Tigris-Euphrates course, a series of marshes has maintained a distinctive environment and culture for millennia (now threatened). Apart from water and fertile soil (and later oil), Mesopotamia contains few natural resources, and has depended on trade with people in the mountainous regions to the north and east for stone, copper, and timber.

Mesopotamia is bordered on the east by the Zagros Mountains

of western Iran and eastern Turkey (elevation up to nearly 5 000 m) whose highland valleys were home to Elamite and Persian civilizations as well as later powerful nomadic confederations including the Bakhtiari. The Zagros have been a rich source of stone and timber.

As this outline suggests, geography plays a significant role in the formation and maintenance of cultures. The earliest civilizations with large population centres developed near abundant sources of water and agricultural land, rather than in areas of other valuable raw materials, like metals, semi-precious stones, building stone, or timber. Geography also provides a basis for distinctive attributes of regional cultures, like the importance of olive oil and wine in the cuisine of the eastern Mediterranean region (where grapes and olives can easily be cultivated), or the extensive use of incense in daily life, ritual practice, and in economic exchange in the cultures of south Arabia.[7]

Climate.

The climate of the Middle East ranges from the warm summers and cold winters of highland Turkey and Iran, through hotter summers and cool winters of northern Mesopotamia and the Mediterranean coast, to the extreme temperatures of the Arabian desert. Much, but not all, of the region is arid.

It is difficult to be precise over the current climate because it has become very variable over the last few years. Temperatures have tended to be much higher in the summer than traditionally the case, and lower in the winter. Flooding has been a feature of the last few years across the Gulf, North Africa, and much of the north of the region. This, too, is a difference to traditional climate.

There is much climate related damage ranging from the destruction of traditional and new buildings by rain to the wadi floods that have swept all before them, including the buildings built within them in the dry times.

Sandstorms remain a common occurrence, and their strength has increased. A bit like thunderstorms elsewhere they leave clear, fresh, air in their wake.

Unlike in previous times it is not possible to be specific about climate now in the Middle East. It varies. Traditional views can be found in older texts.[8]

Soils, Vegetation and Agriculture

Soils and vegetation have, historically, followed the seven regions noted above. These days, like climate, things vary more than they did. Broadly speaking they divide as follows:

Desert Soils

Desert soils are mostly lithosols. These are a group of shallow soils lacking defined horizons, especially an entisol (recent fertile soil, natural or artificial) consisting of partially weathered rock fragments, usually on slopes. Salt deposits can be common. Sand is a common occurrence is some areas.

Arid Steppe Soils

Arid steppe soils can be immature, basically sandy in texture, or loams, In less arid areas sierozems are more likely, these are any of a group of calcareous, brownish grey soils based in a carbonate or hardpan layer, found in arid climates.

Semi – Arid to Humid Areas

As aridity becomes less pronounced different soils are evident. Brown and yellow-brown soils from various parent rocks. The soils may range from silty clays to clay loams with frequent stoniness. Terra Rossa soils are evident by their bright colour and heavier texture. Terra Rossa soils can store much water. In other areas significant crusts can be evident, usually a few centimetres below the surface and sometimes very thick (up to 4 m in some parts of the Lebanon). These crusts restrict growth of trees. Often cultivated with cereals and fruit trees; the latter usually doing well through a breached crust. Infill and bench soils are evident in areas of accumulation and downwash. These are often key to human settlement. Alluvial soils are soils in which temporary waterlogging occurs due to seasonal flooding, such as in the Nile Valley. (Although this is under threat from upstream dams in many areas. In the Upper Nile of Sudan, the alluvial soils were deposited at earlier times, prehistoric).

There is a widespread lack of humus due to high temperatures and a lack of leaf litter because of the predominance of evergreen trees.

Irrigation

Many crops are aided by irrigation. However, care must be taken as ground temperatures can rise to 75 °C in the summer relatively easily and this encourages salinity. Salinity is also an issue in the major rivers as they near the sea, with increased saline loads the closer they get to the sea. This is destructive of irrigated lands and there is an annual shrinkage of arable land because of this.

Natural Vegetation

Climate is the main driver of vegetation types. Temperature and aridity mean that dry seasons see many plants defoliate or die back; other plants develop extensive or deep root systems to counter the lack of water. Variations on these two key themes are also noticeable. In the mountains or the river valleys rainfall can be more plentiful, as such lusher vegetation types can be seen until the tree lines are reached in the mountains.

Mediterranean Vegetation

The coastal plains of Cyprus, Israel, Lebanon, Syria and Turkey together with the lower flanks of the mountain ranges immediately inland define the narrow areas of Mediterranean vegetation with the Jebel Akhdar of Cyrenaica, parts of the Jefara and Jebel of Tripolitania. These areas are characterised by vines, wheat, olive and fruit trees with many shrubs and herbs. Garrigue and phrygana are also common.

Steppe Vegetation

On the lower slopes of flanking mountains carob, juniper, terebinth, thorn, plum, sage, thyme etc. can be found.

On the true steppe trees are absent and various species of grass appear; many of which have adapted to the semi-arid conditions. More than half of the plants of the steppe disappears in the summer. Small changes in rainfall can have disproportionate effects on the sustainability of nomadic livestock. The Indo – Aryan invasion of Europe and the Middle East during the second millennium BCE; the Jewish occupation of Palestine and the rise of Islam in the 7th century CE can all be traced to slight changes in environmental conditions in Eurasia.

Desert Vegetation

Desert vegetation is limited. Camel thorn and certain tamarisks exude a sweetish sap which when hardened by atmospheric contact becomes the 'manna' of biblical fame. Otherwise much of the desert is usually barren except for short-lived bursts of flowers and vegetation after rains.

Mountain Vegetation

Mountain vegetation consists of three forest growths and alpine pasture or heath. The forest growths are characterised by, firstly, evergreen, coniferous and deciduous trees at lower levels then, the cedars, maple, juniper, oak and pine at higher levels; the second type of forest are oaks, hazel, alder, maple, hornbeam, hawthorn, plum, and wild pear typical of the Elburz and containing no conifers; thirdly in the southern Caucasus are beech, oak, hazel, walnut, maple and hornbeam.

Savannah

In the Sudan broadly south of 15 $^\circ$ North are the savannah lands. Grass and acacia are typical with some deciduous trees.

Riverine Vegetation

The extensive alluvial lowlands of the great rivers have a special type of vegetation. Aquatic grasses, papyrus, lotus and reeds that sometimes attain a height of 8 m. The most common tree is the date palm, tolerant of high volumes of water. Cultivated palms and liquorice were staples.

Changes In Vegetation

The climate change of the Quaternary period where ice ages have come and gone interspersed with warmer periods, such as current one, has had an impact on vegetation[9]. Snowlines have descended but they seem to have had little overall effect on vegetation types.

Agriculture

The principal food crop grown throughout the region is wheat. Wheat was probably first cultivated in the Middle East and certainly during Roman Times both wheat and barley were crops grown around the littoral of the Mediterranean. Turkey is the major wheat producer, although it is a mainstay in all countries. Barley is the second most important food crop, known in the region since Neolithic times. The pattern of barley distribution, like that of wheat, is concentrated in the north, with crops becoming increasingly sparse towards the Empty Quarter of the Arabian Peninsula, before the lush areas of the south Arabian, Yemeni and Omani coasts. Most other grains like corn and rye and the drought resistant crops such as the millets and sorghums are also grown. Rice is a favoured crop, especially in the desert, and is grown with the aid of irrigation especially in Egypt, Iran and the marshlands, such as they now are, of Iraq.

The region does not produce enough food to sustain itself, despite this widespread grain distribution. It is a net importer of grain, although some rice and barley are exported. Turkey, Iraq, and Syria used to have wheat surpluses, but these are rare these days. Most countries now must import grain.

Tree crops are olives, citrus fruits, and dates. Turkey leads in olive production. The coastal regions of Syria, Lebanon, and Israel also produce olives. Iran is a minor producer. The citrus probably originated in the area and was introduced to Europe by the Crusaders in the 11th century CE. Oranges, raised in the Levant, southern Turkey, and northern Iran, are the leading citrus crop. They are also one of Israel's leading exports, having supplied more than half of its foreign exchange earnings during the country's first decade or so.

Dates, historically the chief diet of the Bedouin and other nomads are the one important crop in which the Middle East leads. Until recently Iraq grew three quarters of the world's supply of dates. Dates still have many uses. They are a food staple, it produces an alcoholic liquid, arak. The pits are ground for animal fodder, fibres produced rope, and the trunk fuel. Date palms used to occupy up to 90% of most Arabian Peninsula oases, but today many have fallen into disrepair. Bahrain had over a million date palms until many were cut down to make way for development.

Many varieties of fruits and nuts are grown. Almonds, walnuts, and pistachios are common. Turkey leads the world in hazelnut production. Lebanon produces apples, apricots and melons in Iran, and Turkish figs are world famous. As in all Mediterranean lands' grapes are produced, but rarely for alcohol, usually for raisins.

The leading industrial crop is cotton. Until some diversification and the arrival of oil and gas from the Mediterranean, long fibre cotton was Egypt's largest export. Turkey follows Egypt in the production of cotton, but its total crop is less. Syria, Iraq, Israel, and Iran have experimented with cotton, but they have not really competed with Egypt. Flax, hemp and silk are grown in the fertile crescent but not in large enough quantities to become major exports. All countries have experimented with different types of technical agricultural techniques with

17

possibly Saudi Arabia leading in large scale production (now under revision because of the cost), and Israel in smaller scale but high-quality production.

Coffee is produced in Yemen; at one time exported from the port of Mocha. Tea is grown in small quantities along Turkey's Black Sea coast and the Caspian shore of Iran. Turkey also produces beet, sugar cane, and tobacco. Tobacco, poppies, qat, and marijuana is grown at different scales throughout the region.

Camels were once the dominant livestock and used for transport, turning water wheels, ploughing, meat, milk, fibre, fuel, urine, and as a measure of personal and bridal wealth. These days many are used for the sport of camel racing, where much money can be made. Some nomadic people keep to the traditional ways, often subsidised by the state. Traditionally cows were s; mall, but cattle farms and ranches have been created by Saudi Arabia and the UAE in particular to produce milk and beef. Goat and lamb are both produced for meat and milk; goats have destroyed great swathes of pasture across the region (they eat the roots too). Much lamb is imported from New Zealand, live. Pigs are not usually seen, as eating pork is prohibited across the region. (Historically pigs carried many parasites that could transfer to man, including tape worm; so a good scientific basis exists for the ban in such a climate, although it is now tied to Islam and Judaism religion).

Horses, once common, are now luxury items as they are, for example, in Europe and North America.

The region's mountainous areas have been a great source of timber.

The lower reaches of mountains and the less fertile valley areas are a great source of nuts, herbs and berries. The semi-arid lands are more productive than often acknowledged.

Over the last twenty-five years production has declined in general because of the significant damage done by warfare. ISIL used a scorched earth policy that had a significant impact on agricultural production across the region. [10][11]

Water

A survey of the popular and specialist press over the last half century would indicate that the most valuable, and vital, commodity in the Middle East is oil. A similar look at the catalysts of regional warfare would indicate the pre-eminence of the Arab- Israeli conflict. These views are substantially incorrect. It is water, and the control of water resources that are the key commodity and the key driver of conflict.

The controversy over the Israeli control occupied southern Lebanon water resources, and the Saudi belief that drilling for water is as important as drilling for oil, give a foretaste of the status of water may achieve in the political balance of the Middle East.

The Middle East is largely arid. It has only four rivers of major international significance: the Nile, the Euphrates, the Tigris, and the Jordan – and the last of these is a very dubious contender. Over 50% of the area is desert, much of the remainder of marginal agricultural potential and most of the population and food supply is concentrated in oases, valleys or on the coast. Aridity is alleviated in part by groundwater resources; but these are increasingly 'dry' or 'saline', not equally distributed between states and do not respect international boundaries.

Historically, the population of the region was divided, crudely, between the nomadic tribes of the deserts and the sedentarists of the fertile valleys. For the most part these two groups lived in relative, symbiotic, harmony. The emergence of new states, and a growing population cut across this relationship. The process was reinforced by the increased nationalism of the new states. Water resources became either over-abundant or restricted by the new boundaries. Disproportionate population growth and industrial/technical/agricultural development exacerbated the differences in water resources and requirements between states.

In general water requirements per capita in the region reach a critical level at between 1 000 and 1 500 litres per day for all purposes (in the UK the population uses an average of 4 500 litres per day for all purposes, including the water used by imports) and around 100 litres per day for personal requirements (Abu Dhabi 250 litres per day, the UK 145 litres per day; 2015 approx.). A survey of the major countries in the region showed that critical levels had been reached by 1986 in Israel, Syria, Libya, Egypt, and the Saudi Peninsula; by 2000 in Iraq and Turkey. Desalination has provided some respite, but it is expensive, and the increased salinity of seawater caused by the effluent from water treatment plants has had a deleterious effect on fishing, tourism, sea life fauna and flora, and sea temperature.

Water is the life giver. Despite a myriad of technological developments, it is unlikely that these, or improvements in distribution, can stave off the deterioration of an already critical position. A shortage of water stems the flow of oil and foreign exchange; it is essential to both the extraction and treatment of the mineral. Water can thus be said to be the most valuable commodity in the Middle East.

Several historical, current, and possible confrontations over water emphasise the politico-military implications. Water related confrontations have been part of the Arab – Israeli conflict, particularly about the Litani; Egypt has disagreements with its neighbours over the use of the Nile; the Buraimi Oasis has been a source of conflict between Saudi Arabia and the UAE; Iraq has disputes with neighbours over the Tigris and Euphrates. These are just the major headlines. That further confrontations can be expected is highlighted by recent disagreements between Egypt and Sudan; between Turkey and Iraq; Turkey and Greece; Israel and Lebanon.

It would be inadequate to suggest that the stability of the Middle East rests solely on the provision of an adequate supply of water for all countries in the region. Statistics showing critical levels are open to varying interpretations; and political statements relating to water may be surrogates for more subtle signals. Nevertheless, water is in short supply.

Today the competition is not between desert nomads and valley dwellers but between urban and rural and between nation and nation. The legacy of colonialism in the shaping of international boundaries has not been helpful. Several of the most powerful countries of the Middle East, all of whom have large and growing populations, do not have sufficient renewable resources within their boundaries to provide enough water for their own populations today, let alone in the future.

Would Egypt invade Sudan, or Ethiopia? In the general run of international relations this would be unthinkable; as would, until relatively recently, Israeli retention of the Litani. History is littered with invasions provoked by lesser issues. The simplicity of the need must not be obscured by the overtones of either current international diplomatic discussions or language. Yet the subtlety of relations over water must not be underestimated either. The complex political, diplomatic, economic, religious, and social ties of the Middle Eastern states make discussions about such a basic human need difficult.[12]

CHAPTER 3: TRIBE AND LANGUAGE

Tribe

The term tribe refers to a group of persons forming a community and claiming descent from a common ancestor. In the Middle East and North Africa, unlike many other parts of the world, claiming tribal affiliation often positively affirms community, identity, and belonging. In the mid-to late 20th century CE, nationalist leaders in some regions rejected claims to tribal identity as 'primitive' or potentially divisive to national unity.

In the early 21st century CE in Morocco, Yemen and Jordan, tribal affiliations figure implicitly in electoral politics in many regions, although other aspects of personal and collective identity also come into play. In the Iraq ruled by Saddam Hussein (1979–2003 CE), the mention in public of one's tribal identity, outlawed in the 1980s CE to forge national identity, crept back into common usage and regime practice by the mid-1990s CE.

Tribal identities remain important in many regions of the Middle East. They provide the basis for many forms of communal and political solidarity, although never exclusive ones, in many parts of the Arabian Peninsula, Iraq, Jordan, Syria, among Arabs in Israel, and in the Palestinian areas.

Tribes At The Time Of The Prophet Muhammad (pbuh)

Tribal identities in the Middle East are best seen in the context of the wider social and economic networks in which they played a part, from ancient empires to the present. Tribal, kinship, and genealogical identities also profoundly influenced religious and political formations in earlier periods of the Middle East. For example, studies of ancient Judaism now also take tribal relations more into account than did earlier accounts that relied primarily on textual exegesis. In all these cases, however, alternative forms of social and political identity were never entirely absent.

For example, in the Arabian peninsula at the time of the advent of Islam in 622 CE social position in both oasis towns and their hinterlands depended foremost on overlapping ties of family, kinship, and tribe. In this context, Islam offered a new form of belonging, the 'firmest tie' in the language of the Holy Quran (2: 256), binding believers to God and giving them a sense of individual responsibility. The Holy Quran morally sanctions ties to family, kin, and tribe but the community of Muslims (in Arabic this is called *umma*), united in submission to the one God, takes precedence.

The sense of belonging, as individuals, to the community of Muslims as the principal social and religious identity broke with the primary loyalties of the pre-Islamic era, but in practice tribal structure and claimed descent remained essential to understanding political, social, and economic action from later historical periods to the present.

Thus, there are many early references to the Prophet Muhammad (pbuh) as an arbitrator among feuding tribes, a role traditionally played by members of his descent group, the Quraysh, prior to the advent of Islam. Many tribal groups decided that their adherence to the community of Muslims ceased with Prophet Muhammad's (pbuh) death in 632 CE, leaving them open to forge new alliances.

Tribal Identity and Political Metaphor

Tribal genealogies and identities often employ metaphors such as the parts of the human body and the branches of a tree to symbolize stability, obligation, and belonging, but tribal and lineage identities in the Middle East are social constructs that change and are manipulated with shifting political and economic circumstances. Ibn Khaldun (1332–1406 CE), the medieval North African historian and advisor to kings, recognized the flexible shape of tribal identities.

For Ibn Khaldun, *'group feeling'* (In Arabic: *'asabiyya'*) exists when groups act cohesively, as if compelling ties of obligation hold them together to achieve common interests over extended periods of time. Thus, belonging to a tribe does not depend on kinship or descent alone. In certain circumstances, individuals can change tribal, lineage, and clan affiliations.

Dynasties and political domination were hard to sustain without such cohesiveness, especially present in tribal contexts. Group feeling is expressed in terms of presumed 'blood' relationships, but in tribal contexts these are strong and compelling social metaphors for bonds of solidarity that take precedence over all other bonds of association. In Jordan, Iraq, Egypt, and elsewhere, tribal codes of responsibility and justice based on such cohesion often parallel the civil and criminal codes of state justice, and those of Islamic law, the Sharia.

The Multiple Meanings of Tribe

The fact that one word, tribe, describes a range of ideas about society and social forms throughout the Middle East, as elsewhere in the world, does not make these meanings intrinsically related. For example, take the notion of tribe, still prevalent in many archaeological discussions, as an organizational level between 'band' and 'state'. This formulation implies that tribes are on an evolutionary ladder and independent of states. Yet in earlier historical periods and in the present, tribes and states coexist and overlap. The problem of properly understanding tribal identities is compounded by the views of some

Middle Eastern urban intellectuals who have adopted 19th century CE evolutionary views and assume that tribes exist only at the fringes of states or are residues of pre-state formations.

Both now and in the past, however, ideas of tribe share 'family resemblances', possessing partial and overlapping similarities and a shared cultural logic. Far from being a relic of the past, 'tribe' in the Arabian Peninsula and the modern Middle East can even sustain modern national identity. That said in Saudi Arabia, for example, there is an effort being made to subvert tribe to nationalism. This is a common theme in conversation.

Tribal identity, like other bases of social cohesion, including kinship, citizenship, and nationalism, is something that people (and sometimes ethnographers and state officials) create, and it changes with historical and political context. The first form that the notion of tribe can take is the elaboration and use of explicit ethnopolitical ideologies by people themselves to explain their social and political organization.

These locally held ideologies of tribal belonging in the Middle East are generally based on a concept of political identity formed through common father to son descent. A major exception is the Tuareg of the Sahara, where tribal identity is based on mother to son descent.

People in such tribes sometimes hold that how groups align themselves in time of dispute is explained by tribal and lineage identities alone, but other grounds for political action coexist and overlap. In precolonial Morocco as elsewhere, coalitions did not necessarily occur along the lines of tribe or lineage.

This is demonstrated by the patterns of resistance in which people from various sections and tribes aligned themselves against the French in the early 20th century CE. Pre-colonial accounts of disputes in western Morocco also suggest that alliances followed more flexible lines than those predicted by formal classification.

In general, tribal names and chains of patrilineal genealogies provide a range of potential identities rather than a basis for sustained collective action in itself. Often there is strong resistance to efforts to write down genealogies or claims to tribal descent because writing, by fixing the relationships among groups, distorts the ongoing process by which groups rework alliances and obligations and "re-imagine" the past in order to legitimise actions in the present.

For example, when Moroccan tribespeople discuss tribe (In Arabic: *qabila*), they elaborate the notion in different ways depending on their generation and social status. Socially and politically dominant individuals use ideas of tribe and lineage to fix political alliances with members of other tribal groups and to enhance their own position vis-à-vis state authorities and their followers. Ethnographers working in tribal societies have frequently based their accounts of kinship relations and tribal organization on information provided by such socially and politically dominant individuals. In contrast, the notions of tribal identity maintained by ordinary tribesmen, not to mention tribeswomen, often differ significantly from such formal ideologies of politically dominant tribal leaders.

A second notion of tribe is based on its use as an administrative device in contexts as varied as the Ottoman Empire, Morocco, Iran and other countries prior to, during, and after colonial rule. Administrative assumptions concerning the nature of tribes are generally based, to some degree, on locally maintained conceptions modified for political purposes. Thus, administrative concepts of tribe frequently assume a corporate identity and fixed territorial boundaries that many 'tribes' do not possess and give privileges and authority to tribal leaders that are dependent on the existence of a state organization and not derived from leadership as understood by tribal people themselves. In cases such as Morocco and the Sudan, colonial authorities formally promoted 'tribal' identities and developed tribal administration to a fine art to retard nationalist movements. In reaction, the post-colonial governments of these and other countries signalled an ideological break with the colonial past by formally abolishing tribes as an administrative device, although such identities remain politically significant.

A third meaning of tribe refers to the practical notions that tribal people implicitly hold as a guide to everyday conduct in relating to their own and other social groups. These notions emerge primarily through social action. Tribal people do not always articulate such notions in ordinary situations because they are so taken for granted and because the social alignments based on these notions frequently shift. Practical notions of tribe and related concepts of social identity implicitly govern crucial areas of activity, including factional alignments over land rights, pastures, and other political claims, marriage strategies (themselves a form of political activity), and many aspects of patronage. In Jordan and among Palestinians in the occupied West Bank and in Israel, for example, Arabic newspapers are filled with announcements indicating the settlement of disputes among lineage and tribal groups precipitated by disputes or even automobile accidents resulting in personal injury in which tribal leaders mediate a settlement that is then publicly announced.

A fourth meaning of tribe relates to the analytical conceptions of the term held by anthropologists. Anthropological conceptions are intended primarily to make sociological sense of tribal social relations and often parallel those held by tribal people themselves. They are not more real than tribal people's conceptions of tribe or superior to them; they are a more explicit form of knowledge intended to explain how societies work. The anthropologist's objective is to achieve as adequate an understanding as possible of how people in each society conceive of social forms, use this knowledge as a basis for social action, and modify these conceptions in practice and over time.

Language

Writing, or the representation of meaning through symbols and images, is an artifact of great historical and cultural importance. The Middle East is the birthplace for many forms of written language, including several phonetic alphabets which provided the breakthrough of representing sound through visual symbols. Artifacts of various scripts show the diversity of the cultural influences and how they have evolved over time. In addition to writing systems now strongly associated with the Middle East, such as Arabic and Hebrew, scripts developed by Assyrians, Egyptians, Babylonians, Sumerians, and Ancient Greek systems, such as linear B, are included. These samples demonstrate the widespread geographic influence these civilizations have had from North Africa to West Asia, and to the Indian subcontinent.

The Rosetta Stone has inscriptions in Hieroglyphics, Egyptian Demotic and Greek. The inscriptions were of the same message, but in different languages and writing systems. It was the most critical artifact in the scholarship which finally would decipher Ancient Egyptian Hieroglyphics. Discovered by Napoleon's team of scholars in Rosetta, Egypt, in 1799 CE, this artifact now symbolizes the act of decoding and uncovering lost knowledge.

Arabic, Hebrew, and Greek have survived as living languages, still spoken by significant numbers of people. There are still people in Syria who speak Aramaic, also known as Syriac, as their native tongue. Ancient Egyptian continues through to the present day as the liturgical language used in the Coptic church. Arabic and Hebrew outlived the others, however, as the most actively used writing systems.

The primary living languages of the Middle East today are Arabic, Hebrew, Kurdish, Persian and Turkish. Pashto is another language spoken by a significant number in bordering Afghanistan, while other Turkic languages closely related to

Turkish, such as Turkmen, Uzbek, and others are important. Tajik and Dari are forms of Persian spoken in bordering Afghanistan and Tajikistan. Arabic has a unique place amongst the writing systems due to its place in Islam, and Islam's impact on the region. Many of these languages use, or have used Arabic script in the past, as their writing system.

CHAPTER 4: RELIGION

The Monotheistic Religions: Judaism,
Christianity, Islam and latterly Hindu

In Judaism, Abraham was born in around 1813 BCE and creates his covenant with God by 1713 BCE. In 1280 BCE Moses led the exodus of Jews from Egypt. By 500 BCE the Israelites had the well-established religion of Judaism based on the revelation of the word of God to Abraham. Judaism and Jews pre-date both Christianity and Islam. By 140 BCE the Maccabean uprising established an independent Jewish state in what is now Palestine. It is worth remembering this in the modern Israel/Arab context.

In Christianity, the birth of Christ defines the religion and his birth date the beginning of the Common Era, or Anno Domini. The period before the birth of Christ is Before the Common Era or Before Christ. Despite some initial persecution by Rome, and antagonism from Jews, the Roman Empire was Christian by the year 306 CE. Many Jews did not like Christianity. Christianity predates Islam. Judaism predates Christianity.

In Islam, most historians accept that Islam originated in Mecca and Medina at the start of the 7th century CE. Muslims regard Islam as a return to the original faith of the prophets, such as Jesus, Solomon, David, Moses, Abraham, Noah and Adam, with the submission (Islam means submission) to the will of God.

In his early teens, Prophet Muhammad (pbuh) worked in a camel caravan, following in the footsteps of many people his age, born of meagre wealth. Working for his uncle, he gained experience in commercial trade traveling to Syria and eventually from the Mediterranean Sea to the Indian Ocean. In time, Prophet Muhammad (pbuh) earned a reputation as honest and sincere, acquiring the nickname 'al-Amin' meaning faithful or trustworthy.

In his early 20s, Prophet Muhammad (pbuh) began working for a wealthy merchant woman named Khadijah, 15 years his senior. She soon became attracted to this young, accomplished man and proposed marriage. He accepted and over the years the happy union brought several children. Not all lived to adulthood, but one, Fatima, would marry Prophet Muhammad (pbuh)'s cousin, Ali ibn Abi Talib, whom Shi'ite Muslims regard as Prophet Muhammad (pbuh)'s successor.

The Prophet Muhammad (pbuh) was religious, he visited sacred sites near Mecca. On one such pilgrimage in 610 CE, he was meditating in a cave on Mount Jabal aI-Nour. The Angel Gabriel appeared and revealed the word of God: *"Recite in the name of your Lord who creates, creates man from a clot! Recite for your lord is most generous.'"* These are the opening verses of Surah (Chapter) 96 of the Holy Quran. Most Islamic historians believe Prophet Muhammad (pbuh) was equivocal and disturbed by the revelations and that he did not reveal them publicly for several years. However, Shia tradition states he welcomed the message from the Angel Gabriel and was inspired to share his experience with other potential believers.

The divine revelations called for submission to the one God, the expectation of the imminent Last Judgement, and caring for the poor and needy. The five pillars of Islam thereby became: profession of faith, prayer, concern for the needy, self-purification, and the pilgrimage, if one is able. One can become a Muslim by adopting and practising these five pillars, or even more simply by saying one is Muslim and then acting accordingly. the use of 'Peace Be Upon Him' (pbuh) is intended to remind people of a (the) prophet's special place in the practice of Islam,

Islamic tradition holds that the first persons to believe were the Prophet Muhammad's (pbuh) wife, Khadija and his close friend Abu Bakr (regarded as the successor to the Prophet Muhammad (pbuh) by Sunni Muslims). Soon, the Prophet Muhammad (pbuh) began to gather a small following, initially encountering no opposition. Most people in Mecca either ignored him or mocked him as just another prophet. However, when his message condemned idol worship and polytheism, many of Mecca's tribal leaders began to see Prophet Muhammad (pbuh) and his message as a threat. Besides going against long standing beliefs, the condemnation of idol worship had economic consequences for merchants who catered to the thousands of pilgrims who came to Mecca every year. This was especially true for members of the Prophet Muhammad's (pbuh) own tribe, the Quraysh, who were the guardians of the Kaaba (what became Islam's Holy Shrine). Sensing a threat, Mecca's merchants and leaders offered Prophet Muhammad (pbuh) incentives to abandon his preaching, but he refused.

There was increasing resistance to Prophet Muhammad (pbuh) and his followers, and they were eventually forced to emigrate from Mecca to Medina, a city 400 km to the north in 622 CE. This event marks the beginning of the Muslim calendar. There Prophet Muhammad (pbuh) brought an end to a civil war raging amongst several of the city's tribes. Prophet Muhammad (pbuh) settled in Medina, building his Muslim community and gradually gathering acceptance and more followers. This is why Mecca and Medina are so important in Islam and why the Kaaba in Mecca became the key Muslim shrine.

The Holy Quran is Islam's holy book and guide. It is the revelation by God through the Archangel Gabriel to the Prophet Muhammad (pbuh). This revelation began in the month of Ramadan and extended over 23 years. As the Prophet Muhammad (pbuh) could not write associates wrote down the revelations. The Caliph Uthman (qv) established the standard work, known as the Uthman Codex. The Holy Quran additionally assumes awareness of biblical and apocryphal works. It provides the basis for Sharia Law. Hadiths are oral and written traditions believed to describe words and actions of the Prophet Muhammad (pbuh) and are almost equally important.

So, just as the Christian religion incorporated many Pagan dates, traditions and works into Christianity so Islam included many Christian and Jewish traditions. In the Islamic case it was more formal, even consequent, and clearly centred on the belief and will of God as revealed to the Prophet Muhammad (pbuh). However, it is important to understand that Islam became *primus inter pares* amongst a number of competing religions at the time, including Judaism.

The Prophet Muhammad (pbuh) and his teachings gradually started to bring together a number of diverse tribes and peoples so that by the time of his death in 632 CE there was a substantial following around Medina and Mecca in what is now Saudi Arabia. His successor, the first Caliph, was elected that year. The Caliphates continued until 1258 CE. A period of 600 years, the equivalent in the UK of the period between Henry VII and Elizabeth II today. An extraordinary period of time brought to an end by the Mongol sacking of Baghdad, and partly reinstated by the Ottomans.

According to most commentators the separation of Sunni and Shia is as old as Islam. Islam split into two divisions immediately after the Prophet Muhammad's (pbuh) death in 632 CE. Later, these two groups became known as Sunni and Shia. Sunni means the individual or a group who follows the path and tradition of the Prophet. It is rooted in the word Sunnah, meaning tradition. The word Shia refers to an individual or a group who follows the path of Ali, the son-in-law of the Prophet and the fourth caliph. The word came from '*sh/y/a*', which means following. Shia goes to the Prophet through Ali. The relationship between Sunni and Shia across the Islamic history is complex. It has shifted from love to hate and from overlap to separation; culture and politics have also influenced the relationship. Throughout history these two groups recognized each other as equally Muslim and showed each other respect.

The groups therefore suggest two interpretations of the same faith.

Sunni and Shia believe in the same God; recite the same holy book, The Holy Quran; confess belief in the same Prophet, Prophet Muhammad (pbuh); understand Judgment/Resurrection Day in the same way; and pray to the same direction, facing Mecca. Both practice the same Five Pillars of Islam: confessing the Oneness of God and the Prophecy of Muhammad (pbuh) (*Shahadah*), Five daily prayers (*Salat*), Fasting (*Sawm*), Almsgiving (*Zakat*), and Pilgrimage to Mecca (*Hajj*).

Sunni and Shia have many things in common, but the list of fundamental differences has only two points. First, Sunnis believe that the Prophet Muhammad (pbuh) did not appoint anybody as his political successor, leaving the issue to the community, while Shia believes that the Prophet declared Ali ibn Abi Talib (the Prophet's uncle) to be his successor. Second, Sunni tends to order religious society in an egalitarian way while Shia tends to a hierarchical view. This is analogous to the egalitarian Protestants and hierarchical Catholics, who place the Catholic Pope atop the religious hierarchy. These two fundamental distinctions have evolved throughout Islamic history. Today, the diversities within both Shia and Sunni are so great that you can find a Sunni nearly indistinguishable from a Shia, and vice-versa, and radical Shia and Sunni who are more like each other than they are to others of their own denomination.

Neither Sunni nor Shia include 'jihad' as one of the five pillars of Islam. This is a misunderstood word in the West...its traditional meaning is struggle but has come to mean either a struggle with oneself against sin or a struggle against the enemies of Islam. In a similar misunderstanding 'fatwa' means a ruling in Islamic law. It has been somewhat misinterpreted following Iranian Shia theocratic 'fatwas' against westerners, themselves radical interpretations. These 'fatwas' have been interpretations of law promoted by anti-western clerics and have no clear foundation within the Sharia (Islamic Law) or the Holy Quran. The Great Satan is a further misunderstanding...the Great Satan has been interpreted as meaning the U.S. by some clerics but within the Holy Quran the phrase, as in other Abrahamic religions, is an entity that seduces humans into sin or falsehood. In Christianity and Islam, he (sic) is usually seen as either a fallen angel or a genie, who used to possess great piety and beauty, but rebelled against God.

In modern times it is important to try and keep these consequential traits in mind. Indeed, any conversation with a senior Sunni Imam (Bishop) would include references to similarity and inclusion; and highlight similarities as opposed to divisions. It is also important to understand that Islam, as noted, is inclusive of the Prophets Abraham, Moses, Gabriel, and Jesus in particular. In the early Caliphates Islam was very tolerant of other religions and their prophets. Given the polytheism into which the revelations to the Prophet Muhammad (pbuh) appeared then such tolerance helped Islam expand. Islam may mean submission, but it is submission to the will of God, and, of course, all humans should submit to the will of God as delivered to the Prophet Muhammad (pbuh) and as subsequently interpreted.

Indian settlers came to live in Oman, creating settlements and practicing Hinduism. Arab sailors were using the monsoon winds to trade with western Indian ports before the 1st century CE. An Arab army conquered Sindh in 711 CE and Arab traders settled in Kerala in the 6th century CE. In the opposite direction, medieval Gujaratis, Kutchis, and other Indians traded extensively with Arab ports including Hormuz, Salalah, Socotra, Mogadishu, Merca, Barawa, Hobyo, Muscat andAden. Arab merchants were the dominant carriers of Indian Ocean trade until the Portuguese forcibly supplanted them at the end of the 15th century CE. Indo-Arabian links were renewed under the British Empire, when many Indians serving in the army or civil service were stationed in Arab lands such as Sudan. The current wave of Indian immigration to the Arab states of the Persian Gulf dates roughly to the 1960s CE. Hinduism is one of the fastest growing religions in the Middle East, mainly due to immigration from the Indian Subcontinent.

In 2001 CE, Belgian speleologists found many inscriptions, drawings and archaeological objects on the Socotra Island off the coast of Yemen left by sailors who visited the island in the 1st century BCE to 6th century CE and most of the texts found were written in the Indian Brahmi script.

The numbers of Indians living and working in the Gulf Sates reached a maximum of around three million at the beginning of the 21st century CE. In the last five years (since 2015 CE) at least a million have returned to India as nationalisation and indigenisation policies take hold in the Arab States.

CHAPTER 5: THE EMPIRES

Greek Empire

The eastern Mediterranean earthquake of 464 BCE led indirectly to the Peloponnesian Wars which in turn led to the expansion of Greek influence across the Mediterranean and the Middle East under the Macedonian Empire Alexander the Great (356 – 323 BCE).

The Seleucid empire, (312–64 BCE), an ancient empire that at its greatest extent stretched from Thrace in Europe to the border of India, was carved out of the remains of Alexander the Great's Macedonian empire by its founder, Seleucus I Nicator.

Seleucus, one of Alexander's leading generals, became Satrap (Governor) of Babylonia in 321 BCE, two years after the death of Alexander. In the prolonged power struggle between the former generals of Alexander for control of the disintegrating empire, Seleucus sided with Ptolemy 1 of Egypt against Antigonus 1, Alexander's successor on the Macedonian throne, who had forced Seleucus out of Babylonia. In 312 BCE Seleucus defeated Demetrius at Gaza using troops supplied by Ptolemy, and with a smaller force he seized Babylonia that same year, thereby founding the Seleucid kingdom, or empire. By 305 BCE, having consolidated his power over the kingdom, he began gradually to extend his domain eastward to the Indus River and westward to Syria and Anatolia where he decisively defeated Antigonus at Ipsus in 301 BCE. In 281 BCE he annexed

the Thracian Chersonesus. That same year, he was assassinated by Ptolemy Ceraunus, the disgruntled son of Ptolemy I.

Seleucus was succeeded by his eldest son, Antiochus I Soter,
who reigned until 261 BCE and was followed by Antiochus
II (reigned 261–246 BCE), Seleucus II (246–225 BCE), Seleucus
III (225–223 BCE), and Antiochus III the Great (223–187 BCE),
whose reign was marked by sweeping administrative reforms
in which many of the features of the ancient Persian imperial
administration, adopted initially by Alexander, were modernized to eliminate a dual power structure strained by rivalry between military and political figures.

The empire was administered by provincial 'strategi', who
combined military and civil power. Administrative centres
were located at Sardis in the west and at Seleucia on the Tigris in the east. By controlling Anatolia and its Greek cities, the
Seleucids exerted enormous political, economic, and cultural
power throughout the Middle East. Their control over the strategic Taurus Mountain passes between Anatolia and Syria, as
well as the Hellespont between Thrace and Anatolia, allowed
them to dominate commerce and trade in the region. Seleucid
settlements in Syria, primarily Antioch, were regional centres
by which the Seleucid empire projected its military, economic,
and cultural influence.

The Seleucid empire was a major centre of Hellenistic culture,
which maintained the pre-eminence of Greek customs and
manners over the indigenous cultures of the Middle East. A
Greek-speaking Macedonian aristocratic class dominated the
Seleucid state throughout its history, although this dominance was most strongly felt in the urban areas. Resistance
to Greek cultural hegemony peaked during the reign of Antiochus IV (175–163 BCE), whose promotion of Greek culture
culminated in his raising a statue to Zeus in the Temple at
Jerusalem. He had previously ordered the Jews to build shrines
to idols and to sacrifice pigs and other unclean animals and

had forbidden circumcision—essentially prohibiting, on pain of death, the practice of the Jewish law. This persecution of the Jews and desecration of the Temple sparked the Maccabean uprising beginning in 165 BCE. A quarter-century of Maccabean resistance ended with the final wresting of control over Judea from the Seleucids and the creation of an independent Judea in what is now Palestine.

The Seleucid empire began losing control over large territories in the 3rd century BCE. Note there was a huge earthquake in 226 BCE that destroyed the Colossus of Rhodes and wrought havoc over a wide area. An inexorable decline followed the first defeat of the Seleucids by the Romans in 190 BCE. By that time the Aegean Greek cities had thrown off the Seleucid yoke, Cappadocia and Attalid Pergamum had achieved independence, and other territories had been lost to the Celts and to Pontus and Bythnia. By the middle of the 3rd century BCE, Parthia, Bactria, and Sogdiana had gained their independence; the conquest of Coele in Syria (Lebanon), and Palestine by Antiochus III (200 BCE) and a brief occupation of Armenia made up to some extent for the loss of much of Anatolia to the Romans. The decline accelerated after the death of Antiochus IV (164 BCE) with the loss of Commagene in Syria and of Judea in Palestine. By 141 BCE all lands east of the Euphrates were gone and attempts by Demetrius II (141 BCE) and Antiochus VII (130 BCE) could not halt the rapid disintegration of the empire. When it was finally conquered by the Romans in 64 BCE, the formerly mighty Seleucid empire was confined to the provinces of Syria and eastern Cilicia, and even those were under tenuous control.

Roman Empire.

The Byzantine Empire, also referred to as the Eastern Roman Empire, or Byzantium, was the continuation of the Roman Empire in its eastern provinces during Late Antiquity and the Middle Ages, when its capital city was Constantinople. It survived the fragmentation and fall of the Western Roman Empire in the 5th century CE and continued to exist for an additional thousand years until it fell to the Ottoman Empire in 1453 CE. During most of its existence, the empire was the most powerful economic, cultural, and military force in Europe.

Several events from the 4th to 6th centuries CE mark the period of transition during which the Roman Empire's Greek East and Latin West diverged. Constantine I (324–337 CE) reorganised the empire, made Constantinople the new capital and legalised Christianity. Under Theodosius I (379–395 CE), Christianity became the state religion and other religious practices were proscribed. In the reign of Heraclius (610–641 CE), the Empire's military and administration were restructured, and Greek was adopted for official use in place of Latin.

The borders of the empire fluctuated through several cycles of decline and recovery. During the reign of Justinian I (527–565 CE), the empire reached its greatest extent, after reconquering much of the historically Roman western Mediterranean coast, including North Africa, Italy and Rome, which it held for two more centuries. The Byzantine–Sasanian War of 602–628 CE exhausted the empire's resources, and during the early Muslim conquests of the 7th century CE, it lost its richest provinces, Egypt and Syria, to the Rashidun Caliphate. During the Macedonian dynasty (10th –11th centuries CE), the empire expanded again and experienced the two-century long Macedonian Renaissance, which came to an end with the loss of much of Asia Minor to the Seljuk Turks after the Battle of Manzikert in 1071 CE. This battle opened the way for the Turks to settle in Anatolia. The empire recovered during the Komnenian restoration, and by the 12th century CE, Constantinople was the largest and wealthiest city in Europe.

The empire was delivered a mortal blow during the Fourth Crusade, when Constantinople was sacked in 1204 CE and the territories that the empire formerly governed were divided into competing Byzantine Greek and Latin realms. Despite the eventual recovery of Constantinople in 1261 CE, the Byzantine Empire remained only one of several small rival states in the area for the final two centuries of its existence. Its remaining territories were progressively annexed by the Ottomans in the Byzantine–Ottoman wars over the 14th and 15th centuries CE. The fall of Constantinople to the Ottoman Empire in 1453 CE ended the Byzantine Empire. The last of the imperial Byzantine successor states, the Empire of Trebizond, would be conquered by the Ottomans eight years later in the 1461 CE siege.

The Caliphates.

After the death of the Prophet Muhammad (pbuh) the Caliphates began, developed, and eventually lost an Islamic golden age.

A caliphate is an Islamic state under the leadership of an Islamic steward with the title of Caliph. Such a person is considered a politico-religious successor to the Islamic Prophet Muhammad (pbuh) and a leader of the entire Muslim world ('umma'). Historically, the caliphates were polities based on Islam which developed into multi-ethnic trans-national empires encompassing multiple religions.

During the medieval period, three major caliphates succeeded each other: the Rashidun Caliphate (632–661 CE), the Umayyad Caliphate (661–750 CE), and the Abbasid Caliphate (750–1517 CE). In the fourth major caliphate, the Ottoman Caliphate, the rulers of the Ottoman Empire claimed caliphal authority from 1517 CE. Throughout the history of Islam, a few other Muslim states, almost all hereditary monarchies such as the Mamluk Sultanate (Cairo) and Ayyubid Caliphate, have claimed to be caliphates.

As noted before the rise of the Prophet Muhammad (pbuh), Arab tribes followed a pre-Islamic Arab polytheism and lived as self-governing sedentary and nomadic tribal communities. Following the early Muslim conquests by the Prophet Muhammad (pbuh), the region became politically unified under Islam.

The first caliphate, the Rashidun Caliphate, immediately suc- ceeded the Prophet Muhammad (pbuh) after his death in 632 CE. The four Rashidun caliphs were chosen through *'shura'*, a process of community consultation that some consider to be an early form of Islamic democracy. The fourth caliph, Ali, who, unlike the prior three, was from the same clan as Prophet Muhammad (pbuh) (Banu Hashim), is considered by Shia Mus- lims to be the first rightful caliph and Imam after the Prophet Muhammad (pbuh). Ali reigned during the First Fitna (656– 661 CE), a civil war between supporters of Ali and sup- porters of the assassinated previous caliph, Uthman, from Banu Umayya, as well as rebels in Egypt; the war led to the establishment of the Umayyad Caliphate under Muawiyah I in 661 CE.

The second caliphate, the Umayyad Caliphate, was ruled by Banu Umayya, a Meccan clan descended from Umayya ibn Abd Shams. The caliphate continued the Arab conquests, incorporating the lands of the Caucasus, Transoxiana, Sindh, Maghreb and Iberian Peninsula (Al-Andalus) into the Muslim world. The caliphate had considerable acceptance of the Chris- tians within its territory, necessitated by their large numbers, especially in the region of Syria. Following the Abbasid Revolu- tion from 746 CE to 750 CE, which primarily arose from non- Arab Muslim disenfranchisement, the Abbasid Caliphate was established in 750 CE.

The third caliphate, the Abbasid Caliphate was ruled by the Abbasids, a dynasty of Meccan origin descended from Hashim, a great-grandfather of Prophet Muhammad (pbuh), via Abbas, an uncle of Prophet Muhammad (pbuh). Caliph al-Mansur founded its second capital of Baghdad in 762 CE, which be- came a major scientific, cultural and art centre, as did the territory as a whole, during the period known as the Islamic Golden Age. From the 10th century CE, Abbasid rule became confined to an area around Baghdad and saw several occupations from foreign powers. In 1258 CE, the Mongol Empire sacked Baghdad, ending the Abbasid rule over Baghdad, but in 1261 CE the Mamluks in Egypt re-established the Abbasid Caliphate in Cairo. Though lacking in political power, the Abbasid dynasty continued to claim authority in religious matters until the Ottoman conquest of Mamluk Egypt in 1517 CE, which saw the establishment of the Ottoman Caliphate.

The conquest gave the Ottomans control over the holy cities of Mecca and Medina, previously controlled by the Mamluks. The Ottomans gradually came to be viewed as the leaders and representatives of the Muslim world and the Gunpowder empires. Following their defeat in World War I, their empire was partitioned by the United Kingdom and the French Third Republic. The Turkish Republic was proclaimed on 29 October 1923 CE, and as part of the reforms of its first president, Mustafa Kemal Atatürk, the Grand National Assembly of Turkey constitutionally abolished the institution of the caliphate on 3 March 1924 CE.

A few other states that existed through history have called themselves caliphates, including the Ayyubid Caliphate during the reign of Saladin (1174–1193 CE), Isma'ili Fatimid Caliphate in Northeast Africa (909–1171 CE), the Umayyad Caliphate of Cordoba in Iberia (929–1031 CE), the Berber Almohad Caliphate in Morocco (1121–1269 CE), the Fula Sokoto Caliphate in present-day northern Nigeria (1804–1903 CE), and the Islamic State of Iraq and the Levant in the 2010s CE.

The Sunni branch of Islam stipulates that, as a head of state, a caliph was a selected or elected position. Followers of Shia Islam, however, believe a caliph should be an Imam chosen by God from the 'Ahl al-Bayt' (the 'Family of the House', Prophet Muhammad's (pbuh) direct descendants).

In the early 21st century CE, following the failure of the Arab Spring and the military defeat of the Islamic State, there has been seen 'a broad mainstream embrace of a collective Muslim identity' by young Muslims, and the appeal of a caliphate as an 'idealized future Muslim state' has grown stronger. It is worth keeping this history in mind as recent events in the Middle East are discussed in later chapters. [13] [14] [15] [16] [17] [18] [19] [20] [21] [22] [23] [24]

Mongols and Tatars

Beginning in the 1240s CE, the Mongols made repeated invasions of Syria. Most failed, but they did have some success in 1260 CE and 1300 CE, capturing Aleppo and Damascus and destroying the Ayyubid dynasty. The Mongols were forced to retreat within months each time by other forces in the area, primarily the Egyptian Mamluks. Since 1260 CE, it had been described as the Mamluk-Ilkhanid War.

During the governorship of Bachu in Persia, the Mongolian army under Yisaur attacked Syria in 1244 CE. The reasons for the attack are unclear, but it may have been in retaliation to the Syrian participation on the Seljuk side in the Battle of Köse Dag; it may have been because of climate change. In the autumn 1244 CE, Yisaur concentrated the Mongol forces in the upper Tigris valley where they subjugated the Kurdish province of Akhlat. Moving across, the Mongolian army encountered no resistance and ravaged the area *en route*. The fortified cities were not taken in this advance because Yisaur was not prepared for siege assault. Passing through the territory of the city of Urfa, he crossed the Euphrates.

He marched directly to Aleppo but went as far as Hailan before the climate impaired his army's movements. Yisaur sent envoys to Aleppo to demand submission of tribute, which Malik agreed to pay. The same demand was sent to Bohemond of Antioch who chose not to fight them instead of defiance.

Yisaur withdrew his force back up the Euphrates valley and

received the submission of Malatia. In Egypt, Sultan as-Salih Ayyub decided to acquiesce to the results and made no attempt to raise an army to encounter the Mongols who had invaded his dominions in Syria.

In 1251 CE, as an expediency to buy peace, Sultan an-Nasir Yusuf sent his representatives to Mongolia for the election of Möngke and agreed to make Syria a vassal state of the Mongol Empire.

In 1255 CE, Hulagu sought to further expand the Empire into the Middle East under orders from his older brother, the Great Khan Mongke. Hulagu's forces subjugated multiple peoples along the way, most notably the centre of the Islamic Empire, Baghdad, which was completely sacked in 1258 CE, destroying the Abbasid Caliphate. From there, the Mongol forces proceeded into Syria.

In 1260 CE, Egypt was under the control of the Bahri Mamluks, while most of the Levant (aside from the Crusader states) was still under the control of Ayyubid princes. The Mongols, for their part, had combined their forces with that of their Christian vassals in the region, the Georgians; the army of Cilician Armenia under Hethum I, King of Armenia; and the Franks of Bohemond VI of Antioch. In what is described by the 20th century CE historians René Grousset and Lev Gumilev as the 'yellow crusade' ('Croisade Jaune'), the combined forces captured the city of Aleppo in January, and then on 1 March 1260 CE, under the Mongol Christian general Kitbuqa, took Damascus. The last Ayyubid king, An-Nasir Yusuf, was captured by the Mongols near Gaza in 1260 CE. However, Hulagu promised him that he would appoint An-Nasir Yusuf as his viceroy in Syria. With the Islamic power centre of Baghdad and Syria gone, the centre of Islamic power transferred to the Mamluks in Cairo.

Hulagu's intention at that point was to continue south through Palestine to Egypt, to engage the Mamluks. However,

Möngke died in late 1259 CE, requiring Hulagu to return to Karakorum to engage in the councils on who the next Great Khan would be. Hulagu departed with the bulk of his forces, leaving only about 10 000 Mongol horsemen in Syria under Kitbuqa. Some of Kitbuqa's forces engaged in raids southwards towards Egypt, reaching as far as Gaza, where a Mongol garrison was established with 1 000 troops.

The Mamluks took advantage of the weakened state of the Mongol forces and, negotiating a passive alliance with the remnants of the Crusader forces in Acre, advanced northwards to engage the Mongols at the pivotal Battle of Ain Jalut in September 1260 CE. The Mamluks achieved a decisive victory, Kitbuqa was executed, and the battle established a high-water mark for the Mongol conquests. In previous defeats, the Mongols had always returned later to re-take the territory, but they were never able to avenge the loss at Ayn Jalut. The border of the Mongol Ilkhanate remained at the Tigris River for the duration of Hulagu's dynasty. Sultan An-Nasir and his brother were executed after Hulagu heard the news of the defeat of Kitbuqa at Ain Jalut.

In December 1260 CE, Hulagu sent 6 000 troops back into Syria, but they were defeated at the First Battle of Homs.

After the fall of Baghdad in 1258 CE, a few of Abbasid princes fled to Syria and Egypt. There, the Abbasids still maintained a feeble show of authority, confined to religious matters, under the Mamluks. But their authority was limited to being figureheads. First of the Caliphs in Cairo, Al-Mustansir II was dispatched to Mesopotamia by Baibars. The Caliph was reinforced with Syrian auxiliaries and the Bedouins. However, he was totally crushed by the Mongol vanguard in South Iraq in 1262 CE. The Mongol protectorate and ruler of Mosul, Badr al-Din's sons sided with the Mamluks and rebelled against the rule of Hulagu. This led to the destruction of the city state and the Mongols finally suppressed the rebellion in 1265 CE. The Mamluks under Baibars fought off the Franks and the Mongols during the Ninth Crusade.

The second Mongol invasion of Syria took place in October 1271 CE, when 10 000 Mongols and Seljuk auxiliaries moved southwards from Rum and captured Aleppo; however they retreated back beyond the Euphrates when the Mamluk leader Baibars marched on them from Egypt.

In the second half of the 13th century CE, civil war had erupted in the Mongol Empire. In the Middle East, this manifested as conflict between the Mongols of the Golden Horde, and the Mongols of the Ilkhanate, who battled over claims on Georgia and Azerbaijan. Both the Golden Horde and the Ilkhanate sought to strengthen their position via trade agreements or other types of alliances with other powers in the area. In 1261 CE, Berke of the Golden Horde allied with the Mamluk Sultan Baibars, against their common enemy the Ilkhanate. This alliance was both strategic, and also important in terms of trade exchanges, as the Egyptians had been the Golden Horde's longstanding trade partner and ally in the Mediterranean.

For their part, the Mongols of the Ilkhanate sought (unsuccessfully) an alliance with the Franks of Europe but did form a Byzantine-Mongol alliance with the Christian Byzantine Empire.[25][26][27][28][29][30][31][32][33][34][35][36][37][38]

The Ottoman Empire

The Ottoman was a state that controlled much of south-eastern Europe, Western Asia, and Northern Africa between the 14th and early 20th centuries CE. It was founded at the end of the 13th century CE in north-western Anatolia in the town of Sogut (modern-day Bilecik Province) by the Turkoman tribal leader Osman I. After 1354 CE, the Ottomans crossed into Europe and with the conquest of the Balkans, the Ottoman Beylik was transformed into a transcontinental empire. The Ottomans ended the Byzantine Empire with the 1453 CE conquest of Mehmed the Conqueror.

Under the reign of Suleiman the Magnificent, the Ottoman Empire marked the peak of its power and prosperity as well as the highest development of its government, social, and economic systems. At the beginning of the 17th century CE, the empire contained 32 provinces and numerous vassal states. Some of these were later absorbed into the Ottoman Empire, while others were granted various types of autonomy over the course of centuries.

With Constantinople (modern-day Istanbul) as its capital and control of lands around the Mediterranean Basin, the Ottoman Empire was at the centre of interactions between the Eastern and Western worlds for six centuries. While the empire was once thought to have entered a period of decline following the death of Suleiman the Magnificent, this view is no longer supported by most academic historians. The empire continued to maintain a flexible and strong economy, society and military throughout the 17th and for much of the 18th century CE. However, during a long period of peace from 1740 to 1768 CE, the Ottoman military system fell behind that of their European rivals, the Habsburg and Russian empires. The Ottomans consequently suffered severe military defeats in the late 18th and early 19th centuries CE, which prompted them to initiate a comprehensive process of reform and modernisation known as the Tanzimat. Thus, over the course of the 19th century CE, the Ottoman state became vastly more powerful and organised, despite suffering further territorial losses, especially in the Balkans, where several new states emerged.

The Committee of Union and Progress (CUP) would establish the Second Constitutional Era in the Young Turk Revolution in 1908 CE, turning the Empire into a constitutional monarchy which conducted competitive multi-party elections. A few years later, the now radicalized and nationalistic Union and Progress Party would take over the government in the 1913 CE coup d'état, creating a one-party regime. The CUP allied the Empire with Germany hoping to escape from the diplomatic isolation which had contributed to its recent territorial losses, and thus joined World War I on the side of the Central Powers. While the Empire was able to largely hold its own during the conflict, it was struggling with internal dissent, especially with the Arab Revolt in its Arabian holdings. During this time, genocide was committed by the Ottoman government against the Armenians, Assyrians, and Greeks. The Empire's defeat and the occupation of part of its territory by the Allied Powers in the aftermath of World War I resulted in its partitioning and the loss of its Middle Eastern territories, which were divided between the United Kingdom and France. The successful Turkish War of Independence led by Mustafa Kemal Atatürk against the occupying Allies led to the emergence of the Republic of Turkey in the Anatolian heartland and the abolition of the Ottoman monarchy. [39] [40] [41] [42] [43] [44] [45] [46] [47] [48] [49] [50] [51] [52] [53] [54] [55]

The British Empire and the Sykes – Picot Agreement

British involvement in the region preceded World War I, but Britain's 'moment' in the Middle East, as it has been called, the period in which it was the dominant power in much of the area, lasted from 1914 CE to 1956 CE. The axis of Britain's Middle Eastern empire stretched from the Suez Canal to the Persian Gulf. At its height between the two world wars, Britain's supremacy was almost unchallenged either by other powers or by indigenous forces. Yet after 1945 CE, British dominance quickly crumbled, leaving few relics of any kind.

The initial impetus toward deeper British involvement in the Middle East arose from the entry of the Ottoman Empire into World War I on the side of the Central Powers at the end of October 1914 CE. The British did not seek conflict with the Turks, seeing it as a diversion from the primary task of defeating Germany; they nevertheless moved quickly both to confront Turkey in the battlefield and to plan post-war dispensation in the Middle East. The 'Eastern question' in its traditional form terminated abruptly, and a new phase began in which the Allied powers struggled over the post-war partition of the Ottoman Empire among themselves.

WWI and British Entry in the Region

The British cabinet decided on 2 November 1914 CE that *"after what had happened we ought to take a vigorous offensive"*. In a public speech at Guildhall in London on 9 November 1914 CE, the Prime Minister, H. H. Asquith, declared: *"It is the Ottoman government, and not we who have rung the death knell of Ottoman dominion not only in Europe but in Asia"*. The next month Britain severed the formal constitutional link between Egypt and the Ottoman Empire, declared a protectorate over the country, deposed the anti-British Khedive Abbas Hilmi II, and installed a successor, Hussein Kamil, as Sultan.

Despite misgivings in the High Command, which favoured concentration of Britain's limited military resources on the western front against Germany, an onslaught against the Ottoman Empire was launched on three fronts: at the Dardanelles, in Mesopotamia, and on the border between Egypt and Palestine; Russian forces, meanwhile, engaged Turkey from the north.

The attack on the Straits resulted in one of the great catastrophes of British military history. An initial naval attempt to force the Dardanelles was easily repulsed. Subsequent landings on the Gallipoli Peninsula by British and empire troops gained no significant military objective and led to a bloodbath. Turkish forces led by Mustafa Kemal (later known as Ataturk) repelled the invaders, causing many casualties. The reputation of Winston Churchill, then First Lord of the Admiralty, who had been the chief political patron of the operation, was damaged.

In Mesopotamia, too, the British were humiliated. An army was dispatched from India to invade the country, from the Persian Gulf. But in April 1916 CE General Charles Townshend's Sixth Division was forced to surrender at Kut al-Amara. The British nevertheless brought in new forces, which advanced to conquer Baghdad by March 1917 CE.

On the Egypt–Palestine front, Turkish raids on the Suez Canal led to British occupation of the Sinai Peninsula. Thereafter, a stalemate developed, partly because of lacklustre leadership, but mainly because of British inability to commit large forces to a front that was regarded as peripheral to the outcome of the war. In 1917 CE, however, the advance resumed under General Edmund Henry Allenby who entered Jerusalem in triumph in December 1917 CE. He moved on the following autumn to win the Battle of Megiddo and to conquer Syria. This was the last great cavalry victory in the history of warfare. By the time of the Turkish armistice on 30 October 1918 CE, British forces were thus in control of most of the Fertile Crescent.

Meanwhile, the British had sponsored and financed a revolt of tribesmen in the Arabian Peninsula against their Ottoman Turkish overlords. Organized by a Cairo-based group of British Middle East experts known as the Arab Bureau, the revolt began in June 1916. It engaged, in particular, the followers of the Hashemite ruler of the Hijaz, Sharif of Mecca (Hussein ibn Ali), and his sons. Among the British officers who advised the rebels was T. E. Lawrence, who fought with bands of Arab guerrillas against targets in Arabia. They blew up Turkish installations along the Hijaz Railroad, captured Aqaba in 1917 CE, and harassed the enemy on the eastern flank of Allenby's army as it advanced north toward Damascus. In recognition of their efforts, and as a sop to Arab nationalist feeling, Allenby stage-managed the capture of Damascus on 1 October 1918 CE, allowing the Arab army to enter the city in triumph, though the victory had been chiefly the work of Australian cavalry commanded by General Sir Harry Chauvel.

The parade fitted into larger British schemes. During the war, the British had given benevolent but unspecific encouragement to Hashemite aspirations toward the creation of a unified Arab state under their leadership. Later Arab claims made much of alleged promises made in correspondence in 1915–1916 CE between the British high commissioner in Egypt, Sir Henry McMahon, and Sharif Hussein, though the exchanges were vague and inconclusive on both sides and never resulted in a formal treaty.

Carving Up the Ottoman Empire

Britain entered into more specific obligations to other allies. In April 1915 CE, it signed a secret treaty promising Constantinople to Russia, thus explicitly jettisoning Britain's long-standing reservations about Russian control of the Straits. (In fact, British governments since the time of Lord Salisbury at the turn of the century had resigned themselves to eventual Russian control of Constantinople.) At the same time, as part of the price of persuading Italy to enter the war on the Allied side, Britain agreed in the Treaty of London that, in a post-war carve-up of the Ottoman dominions, Italy would receive southwest Anatolia.

Under an agreement negotiated in 1916 CE between Sir Mark Sykes and François Georges-Picot, Britain promised France most of Syria, Cilicia, and the oil-bearing region around Mosul in northern Mesopotamia. Much consequence for the British followed the Balfour Declaration of November 1917 CE in which Britain undertook to facilitate the establishment of a national home for the Jewish people in Palestine—with provisos protecting the 'civil and religious rights of the existing non-Jewish communities' and the rights of Jews in other countries. All of these engagements were designed to serve urgent wartime objectives rather than long-term interests. The Sykes

-Picot Agreement is worthy of additional comment.

The Sykes-Picot Agreement, also called Asia Minor Agreement, (May 1916 CE), was a secret convention made during World War I between Great Britain and France, with the assent of Imperial Russia, for the dismemberment of the Ottoman Empire. The agreement led to the division of Turkish-held Syria, Iraq, Lebanon, and Palestine into various French and British-administered areas. Negotiations were begun in November 1915 CE, and the final agreement took its name from the chief negotiators from Britain and France, Sir Mark Sykes and François Georges-Picot. Sergey Dimitriyevich Sazonov was also present to represent Russia, the third member of the Triple Entente.

Background And Provisions

In the midst of World War I the question arose of what would happen to the Ottoman territories if the war led to the disintegration of 'the sick man of Europe'. The Triple Entente moved to secure their respective interests in the region. They had agreed in the March 1915 CE Constantinople Agreement to give Russia Constantinople (Istanbul) and areas around it, which would provide access to the Mediterranean Sea. France, meanwhile, had several economic investments and strategic relationships in Syria, especially in the area of Aleppo, while Britain wanted secure access to India through the Suez Canal and the Persian Gulf. It was out of a need to coordinate British and French interests in these regions that the Sykes-Picot Agreement was born. Its provisions were as follows:

Impact And Legacy

The pact excited the ambitions of Italy, to whom it was communicated in August 1916 CE, after the Italian declaration of war against Germany, with the result that it had to be supplemented, in April 1917 CE, by the Agreement of Saint-Jean-de-Maurienne, whereby Great Britain and France promised southern and southwestern Anatolia to Italy. The defection of

Russia from the war cancelled the Russian aspect of the Sykes-Picot Agreement, and the Turkish Nationalists' victories after the military collapse of the Ottoman Empire led to the gradual abandonment of any Italian projects for Anatolia.

The Arabs, however, who had learned of the Sykes-Picot Agreement through the publication of it, together with other secret treaties of imperial Russia, by the Soviet Russian government late in 1917 CE, were scandalized by it. This secret arrangement conflicted in the first place with pledges already given by the British to the Hashemite dynast Hussain ibn Ali, sharif of Mecca, during the Hussain-McMahon Correspondence (1915–16 CE). Based on the understanding that the Arabs would eventually receive independence, Hussain had brought the Arabs of the Hejaz into revolt against the Turks in June 1916 CE.

Despite the Sykes-Picot Agreement, the British still appeared to support Arab self-determination at first, helping Hussain's son Faisal and his forces press into Syria in 1918 CE and establish a government in Damascus. In April 1920 CE, however, the Allied powers agreed to divide governance of the region into separate Class 'A' mandates at the Conference of San Remo, along lines similar to those agreed upon under the Sykes-Picot Agreement. The borders of these mandates split up Arab lands and ultimately led to the modern borders of Iraq, Israel and the Palestinian territories, Jordan, Lebanon, and Syria.

Even though the borders of the mandates were not determined until several years after the Sykes-Picot Agreement, the fact that the deal set the framework for these borders stoked lingering resentment well into the 21st century CE. Pan-Arabists opposed splitting up the mostly Arab-populated territories into separate countries, which they considered to be little more than imperialist impositions. Moreover, the borders split up other contiguous populations, like the Kurds and the Druze, and left them as minority populations in several countries, depriving their communities of self-determination altogether. Moments of political turmoil were often met with declarations of 'the end of Sykes-Picot', such as the establishment of the Kurdistan Regional Government in Iraq in 1992 CE or the rise of the Islamic State in Iraq and the Levant (ISIL) in 2014 CE. Meanwhile, the Sykes-Picot Agreement is often criticized together with the Hussain-McMahon Correspondence and the Balfour Declaration as contradictory promises made by Britain to France, the Arabs, and the Zionist movement. Whilst no defence of such disingenuity, as will be seen again, the different foci of the British Foreign and Colonial Offices were large contributory factors to such international deception.

These overlapping (many said conflicting) claims came home to roost at the Paris Peace Settlements in 1919 CE, at which all parties presented their claims. Both the Zionists and the Arabs were represented by pro-British leaders: the Zionists by Chaim Weizmann, the Arabs by a Hijazi delegation headed by Amir Faisal (Faisal I ibn Hussein). T. E. Lawrence acted at the conference as adviser to Amir Faisal, who conformed to British desires in all matters; even to the extent of making friendly gestures toward Zionism. The French, however, proved less amenable. They spoke darkly of 'a new Fashoda' (a dispute between Britain and France in East Africa in 1898 CE) and vigorously asserted their territorial demands in the Levant and Anatolia.

In large measure, Britain, as the power in possession, was able to impose its own design on the region. Its forces, commanded by Allenby, were in occupation of the Fertile Crescent and Egypt. Although Allenby's army included French, Italian, and other national units, these were too weak to form a counterweight to British military might. The Bolshevists had in the meantime published the text of the Constantinople convention and renounced their predecessors' claim to the city. The implosion of Russian power and the outbreak of the Russian civil war eliminated Britain's great historic fear of Russian movement south toward the Mediterranean, the Persian Gulf and India.

Consolidation of British Influence

Overwhelming military power also enabled the British to dispose of indigenous challenges to their authority. Rebellion in Egypt in 1919 CE was repressed by Allenby with a dexterous mixture of force and diplomacy. Revolt in Iraq in 1920 CE was put down by General Arnold T. Wilson with an iron fist. Riots in Palestine in April 1920 CE and May 1921 CE were suppressed, in the latter case by bombarding villages from the air and succeeded by political concessions.

The Paris Peace Conference did not, in fact, achieve a resolution of territorial issues in the Middle East. In August 1920 CE, the Treaty of Sèvres, by which Turkey gave up all its non-Arab provinces as well as parts of Anatolia, was signed by the Allied powers and representatives of the Ottoman government, which by this time was little more than a diplomatic ghost. Simultaneous secret agreements among the Allies provided for an additional carve-up of much of what remained of Turkish Anatolia. The treaty never came into effect. As a result of the Kemalist revolt, it was disavowed by the Turks and fell into abeyance.

Following the peace conference, France continued to squabble with Britain over a division of the Middle East spoils. The British conceded control of Syria and Lebanon to their erstwhile ally. They were dismayed, however, when the French, in July 1920 CE, unceremoniously ejected Faisal from Damascus, where his enthusiastic supporters had proclaimed him King of Syria. Faisal arrived in British-controlled Palestine as a refugee with a large entourage. A harried British governor of Haifa complained that they were 'in and out like a swarm of bees' and warned that 'they cannot stay here indefinitely'. There was no disposition, however, on the part of his British patrons to seek to reinstall Faisal in Damascus. As a kind of consolation prize, the British arranged for his 'election' by cooperative Mesopotamian notables as King of Iraq.

The British successfully resisted broader French territorial aspirations. The northern oil-bearing region of Mesopotamia, inhabited mainly by Kurds, was assigned to British-controlled Iraq. This departure from the wartime agreement had been informally agreed to at a meeting of the British prime minister-, David Lloyd George, and the French prime minister, Georges Clemenceau, in November 1918 CE, but the French continued for some time to grumble about the arrangement. French aspirations to a role in Palestine, where they saw themselves as historic protectors of Christian interests, were thrust aside by the British.

Meanwhile, in Transjordan, Faisal's brother, Abdullah I ibn Hussein, had suddenly appeared in October 1920 at the head of a motley army, threatening to attack the French in Syria and to reclaim his brother's 'kingdom' there. The British government saw little advantage in taking over the unfertile hollow of the Fertile Crescent. On the other hand, they could not permit Abdullah to drag them into a war with the French. The foreign secretary, Lord George Nathaniel Curzon, reluctantly sanctioned the dispatch of some British officers to the territory, ostensibly to prevent its 'relapse into anarchy'; in reality to restrain Abdullah from adventures against the French.

In March 1921 CE, Churchill, then Colonial Secretary, convened a conference in Cairo of British officials in the region. This meeting set out broad lines of British administration in the Middle East that were to endure for the next decade. Under this arrangement, Abdullah was established as Emir of Transjordan; the territory was to form part of the British mandate over Palestine without, however, being open to Jewish settlement. While Abdullah formally ruled the country, the British resident and a small number of other officials discreetly steered policy in directions compatible with British interests.

Reduction of Military Presence

Having established their paramountcy, the British rapidly reduced their military establishment in the Middle East. In the early 1920s CE, the conservative press in Britain, particularly newspapers owned by Lords Northcliffe and Beaverbrook, agitated against large military expenditures in the region and called for a British exit from recent acquisitions there. In a general climate of demobilization and budget cutting, the government felt obliged to withdraw the bulk of its troops. Henceforth, except in times of crisis, the British did not maintain a large standing army in any part of the Middle East except at the strategically vital Suez. (The power of press barons is not new.)

For the rest of the period between the wars, the British maintained security in the Middle East mainly with locally recruited forces financed by locally collected revenues. Riots, disturbances, and other challenges to British authority were suppressed by the new tactic of aerial bombardment, demonstrative shows of strength, and limited political concessions.

In the age of Gordon and Kitchener, Middle East empire building had a jingoistic tinge, but after 1914 CE this tendency disappeared. Unlike other parts of the empire (notably regions of white settlement, e.g., East and South Africa) Middle East imperialism had no significant popular constituency in Britain. (France, where there was a strong pressure group on behalf of Roman Catholic interests in Syria, was very different.)

At the same time, the legend of Lawrence of Arabia, stimulated first by public lantern shows in Britain and America and later by T. E. Lawrence's writings on the Arab revolt, encouraged the growth of public interest in Arabia. Although the Arab revolt had only minor military significance, it formed the basis of myth and countermyth. The myth was of a natural affinity between the British Empire and Arab desert warriors. The countermyth was of the betrayal of Arab nationalism by duplicitous British diplomacy. Both myths exercised a powerful subliminal influence on Anglo–Arab attitudes over the next generation. The Arab vogue was further encouraged by the writings of Middle Eastern explorers, travellers, and administrators, such as Freya Stark, Gertrude Bell, and Ronald Storrs. The great Victorian classics of Arabian exploration by writers such as Charles Doughty and Richard Francis Burton were revived and achieved a new popularity.

The official mind of British imperialism, however, was shaped less by sentimental considerations than by hard-headed, realistic calculation of national interest. More than anything, official thinking was predicated on concern about India. Specifically concern about the security of routes to the subcontinent and the Far East and the possible effects of Middle East developments on internal security in India. With the growth of aviation as well as sea traffic, the need for a string of secure air bases was seen as vital. Indian priorities also lay behind British officials' anxiety about the inflammatory threat, as they saw it, of growing pan-Islamic feeling on the large Muslim minority in India. As it turned out, such fears proved exaggerated: Indian Muslims were not greatly preoccupied by Middle Eastern concerns.

The resurgence of Turkey under Atatürk caused some anxiety in Britain and led to a momentary crisis at Chanak (near Constantinople) in the autumn of 1922 CE. As the revived Turkish army advanced on Constantinople, British and French forces, in occupation of the city, prepared to resist. Lloyd George, who had given encouragement to the disastrous Greek invasion of Anatolia, was at first inclined to order British forces to stand and fight. But there was no enthusiasm in Britain for such a war. The episode led to the withdrawal of Conservative support for Lloyd George and his fall from power. With the evacuation British and French forces from Constantinople, the crisis passed. The new Turkish regime signed the Treaty of Lausanne in July 1923 CE, giving up any claim to the Ottoman

Empire's former Arab provinces: but holding on to the Turkish, Kurdish, and former Armenian regions of Anatolia.

With the settlement in 1923 CE of differences over the border between Palestine and Syria, British diplomatic conflict with the French diminished. Disputes with the United States over oil concessions were settled in 1925 CE with a division of interests in the northern Iraqi petroleum industry. For the next decade, Britain could control the region without worrying about any significant great-power competitor.

British policymaking in the Middle East was not centralized in any one government department. The foreign, colonial, India, and war offices all held responsibility at certain periods for different parts of the region. Broadly speaking, the foreign office was responsible for Egypt, the India office for the Persian Gulf, and the colonial office (from 1921 CE) for the mandates in Palestine, Transjordan, and Iraq. Each of these departments refracted its specific angle of vision and concerns in its formulation of policy. Aden, for example, whose importance to Britain was primarily as a coaling station for ships en route to India, was ruled until 1932 CE directly from Bombay; after that, responsibility was taken over by the central government in Delhi, and, beginning in 1937 CE, Aden became a crown colony. In some cases, diffusion of responsibility led to conflict between departments: Palestine, over which the colonial and foreign offices clashed repeatedly, was a case in point.

Indirect Rule and 'Benevolent Paternalism'

Britain's favoured method of rule in the Middle East was indirect and inexpensive: this was a limited liability empire. The model was not India but Egypt, where British advisers had guided government policy since the start of the British occupation. Hardly anywhere did direct rule by a British administration survive intact until after World War II. Typical of British attitudes throughout the region during the period was the comment of the colonial secretary, Lord Cranborne, in 1942 CE: *"We not only disclaim any intention of establishing direct rule, but also quite sincerely and genuinely do not wish to do so"*. Warning against direct British administration of the tribal hinterland of Aden colony, Cranborne added: *"We must keep steadily in front of us the aim of establishing in Aden protectorate a group of efficient Arab authorities who will conduct their own administration under the general guidance and protection of His Majesty's government"*. The characteristic tone of British governance was set by Sir Percy Cox in Iraq and by Allenby in Egypt: benevolent paternalism in time of peace; readiness to resort to brute force in reaction to civil unrest.

The British did not believe in large public investment in this new empire. They nevertheless greatly improved the primitive economic infrastructure bequeathed them by their Ottoman predecessors, established sound public finances, built solid judicial and (though slowly) educational systems, rooted out corruption, and protected minorities. Efficient government was not the primary purpose of imperial rule, but the British installed it almost by reflex.

The mandatory system in Palestine, Transjordan, and Iraq was a constitutional innovation. Formally, the British ruled these territories not as a colonial power but under the ultimate authority of the League of Nations. Mandatory government was to last for a limited period with the specific goal of preparing the countries for self-rule. All this, in the eyes of most observers, was merely a fig leaf to cover the nakedness of imperial acquisition. Although Britain was ultimately responsible to the League for its conduct of affairs in the mandated territories and was obliged to render account annually of its administration, the League exercised little influence over policy. In effect, Britain ruled the mandated territories as if they were colonies, though here too they sought to establish limited local self-government.

As in other parts of the empire, British power ultimately rested on a collaborative equation with local elements. Its exact form varied depending on local contingencies. In some places, the British practised a variant of the politics of notables inherited from the Ottomans. In others, they established mutually beneficial alliances with minorities, as with the Jews in Palestine for a time. Elsewhere, they combined these policies with patronage of dynastic rulers, particularly with the family of Sharif Hussein.

Britain's patronage of the Hashemites was dealt a blow in 1925 CE when Sharif Hussein was driven out of the Hijaz by the resurgent Wahhabi army of Ibn Saud, ruler of Najd. Hussein escaped in a British ship bound for Cyprus. Although Ibn Saud had been granted a British subsidy in 1916 CE, he had not joined in the Arab revolt and had remained jealous of his Hashemite neighbour. Compelled to accept realities, the British quickly came to terms with Ibn Saud. In 1927 CE, they signed a treaty with him that recognized his sovereignty over the Hijaz and, as a result, his leading position among native rulers in the Arabian Peninsula.

Although Ibn Saud employed a freelance British adviser, Harry St. John Bridger Philby, a convert to Islam, the Saudi regime's relations with Britain were never intimate. In the kingdom of Saudi Arabia, which Ibn Saud proclaimed in 1932 CE, U.S. rather than British companies were favoured in the scramble for oil concessions, after Britain had turned down a request from Ibn Saud for a loan to develop the oilfields. At the time, this seemed of minor importance; later, when vast oil reserves were discovered, the British regretted the failure. Oil production on a large scale, however, did not begin in the country until after World War II.

Until the late 1930s CE, the limited liability system survived more or less intact. The independence granted to Egypt in 1922 CE and Iraq in 1932 CE did not fundamentally affect Britain's paramountcy. In each case, Britain retained effective control over vital strategic and economic interests. The continuation of this 'veiled protectorate', as it became known in the Egyptian case, exacerbated nationalist frustrations and resentments, but these posed no imminent threat to Britain. Independence in Iraq was followed by the mass killing of members of the Nestorian Christian community, known as Assyrians. Thousands fled overseas. Like other minorities, they had looked to the British for protection; the failure to assure their security left a dark stain on Britain's imperial record in the country. (Not for the first or last time.).

Increasing Threats to British Control

From 1936 CE onward, Britain's dominance in the Middle East was increasingly threatened from within and without. Mussolini's determination to create an Italian empire around the Mediterranean and the Italian conquest of Ethiopia in 1935 CE posed a sudden danger to Britain. The powerful Italian broadcasting station on the island of Bari began broadcasting anti-British propaganda to the Middle East. The Italian dictator wooed Ibn Saud and other Middle Eastern rulers and gave covert support to anti-British elements in the region, including the anti-British leader of the Palestine Arab nationalist movement, Hajj Amin al-Husseini. The Palestine Arab Revolt between 1936 CE and 1939 CE tied down large numbers of British troops at a time when, with the Nazi threat looming in Europe, the British could ill afford such a diversion.

Conscious of their limited resources, particularly of military manpower, the British faced unpalatable policymaking dilemmas in the final months of the peace and felt compelled to subordinate all other considerations to the imperatives of imperial security: hence, the White Papers on Palestine of May 1939 CE, which reversed the Balfour Declaration policy of support for a national home for the Jewish people and restricted Jewish immigration to Palestine at a time of mounting danger to Jews in Europe.

World War II

During World War II, the Middle East played a vital part in British strategic calculations. As prime minister from May 1940 CE, Churchill placed a high priority on bolstering British power in the region. At a critical phase in the war, he insisted on dispatching large numbers of tanks and men to reinforce British forces confronting the Italians, and later the Germans, on the border between Egypt and Libya.

The British could no longer afford the luxury of a piecemeal bureaucratic approach to the Middle East. Economic planning and supply questions for the entire region were coordinated by the Middle East Supply Centre in Cairo. A British minister resident was sent to Cairo to take charge of overall policy making. (One incumbent, Lord Moyne, a close friend of Churchill, was murdered in November 1944 CE by Zionist terrorists as a protest against British policy in Palestine.)

After Italian entry into the war in June 1940 CE, the danger of attack in the Mediterranean precluded use of the Suez Canal by British ships carrying supplies to and from India and the Far East. Ships carrying reinforcements to British forces in Egypt had to take the Cape of Good Hope route before passing through the canal from south to north. Except in Egypt, where they built up their forces to confront the Italians and later the Germans, the British could not afford to maintain more than a thin crust of military control in most of the region during the war. Yet by a mixture of diplomacy, guile, and occasional demonstrative concentrations of force, they succeeded in averting serious challenge from nationalist opponents. The two most dangerous threats came in Iraq and Egypt. A pro-Axis coup erupted in Iraq in April 1941 CE, headed by Rashid Ali al-Kaylani, aided by Italian and Nazi agents and by the ex-mufti of Jerusalem, Hajj Amin al Husseini. With pro-Vichy forces in control of Syria and Lebanon, British power throughout the Fertile Crescent seemed for a moment on the verge of toppling.

But in May, a small British force from the Habbaniya air base moved into Baghdad. Al Kaylani and the ex-mufti fled to Germany where they devoted themselves to anti-British propaganda. The following month, British and Free French forces, operating from Palestine, advanced into Syria and Lebanon and installed new French administrations sympathetic to the Allied cause.

The other threat appeared in Egypt, where nationalist elements, particularly in the Egyptian army, were impressed by Axis military successes and sought to take advantage of Britain's moment of weakness. The British reacted firmly. In February 1942 CE, British tanks surrounded the royal palace as a weeping King Farouk was forced by ultimatum to appoint a prime minister acceptable to the British, Mustafa al-Nahhas, head of the Wafd party. From the British point of view, the Abdin palace coup, as the episode became known, gave a salutary demonstration of British resolve at a time of acute military pressure from the Germans in the western desert.

The battle in the western desert swung to and fro. In the initial phase, between June 1940 CE and February 1941 CE, a British army under General Archibald Wavell beat back an offensive by Italian forces under Marshal Rodolfo Graziani and advanced into Cyrenaica. In the spring of 1941 CE, however, Axis forces were bolstered by the arrival of the German Afrika Korps commanded by General Erwin Rommel, a brilliant strategist. The tide was reversed: the British were routed from Libya, and the British garrison at Tobruk was besieged and captured. By mid-1942 CE, the Germans had advanced deep into Egypt. Government departments in Cairo began burning secret documents, and emergency evacuation plans were prepared.

In November 1942 CE, the critical battle of the campaign was fought against Rommel at al-Alamayn by the British Eighth Army under General Bernard Montgomery. Months of careful planning coupled with imaginative mobile tactics, intelligent exploitation of Ultra-signals intelligence, as well as British superiority in numbers of men and machines, brought a decisive victory. This was, in Churchill's phrase, 'the end of the beginning'. Thereafter, the British strategic position in the region eased. Almost simultaneously in Morocco and Algeria, Operation Torch, the landing of U.S. and British forces commanded by General Eisenhower, had opened a new front against the Axis. By May 1943 CE, the Germans and Italians had been cleared out of northern Africa.

Churchill's preoccupation with the Mediterranean led him up some blind alleys. He tried repeatedly to draw Turkey into the war on the Allied side but without success. Turkey remained neutral until early 1945 CE, when it declared war on Germany at the last moment in order to qualify for membership in the United Nations (UN). The United States opposed Churchill's Mediterranean strategy both on military grounds and because the United States did not wish to give the appearance of propping up British imperial interests. Ibn Saud, too, remained neutral until the last moment, though he received handsome subsidies from the British and the United States and made some gestures of support for the Allied cause.

Britain did not seek territorial acquisition in the Middle East in World War II. It nevertheless found itself drawn into new responsibilities. Following the German attack on the Soviet Union in June 1941 CE, Britain joined the U.SSR in occupying Iran. Arms and other supplies to the Soviet Union were sent by rail through Iran. With the expulsion of the last Axis forces from Libya in 1943 CE, that country was placed under military administration: French in the Fezzan and British in Tripolitania and Cyrenaica. British forces also occupied the former Italian possessions of Eritrea, Abyssinia, and Italian Somaliland. Abyssinia was restored to its indigenous imperial ruler. Eritrea remained under British rule until 1952 CE when it was annexed by Abyssinia. Italian Somaliland was returned to Italy as a UN trusteeship in 1950 CE. Libya became independent in December 1951 CE, though Britain was granted the right under the Anglo–Libyan Alliance Treaty of 1953 CE to maintain military installations there.

During the war, large reserves of oil in the Arabian Peninsula had come onstream. Because of the closure of the Mediterranean to British commercial shipping, British use of Middle East oil during the war was mainly restricted to the area east of the Suez. Elsewhere, Britain mainly relied on imports from the Americas. After the war, the balance changed. Over the next three decades, Britain became steadily more dependent on oil imports from the Middle East, especially Kuwait.

Post-war Loss of Empire and the Cold War

In the later stages of the war, the British government, seeing the nationalist mood in many Arab countries, tried to move toward a new relationship with the Arabs. Following a speech by the British foreign secretary, Anthony Eden, in which he indicated British sympathy for the idea of Arab unity, a conference of Arab states at Alexandria in October 1944 CE approved the foundation of the League of Arab States. The effort to ride the tiger, however, had only limited success; the British soon found that Arab nationalism turned strongly against them.

During the war, the Soviet Union had cautiously raised its diplomatic profile in the Middle East. After 1945 CE, the region became a secondary arena of great-power conflict in the Cold War. In 1945 CE and 1946 CE, the U.SSR signalled its newly aggressive posture by attempting to establish pro-Soviet administrations in northern Iran. Eventually British and American, as well as Russian, forces withdrew from Iran and a pro-Western regime was consolidated under Mohammad Reza Pahlavi.

Elsewhere, Soviet influence was exercised by propaganda and subversion rather than direct military intervention. Although Communist parties remained weak in the region, Soviet sponsorship of Arab nationalist movements posed a growing threat to Western interests in general and the British in particular.

The end of British rule in India in 1947 CE lessened the strategic argument for a major British military commitment in the Middle East. But oil, both investments and supply, and the security of the Suez Canal remained central British concerns. British policy now faced acute difficulties in the Middle East: on the one hand, Britain retained vital interests there; on the other, its post-war economic debilitation left it unable to muster the military forces required to meet any serious challenge to control those interests.

As a result, Britain was increasingly overshadowed by the U.S. in the Middle East. Under the Truman Doctrine, enunciated in 1947 CE, the U.S. replaced Britain as the main provider of military and economic assistance to Greece and Turkey. The United States had already begun edging the British out of monopolistic control of oil concessions. Now, the U.S. became the dominant external diplomatic power, particularly in Saudi Arabia. It established a large air base in Saudi Arabia, built the Trans-Arabian Pipeline, and became the major external source of arms and other aid. As an aside Britain was identified by the U.S. as a potential enemy up to 1938 CE: with a particular concern regarding invasion from Canada.

Saudi relations with Britain were meanwhile clouded by the Buraimi Oasis Dispute (claimed by Abu Dhabi and Oman, which were both under British protection). The dispute flared into military conflict in 1952 CE and again in 1955 CE; it led to a breach in Anglo–Saudi diplomatic relations between 1956 CE and 1963 CE.

British military and political weakness was damagingly demonstrated to the world by the collapse of the British mandate in Palestine. Despite the presence of substantial British forces and the experience gained in crushing Arab insurgency between 1936 CE and 1939 CE, the mandatory government proved unable to assert its authority in the face of a revolt by the half million Jews in the country.

The international ramifications of the Palestine conflict created serious difficulties for the British between 1945 CE and 1948 CE. In the British-occupied zones of Germany and Austria, the military authorities were faced with growing numbers of Jewish displaced persons, the majority of whom demanded to be allowed to proceed to Palestine. In the U.S., on which Britain depended for economic aid, the assertive and electorally significant Jewish community pressed Congress and President Harry Truman to secure a pro-Zionist outcome in Palestine. Meanwhile, British diplomats throughout the Arab Middle East reported that the Palestine question had become a central mobilizing issue for Arab nationalists and anti-British agitators.

Although the colonial office remained formally responsible for Palestine, these international complications led the foreign office to take effective control of British policymaking on the issue after 1945 CE. The Labour Government's foreign secretary, Ernest Bevin, adopted an anti-Zionist position, which at times tipped over the edge into antisemitism; his undiplomatic outspokenness secured applause from frustrated officials but was bitterly resented by many Jews. In the final stages of the crisis (1947 CE–1948 CE), the British publicly washed their hands of the matter, professing to leave it to the decision of the United Nations. Yet, following the decision of the UN General Assembly on 29 November 1947 CE to partition Palestine into Jewish and Arab states, the British barely cooperated in implementing the decision. Privately, Bevin encouraged the government of Transjordan to reach a modus vivendi with the Zionists on the basis of a different kind of partition, one in which the Transjordanians would take over the Arab-inhabited hill regions of the country and coexist with a Jewish state in the rest of Palestine. In the end this was, broadly speaking, the outcome.

The Arab Israeli War, which lasted from 1947 CE to 1949 CE, tightened the British connection with Transjordan. Although the country had been granted independence in 1946 CE, it remained under British tutelage. In March 1948 CE, an alliance treaty was concluded in which the two countries promised each other military assistance and Transjordan agreed to the stationing of British forces in the country 'until such a time . . . that the state of the world renders such measures unnecessary'. Britain was the only country in the world to recognize the Jordanian annexation of the West Bank.

The Zionists' feat in driving the British out of Palestine in 1948 CE depressed British prestige throughout the region. The British government after 1945 CE made strenuous efforts to dissociate itself from Zionism; Arab nationalists for the next generation nevertheless attributed the creation of Israel in large measure to Britain's earlier support of a national home for the Jewish people.

British Influence in Decline

After Palestine, the second significant test of British political will in the Middle East came in Iran. In 1951 CE, the Anglo–Iranian Oil Company, in which the British government owned 51 % of the shares, was nationalized by legislation in the Iranian parliament. A nationalist government, headed by Mohammad Mossadegh, defied British attempts to secure a reversal of the nationalization. With the support of major international oil companies, the British government organized a boycott of Iranian oil. Diplomatic relations between the two countries were broken. The departure of foreign oil exports led to closure of the Abadan oil refinery. As the oil companies refused to process, ship, or purchase Iranian oil, the entire petroleum industry in the country ground to a halt. At the height of the crisis in 1953 CE, the Shah, who strongly opposed Mossadegh, fled the country.

Meanwhile, in November 1952 CE, the British had approached the United States about the possibility of organizing a joint covert operation to protect western interests in Iran. Shortly afterward, an Iranian army coup, engineered by the U.S. Central Intelligence Agency with British help, overthrew Mossadegh and brought about the return of the Shah. The Iranian oil industry was reorganized: The British granted formal recognition of Iranian ownership of the oil industry in exchange for the lease of its operations to a multinational consortium. The British share in this consortium was reduced to under a half, with the remainder held mainly by U.S. companies.

Of even greater concern to British governments was the deterioration of the British position in Egypt. Egyptian nationalists, chafing under what was seen as continued behind-the-scenes British influence, demanded the renegotiation of the Anglo–Egyptian treaty of 1936 CE and the closing of British bases. There was also conflict with Britain over the Sudan, which was ruled by Britain though it was formally an Anglo–Egyptian condominium; the Egyptian government now sought to annex the country to Egypt. In January 1952 CE, anti-British riots broke out in Egypt and paved the way for the revolution of July 1952 CE in which a group of military officers, headed by Muhammad Naguib and Gamal Abdel Nasser, seized power, deposed the king, and declared a republic.

The British now began to consider moving the centre of gravity of their Middle East operations to a more secure point. A first step was the decision in December 1952 CE to move the Middle East headquarters of the British armed forces from Egypt to Cyprus.

In the hope of constructing a bulwark against Soviet subversion and of limiting the growth of anti-Western influences in the region, Britain and the United States had proposed in October 1951 CE the creation of the Middle East Defence Organization. Turkey, which was concerned about Soviet pressure for a new regime at the Straits, expressed willingness to join such an alliance; but Egypt rejected it, and no other Middle Eastern state expressed interest, whereupon the scheme was abandoned.

Other such proposals met similar fates. The Baghdad Pact of 1955 CE represented a final attempt by the western powers, with the U.S. by this time playing the leading role, to create a regional framework under their auspices. The core of the scheme was a multilateral military aid treaty signed by Britain, Iraq, Turkey, Iran, and Pakistan, with the U.S. acting as an interested outside party. No Arab state apart from Iraq could be induced to join the pact, and Egypt, in particular, opposed it vigorously. The failure to attract Arab members was a further sign of the decline of British authority in the region.

In Jordan, the young King Hussein ibn Talal, educated at Harrow and Sandhurst, became the most pro-British of post-war Middle East rulers. His cultural formation was as much British as Arab; he maintained a home in Britain and was the one Arab ruler who was a popular public figure in Britain (his second wife was British). Such personal predilections, however, could not overcome the larger forces shaping events. Hussein, whose long career was marked by frequent shifts of policy consummated with supreme manoeuvring skill, found himself compelled to bend to the anti-British wind. In March 1956 CE, responding to external and internal political pressures, he dismissed the British commander of his army, Sir John Bagot Glubb. Since the formation of the Transjordanian emirate in 1921 CE, the state's army, the Arab Legion, had always been commanded by a British officer. In his ability to reconcile loyalties to the British and to his Arab employer, Glubb had been characteristic of a fading type of British officer in the Middle East. While commanding the Arab Legion he had routinely supplied the British government with secret copies of Jordan's war plans. The dismissal of 'Glubb Pasha' was generally regarded as the end of an era and a telling sign of the decline of British influence.

The Suez Canal

The supreme crisis of British power in the Middle East came later that year, appropriately at the focal point of Britain's interests in the region and the *'raison d'être'* of its presence there—the Suez Canal. In spite of its gradually diminishing economic position relative to other powers, Britain remained the world's foremost shipping nation, and the British merchant fleet was by far the largest user of the canal. With the growth of motor transport and the switch from coal to oil as the main industrial fuel, Britain had become overwhelmingly reliant on the importation of Middle East oil carried through the canal in tankers. Pressure from the Egyptian government for a British evacuation of the Suez Canal zone, therefore, encountered stiff resistance.

In October 1954 CE, Britain had promised to withdraw all its force from the canal zone by mid-1956 CE. The agreement, however, was hedged with several provisos reminiscent of the veiled protectorate, among them a stipulation that Egypt continue to offer Britain *'such facilities as may be necessary to place the Base [in the canal zone] on a war footing and to operate it effectively'* if any outside power attacked a member of the Arab League or Turkey. In November 1955 CE, British troops withdrew from the Sudan as the country moved toward full independence in January 1956 CE. The following July, in accordance with the 1954 CE agreement, Britain withdrew the last of its troops from the canal zone.

Hardly had the last British soldiers packed their bags, however, than the Egyptian president afforded the British a pretext to return. On 26 July 1956 CE, Nasser, infuriated by the withdrawal of an offer by the United States, Britain, and the World Bank to finance the construction of a new dam at Aswan (eventually financed by the U.SSR), announced the nationalization of the Suez Canal Company, which operated the canal. The British standing in the matter was doubtful. The British government owned a minority stake in the company, but nationalization in itself was no offense against international law, provided compensation was paid, and the Egyptians insisted that they would continue to operate the canal as before.

The nationalization was, nevertheless, regarded by the British prime minister, Anthony Eden, as an intolerable affront. When diplomacy failed to secure an Egyptian retreat, the British prepared for war. They were joined by France, which had its own reasons for opposing the Nasser regime on account of Egypt's support of Algerian rebels. Israel, which had suffered a series of border incursions from Egypt, was also drawn into military and diplomatic planning. Conspiratorial discussions among representatives of the three countries at a villa in the Paris suburb of Sèvres from 22 to 24 October 1956 CE culminated in a secret treaty. The agreement mapped out a scenario for war with Egypt. Israel would attack first across the Sinai Peninsula. The British and French would then enter the conflict, ostensibly to secure the Suez Canal, in fact to destroy Nasser's regime.

The Israelis attacked on 29 October 1956 CE, and the British and French duly issued an ultimatum the next day calling on Israel and Egypt to withdraw to positions 10 miles east and west of the Suez Canal (the Israelis had not yet, in fact, reached the canal). In the absence of Egyptian acquiescence, British and French planes began bombing Egyptian military targets on 31 October 1956. On 5 November 1956, the two powers landed paratroops. The next day, however, British policy went into reverse as a result of U.S. opposition to the invasion and of growing market pressure on sterling. Britain and France were humiliatingly obliged to agree to a cease-fire, and by Christmas they had withdrawn their forces from Egypt.

Britain's collusion with France and Israel in the events leading to the Suez war became the subject of bitter controversy in Britain. The issue is said to have divided the nation more than any foreign-policy question since Munich. The Labour Party, a small part of the Conservative party, some foreign office officials, and most enlightened opinion were hostile to Eden's policy. For the British government, Suez was an unmitigated catastrophe; not least in the severe strains it placed on relations with the U.S. Eden resigned a few weeks later, complaining of ill health.

Although Suez is generally regarded as a watershed in British history, heralding a wider imperial withdrawal, Britain continued for another decade to maintain a substantial military presence in the Middle East and to be ready on occasion to use it forcefully in defence of its interests.

Last Vestiges of Empire

The next flashpoint was Jordan. In March 1957 CE, a nationalist government in Jordan abrogated the Anglo–Jordanian Treaty. In July 1958 CE, the Jordanian regime was severely shaken by the revolution in Iraq, in which the Hashemite regime was ousted and the young King Faisal II ibn Ghazi and the pro-British Prime Minister Nuri al-Said were both murdered. British paratroopers were sent, at the request of King Hussein, to prevent a similar revolution in Jordan. Two aspects of this intervention, code-named Operation Fortitude, illustrated the changed political environment within which the British, perforce, now operated. First, the cabinet refused to commit British forces until the approval of the U.S. government had been secured. Second, the British requested and received permission from Israel to overfly Israeli territory in order to transport troops from bases on Cyprus. The British force succeeded in bolstering the Hashemite monarchy without firing a shot. The pro-British Jordanian monarchy survived, but Britain lost its bases in Iraq as well as its oil interests there.

In 1961 CE, when Kuwait, hitherto a British protectorate, secured independence, the military regime in Iraq threatened a takeover of the oil-rich principality. As at the time of the intervention in Jordan in 1958 CE, the British made sure that they had U.S. approval before taking military action. 8 000 British troops were sent to Kuwait and remained there as a deterrent against Iraqi invasion until 1963 CE.

In Aden in the mid-1960s CE, British forces conducted a miserable campaign against nationalist insurgents supported by Egypt. The British military headquarters at Aden were evacuated in November 1967 CE when the Federation of South Arabia achieved independence as the People's Democratic Republic of Yemen. Although the writing was on the wall for what remained of British power in the Middle East, there was no complete pull-out. With the liquidation of the base at Aden, Britain expanded its military presence in Bahrain and other Gulf principalities.

In the crisis prior to the outbreak of the Arab–Israel War of 1967 CE, the British government of Harold Wilson briefly considered participating in the dispatch of an international naval flotilla to assert the right of passage to Israel through the Strait of Tiran, which the Egyptian government had declared closed against Israeli and Israeli-bound ships. But no other country was prepared to join in the effort, and the idea was dropped. Although both Wilson and his foreign secretary, George Brown, were sympathetic to Israel, their attitude was not governed by any pro-Zionist altruism. The British remained vitally interested in free passage through the Suez Canal. Upon the outbreak of war with Israel in June 1967 CE, Nasser closed the canal to all shipping; it did not open again until 1975 CE. The closure severely affected the British balance of payments. The British economy was blown off course, and the government was compelled, against its wish, to devalue sterling in November of that year.

Only in 1968 CE did the Wilson government abandon pretensions to world-power status by dropping the east-of-Suez defence policy. In March 1970 CE, the revolutionary government in Libya, headed by Colonel Muammar al-Qaddafi who had attended an officers' training school in Britain, ejected the British from their bases in the country. British forces withdrew from Bahrain in 1971 CE but retained naval facilities there. Also in 1971 CE, British forces left Abu Dhabi, whereupon the seven Trucial Coast sheikhdoms formed the Federation of the United Arab Emirates. The British retained troops in Oman, where they helped suppress a leftist rebellion in the Dhofar region. Although British forces were formally withdrawn in 1976 CE, many senior British officers remained on individual contracts as commanders of the Omani army. Only in 1984 CE was the British commander in chief of the country's armed forces replaced by an Omani. After that, the sole remaining permanent British military presence in the Middle East was in the sovereign bases in Cyprus.

With the elimination of its military power in the region, Britain found itself relegated to a secondary role in Middle Eastern politics. More and more, Britain was buffeted and unable to deflect ill political and economic winds blowing from the Middle East.

Oil, Terrorism, and the British Economy

During the 1970s CE, the exploits of Palestinian Arab terrorists and the anti-Western rhetoric of Middle East leaders like Qaddafi evoked some admiration on the radical left of the political spectrum in Britain as elsewhere in Europe. Episodes such as the hijacking by Palestinian terrorists of two planes to a desert aerodrome in Jordan—the episode that occasioned the Black September conflict between the Jordanian government and the Palestine Liberation organization in 1970 CE riveted television audiences in Britain. In that instance, the government of Prime Minister Edward Heath decided to give way to terrorist demands and released an imprisoned Palestinian, Leila Khaled, who became a folk hero of the revolutionary left.

The Arab–Israel War of 1973 CE and the ensuing international energy crisis had dramatic and damaging effects on the British economy. The sudden huge increase in the price of oil and the restriction of supply by the oil producers' cartel, the Organization of Petroleum Exporting Countries (OPEC), were the major causes of the stagflation that afflicted Britain in the mid-1970s CE. The coal miners' union attempted to seize the opportunity offered by the general rise in energy prices to secure a large increase in wages paid by the nationalized coal industry. The miners' strike ushered in a bitter confrontation with the Conservative government of Heath, which called a general election on the issue in February 1974 CE and narrowly lost to the Labour Party.

As a member of the European Economic Community (EEC) from 1974 CE onward, Britain generally sought to adjust her diplomacy in the Middle East to conform to a consensus of EEC members. In the aftermath of the 1973 CE and 1979 CE oil crises, this resulted in a suddenly humble attitude by former imperial powers to sometime protégés such as Iran and the Gulf emirates. A case in point was the Venice Declaration, issued by the EEC in June 1980 CE, which marked a significant shift in diplomatic posture toward the Arab position in the conflict with Israel.

The power of OPEC enabled the producing states at last to seize effective control over their oil industries. During the 1970s CE and 1980s CE, they moved toward vertical integration of the industry, nationalizing the extraction installations, establishing refineries and petrochemical industries, investing in their own transportation of products by tanker or pipeline, and creating their own marketing mechanisms. The power of the international oil companies in the region consequently dwindled. The British government's direct interest in Middle East oil evaporated in the 1980s CE when the government of Prime Minister Margaret Thatcher sold off government shareholdings in British Petroleum and Anglo–Dutch Shell.

Unlike most western industrial countries, however, Britain enjoyed fortuitous good fortune in the discovery and successful development of indigenous oil resources. Its dependence on Middle East oil imports ended after 1980 CE with the arrival onstream of large oil reserves from the North Sea. As Britain's oil production grew, it was able to play a major role in weakening and ultimately destroying the effectiveness of OPEC. Although oil production costs were much higher in the North Sea than in the Middle East, the British, in concert with other non-OPEC producers, proved able to undercut the floor prices set by OPEC. Several OPEC members, desperate for revenues to sustain their commitments to large expenditures on armaments or social programs, broke cartel discipline and secretly sold at lower prices. With demand flagging, this led in 1986 CE to a sudden collapse in oil prices.

In the 1980s CE, Middle Eastern politics spilled over onto the streets of London with a spate of terrorist incidents, including assassinations, bombings, and embassy seizures. In 1984 CE, a British policewoman, PC Yvonne Fletcher, was murdered in the street during a demonstration in front of the Libyan People's Bureau in Saint James's Square in London. The gunshots were fired by a Libyan diplomat from within the embassy. There were also attacks on several Israeli and Zionist targets in Britain, as well as on Jewish institutions that had nothing to do with Israel. The most shocking terrorist incident was the mid-air explosion in 1988 CE aboard a Pan Am plane over Lockerbie, Scotland, in which all the passengers and crewmembers were killed. Scottish and U.S. prosecutors sought to secure the extradition of two Libyan citizens suspected of responsibility for planting the bomb. But the Libyan government long refused to yield up the men, in spite of the imposition of economic sanctions by the United Nations in 1992 CE. Although an alleged participant was extradited, imprisoned, and compassionately released it is still not entirely clear who planted the bomb.

Perhaps the most bizarre of all these episodes was the *fat-*

wa (legal opinion) issued in 1989 CE by the leading Iranian cleric, Ayatollah Ruhollah Khomeini, pronouncing a death sentence against the British novelist Salman Rushdie, who is of Indian Muslim background. Rushdie's novel 'The Satanic Verses' was held by some, but not all, devout Muslims to contain blasphemous libels against Islam. Rushdie was forced to live in hiding for several years, protected by the British security services. In spite of pressure, at first private and discreet, later public and emphatic, from the British and other western governments, the Iranian theocracy proclaimed itself unable to rescind the decree even after Khomeini's death in 1989 CE.

By the 1990s CE, the Middle East occupied a relatively lower place in British diplomatic preoccupations than in any other decade since World War I. British economic interest in the region became focused primarily on trade rather than investment. But with their reduced purchasing power following the collapse of the oil cartel, the Middle East oil producers no longer offered such abundant markets. British arms and engineering exports to the Middle East assumed greater importance as the balance of oil imports decreased. During the long-drawn-out Iran–Iraq war between 1980 CE and 1988 CE, Britain, like other western countries, sold arms to both sides.

This policy rebounded against the British government in 1990 CE when Iraq invaded and occupied Kuwait. The British joined the United States and twenty-six other countries in sending forces to the Gulf to eject the Iraqis from Kuwait in 1991 CE. Although Britain played only a secondary role in the war, the crisis lit a slow-burning fuse in British internal politics in the shape of a scandal concerning the authorization of earlier British arms sales to Iraq. The Conservative government was gravely discredited by the affair and several senior politicians and civil servants were strongly criticized by a committee of inquiry in 1995 CE.

Britain's Legacy in the Middle East

The cultural and social residue of Britain's Middle East empire was slight. Unlike France, Britain left behind no significant network of religious or educational institutions. Anglican Christianity had found few adherents in the region. Its mainly British clergy in the Middle East was gradually replaced at all levels by indigenous priests. The British Schools of Archaeology in Jerusalem, Ankara, and Baghdad continued to make a central contribution to excavations; but the one in Baghdad was defunct by the 1990s CE, and the Jerusalem school was largely inactive after the 1967 CE War (it later opened an Amman branch). In the Sudan, the Christian population in the south retained some links with the Church of England, but the University of Khartoum (formerly Gordon College) no longer looked to the English university system as a model. In Jordan, the royal court and the army maintained intimate links with Britain and copied British styles. Elsewhere, few relics of British cultural influence remained. Unlike most other parts of the former British Empire, the imperial language did not survive into the post-colonial era in the Middle East as the primary means of communication. Insofar as English continued to be spoken, this was a reflection of new American, not old British, influence. Probably the most significant British cultural export was the World Service of the BBC: Its broadcasts in English, Arabic, and other languages commanded a wide audience in the region.

At no time in the twentieth century did the Middle East take priority over the rest of the world in British diplomatic or strategic preoccupations. Yet the most striking land victories of British arms in both world wars were won respectively at Megiddo in 1918 and at al-Alamayn in 1942 CE; the resignations of three British prime ministers (Lloyd George, Eden, and Heath) were occasioned by Middle East conflicts; and Britain's most severe economic recession after the 1930s CE came about as a direct result of the interlinked political and energy crises in the Middle East in 1973 CE. For all these reasons, the Middle

East occupied a central position in the history of British exter-
nal   relations   in   the   20th   century
CE.[56] [57] [58] [59] [60] [61] [62] [63] [64] [65] [66] [67] [68] [69] [70] [71] [72] [73] [74]

CHAPTER 6: POST WORLD WAR TWO

The American Hegemony

Hegemony is an idea that argues for the indispensable role of a hegemon to sustain an international liberal order (ILO), and the standard way of defining this role is within the context of the Hegemonic Stability Theory (HST). The HST refers to a cluster of approaches interested in the role of dominant power in global politics. The underlying claim of these approaches is that the international political and economic system is at its most stable when it is under the control of a single state or '*hegemon*' The hegemons usually fall one of the three categories by their behaviour. First is a '*benign hegemon*', which provides global leadership and absorbs the cost of sustaining the order. Second is a '*coercive hegemon*', which forces other states to pay for its hegemony. Lastly, third is a 'transactional hegemon,' which recovers the cost without coercion simply by reaping the benefits of its global position. The U.S. has shown aspects of all three and, so far, China has kept to the latter outside its own borders.

The United States of America has been the hegemonic state since 1945 CE. It has shaped the contemporary global liberal international order. It has provided some of the public goods and supported the post-Second World War Europe (Marshall Plan) recovery process for Europe. It provided the Breton Woods system of institutions to establish global financial

DR MAITLAND PETER HYSLOP

order; and ensured the security and stability of the global oil market, by extending security cover to the Gulf oil-exporting states and security to sea-lanes of communication in the global commons. The U.S. supported stability through its values but also worked with the existing non-democratic ruling regimes in the Middle East. The precedence of realism over idealism paid the U.S dividends, as it was successful in forming a large coalition of the states that jointly shared a threat from the Soviet Union and communism.

The second face of the U.S. hegemony became evident in its approach to the Arab-Israel conflict. The U.S. provided unparalleled economic, military and diplomatic support to Israel. This support represented, in many ways, the U.S domestic choice and its civilizational connection with the land of Israel. Its strategy was to maintain Israel's qualitative military edge over other regional powers; this avoided the need for a direct American confrontation with the Arab states. However, by the time the Cold War came to an end, the U.S. establishment had developed a position that the Middle East was a geopolitical gap, which either failed or was reluctant to integrate into the American sphere of influence. Its discourse on the danger to the American way of life was linked with Iran, Iraq, and terrorism. It used the opportunity provided by Saddam Hussain's decision to invade Kuwait in 1990 CE to warn the Arab world that the territorial *status quo* was the permanent position of the American hegemony. Thereby the U.S. legitimized the application of a pre-emptive strike strategy, setting up more military bases and pursuing a policy of regime change in the Gulf region. Thus, a close link was developed between the American heavy military presences in this part of Asia with the survival of the American Empire.

While the third face of the U.S. hegemony was evident from the historic meeting between the U.S. President Franklin D. Roosevelt and the Saudi King Abdulaziz, in 1945 CE, and culminated into the 1974 CE agreement, in which the kingdom agreed to sell all its oil resources in U.S. dollars. The U.S. thereby cemented the American dollar hegemony over the global oil market.

Still, to a large extent, the U.S. image in the Middle East had been benign, except in Iran and later Iraq. Most ruling regimes in the region had multifaceted ties with the U.S. Despite the U.S. maximum pressure strategy on Iran, the latter has gained progress in the domestic defence industry and received Russian and Chinese support. Iran's regional rise received new impetus after the U.S. removed two anti-Iran regimes (the Taliban, for a while, and Saddam Hussain) from power. This in turn, affected the U.S. hegemonic role and relations with the other regional powers of the Middle East.

Offshore Balancing in the Middle East

After the global financial crisis of 2008 CE, the U.S. also felt the Chinese geopolitical weight in the Indo-Pacific region. China had expanded its influence, and there was limited U.S. resistance to it. In this context, President Obama became the first American president that called for an Asia pivot or balancing strategy towards the Asia-Pacific region. In the Middle East, the U.S. wields significant military influence and has a long-existing security alliance structure; but in other areas, such as trade, oil, finance, and technology, most of the region's demands have been satisfied by the emerging global powers such as China.

The shift in the U.S. strategic focus overshadowed the U.S. military role In the Middle East. When the Arab Uprising erupted, President Obama withdrew backing to the Egyptian military regime and in other places engaged with a light military footprint. The Obama strategy was to externalize the strategic and operational burden of war to human and technological surrogates. This was despite pressure from the allies and growing human rights violations. Obama approached the Libya crisis and the Syrian civil war with prudence and declined military commitment. Instead, the U.S. joined the other global powers and signed with Iran the Joint Comprehensive Plan of Action (JCPOA), otherwise known as the Iran Nuclear Deal, in July 2015 CE and allowed Russia to fight rebellions and terrorist outfits in Syria.

Donald Trump Era

President Trump's foreign policy was disruptive because it sought to revise this ILO with which American hegemony had been associated since 1945 CE. It has, in his world view, given America a raw deal. Consider his inauguration speech in 2017 CE, where he vehemently argued that *"we have enriched foreign industry at the expense of American industry. Subsidized the armies of other countries while allowing for the very sad depletion of our military. We have defended other nations' borders while refusing to defend our own"*; or that, *"we have spent trillions of dollars overseas while America's infrastructure has fallen into despair and decay"*.

To correct these imbalances President Trump resorted to transactional bilateralism or transactional hegemony. He put forward the 'America First' strategy which promoted bilateral engagements at the expense of multilateralism. Thus, Trump's rise represented a revolt against American international liberalism. He echoed the apprehension of white middle classes who have witnessed their economic prosperity decline; and believed that the U.S. policy of acting as a global policeman had not benefited its interests.

While the other regions seem to be able and capable of sustaining the American disengagements in various areas, the Middle East especially seems to witness greater regional division and the intervention of other global powers. For instance, after the U.S. came out of Trans-Pacific Partnership (TPP), it did not result in the end of the process; rather, it propelled other regional actors to come together and transform it into the Comprehensive and Progressive Trans-Pacific Partnership (CPTPP).

Although Japan has retained its cautious and critical views toward China's global and regional economic initiatives, this did not prevent Japan from working with China to build a regional economic order as a way of reducing negative impacts of American high tariff policy on its trade and investment.

Likewise, Trump's repeated questioning of NATO's relevance forced the Europeans to embrace the old idea of defence of Europe. The European Commission (EC) wrote in June 2017 CE, *'we have moved more in the last 2 years than in the last 60'*. It has made an entry into the defence area with the launch of the European Defence Action Plan (EDAP) in November 2016 CE and a proposal for the European Defence Fund (EDF) in June 2017 CE. The EC will also have a new Directorate General for Defence Industry and Space that will be tasked with building an open and competitive European defence market.

All these policy initiatives aimed at achieving a strategic autonomy for the EU through an industrial dimension, by establishing a defence industry that can single-handedly produce the equipment and the capabilities that European countries require to defend their territory and their interests. Although those developments better indicate the EU attempt to create a degree of hedge against U.S. uncertainties, it does not mean divorce in the trans-Atlantic alliance. On the occasion of the 70th anniversary of NATO in London, there emerged a new consensus among allies to take more action to balance Beijing's growing power.

Middle East Policy

When President Trump came into office the traditional U.S.-Saudi strategic alliance based on oil and security was no longer a defining link. The shale revolution in the American oil industry made the U.S, the world's largest oil producer. Now the U.S. oil industry was a competitive player in the global oil market and domestically linked with the livelihood of the millions of American citizens. The U.S. demand to the kingdom became cooperation and reciprocity. This became evident when global oil prices collapsed, and the U.S. shale industry was losing market share. Then, many in the U.S. called the Saudi oil strategy harmful to American oil interests.

It was in this context; President Trump stated that *"I will do whatever I have to do... to protect... tens of thousands of energy workers and our great companies" and* added that plans to impose tariffs on Saudi Arabia's oil exports into the U.S. were *"certainly a tool in the toolbox".* Later, when he sensed a lack of understanding on the part of Saudi Arabia, he said that the ruling regime would not last in power for two weeks without the backing of the U.S. military. The U.S. lawmakers expressed similar sentiments, as Senators Kevin Cramer of North Dakota and Dan Sullivan of Arkansas introduced the Strained Partnership Act calling for the removal of U.S. troops and military equipment from Saudi Arabia unless it slashed output. Earlier, Trump advocated arms diplomacy when he picked Saudi Arabia for his first foreign official destination. At the conclusion his trip, the U.S. signed arms deals worth U.S. $110 billion with Saudi Arabia, and later multi-billion arms deals were signed with other Arab Gulf states.

When the U.S. signed the JCPOA, Iran had a favourable geopolitical status in the region. The Iran-backed regional proxies were dominating scenes in Iraq, Syria, Lebanon, Gaza Strip, and Yemen. The Obama era strategy of allowing the regional balance of power to flourish was criticized by pro-Zionist and Iran establishments. After taking office, President Trump decertified the JCPOA and termed the Iranian regime as a rogue state in his new strategy on Iran. The U.S. re-activated sanctions on Iran on 4 November 2018 CE. Yet the U.S. withdrawal did not address belligerent geopolitical and sectarian rivalry between Iran and Saudi Arabia. Israel is still concerned with Iran's nuclear program and its growing military capabilities.

By singling out Iran as the only source of regional instability, the Trump Administration, the U.S., further complicated the regional order. Iran has further deepened regional alliances to hedge against the U.S. aggressive behaviour and has extended military ties with Russia and Iraq. The Iran-Russia intervention into Syria successfully saved the falling Assad regime. The effective Russian military intervention and China's geo-economic embedded Silk Road diplomacy attracted and modified the other regional actors of Saudi Arabia and Turkey, and thereafter, they intensified cooperation with both Russia and China.

Similarly, the U.S. settled its long-held reserved political decisions on the Israel-Palestine conflict in favour of Israel. President Trump sided with the Israel and put forward a plan that further disintegrates Palestinians. The U.S. unilaterally recognized Israeli sovereignty over occupied Golan Heights and East Jerusalem. In return, Palestinian President Mahmoud Abbas decided to cut off ties with the Trump administration in December 2017 CE. To force the Palestinian side to comply, the U.S closed down the PLO office in Washington, discontinued its U.S. $200 million assistance for Palestinian Authority, and decreased to zero its contribution to UN Relief and Work Agency.

When Trump unveiled the Middle East Peace deal on 28 January 2020 CE, the Palestinian leadership rejected it. The deal also was rejected by the European Union, Arab League, African Union, and the Organization of Islamic Cooperation. The proposed vision called for setting up the Palestinian state within four years but, the plan has no vision for a contiguous geography for Palestinians and falls short of giving Palestinians a sovereign state.

Thus, the U.S. Middle East policy under Trump continued the Obama era diplomacy of minimizing the costs of its hegemonic presence in the region but followed a different strategy. He emphasized transitional bilateralism while exercising maximum pressure on Iran and Palestinian leadership and concurrently demanded greater coordination of Arab allies and Israel to counter Iranian influence in the region. Consequently, the U.S. is maintaining its military hegemony over a region that is divided both ideologically and in threat perception; and wracked by wars, civil wars, and non-democratic regimes. The Trump administration polarised strategic anxieties among regional actors and has intensified crisis between the U.S. and Iran. Today attitudes are softening on all sides, as will be seen.

The Six-Day War of 1967 CE.

The Six Days War, also known as the June War or Arab-Israeli War, occurred between 5 -10 June 1967 CE. The conflict involved Israel and the Arab countries of Syria, Egypt, Jordan, and Iraq, supported by Kuwait, Saudi Arabia, Algeria, and Sudan. Although Israel was the winner of the war, it was the most consistent Arab response to the founding of the State of Israel.

On the evening of the first day of war half of the Arab aviation was destroyed. On the evening of the sixth day, the Egyptian, Syrian and Jordanian armies were defeated. Even more symbolic than the Arab defeat was the capture of the old city of Jerusalem. Israel considered this city as its capital without the recognition of most of the international community. The results of the Six Days War still influences the current geopolitics of the region.

Overview

The growing tensions between the Arab countries and Israel in mid-1967 led both sides to mobilise their troops. The conflict began when the Israeli air force launched a pre-emptive strike against the Egyptian Air Force bases in Sinai (Operation Focus). Israel claimed that Egypt was preparing to wage war against its nation. Whether the Arab countries were actually mobilising their troops in order to advance against the Israelis, or whether their preparations were merely defensive measures, it is still to this day a matter of debate and controversy.

On 4 June 1967 CE, Israel was surrounded by Arab forces that were far more numerous than their own and their plan of invasion seemed doomed to fail, until the Mossad thought of a solution. War was imminent.

In the face of imminent Arab action, before the invasion began, Israel's government and military leaders had implemented a strategy to break the military blockade imposed by the Arabs. Shortly after, on 5 June 1967 CE, at 0845 hours they launched an air strike against the Arab forces.

This air raid, codenamed 'Moked', was designed to destroy the Egyptian Air Force while it was on the ground. In three hours most of the planes and bases were destroyed. Israeli fighters operated continuously: they returned to refuel and armour in just seven minutes. On this first day, the Arabs lost more than 400 airplanes, whereas Israel lost 20. These air strikes gave Israel the chance to destroy the Arab defence forces. The initial idea was only that of rendering the Egyptian air base inoperative, making it impossible for any military aircraft to take off. Subsequently, Israel's ground forces moved to the Sinai Peninsula and the Gaza Strip where they surrounded the Egyptian units.

The initial actions did not involve the eastern border of Israel. Israel's Prime Minister Levi Eshkol sent a message to King Hussein of Jordan, claiming that the Israelis would not take any action against Jordan unless his country attacked them first. But on the morning of the second day, President Nasser phoned Hussein, encouraging him to fight. He told Hussein that Egypt had been victorious in the morning fight (not in fact true). This claim made by Nasser caused an overwhelming defeat for Jordan.

On the same day, at 1100 hours, Jordanian troops attacked Israel from Jerusalem with mortars and artillery. With full control of the skies, Israeli ground forces were free to invade Egypt and Jordan. The Israelis took much of the Jordanians' west bank in just 24 hours.

On the third day of the war, 7 June 1967, Jordanian forces were driven out of Transjordan, to the other side of the Jordan River. Israel had annexed the whole of Transjordan and Jerusalem, entering and reunifying the city.

The United Nations, under American pressure, initiated calls and negotiations with the Arab countries involved. Fortunately, a cease-fire agreement was reached between Israel and Jordan, and it came into effect that same afternoon. After the ceasefire, Israel's large contingent of troops and tanks was directed against the forces of Egypt in the Sinai desert and the Gaza Strip. The Israel Defence Forces attacked with three divisions of tanks, parachutists and infantry.

Aware of the fact that the war could only last a few days due to the UN's appeals, the belligerent parties understood that a rapid victory and domination of the neighbouring territories was essential. Although they were aware of possible reactions, the Israelis concentrated all their power across the Egyptian lines in the Sinai desert.

On 8 June 1967 CE, the Israelis began their attack on the Sinai desert, and, under the leadership of General Ariel Sharon, they drove the Egyptians to the Suez Canal. At the end of the day, the Israeli Defence Forces reached the channel, and their artillery continued the battle along the front line while their air force attacked the retreating Egyptian forces (which were attempting to retreat using the few roads not controlled by the Israelis). At the end of the day, the Israelis controlled the entire Sinai Peninsula, and thus, militarily, Egypt. Thanks to the intervention of the United Nations, Egypt accepted a ceasefire with Israel.

In the early hours of 8 June 1967, Israel accidentally bombarded the American warship U.S.S. Liberty, off the coast of Israel, which had been mistaken for a ship of Arab troops.

Thirty-four Americans died. This helped to force Israel to accept the ceasefire agreements proposed by the United Nations.

With Sinai under control, Israel began their assault on the Syrians in the Golan Heights on June 9. It was a difficult offensive since the Syrian forces were well entrenched. Israel sent an armoured brigade to the front lines while the infantry attacked the Syrian positions and gained control of the hills.

At 1830 hours on 10 June 1967 CE Syria withdrew from the offensive, accepted the UN's appeal, and signed the armistice.

It was the end of the war on the battlefields and the beginning of the diplomatic bureaucratic war on the UN premises.

The End of the Six Days War

The Six Day War was a defeat for the Arab States, which lost more than half of their military equipment. The Jordanian Air Force was destroyed. The Arabs suffered 18 000 casualties, while on the Israeli side there were 766 casualties.

On the day after the conquest of the Sinai Peninsula, President Nasser of Egypt resigned because of his country's defeat (although he later reconsidered his decision). However, this defeat did not change the attitude of the Arab States towards Israel. In August 1967, Arab leaders met in Khartoum and announced a message of commitment to the world: they were not inclined towards diplomatic negotiations and the recognition of the State of Israel since it had caused their country great harm. Such war greatly amplified the aversion of the Islamic world towards the state of Israel. Many non – Arab countries that had never had friction with Israel ended up severing relations (as did all the other Arab countries).

As for Israel, it had achieved considerable results because of the war. The frontiers over which they had control were now larger and included the Golan Heights (whose control was shared with the Syrians), Transjordan, and the Sinai Peninsula (whose control was shared with the Egyptians). The control

DR MAITLAND PETER HYSLOP

of Jerusalem was of considerable importance to the Jewish people because of the historical and religious value, since the city had a two millennium Jewish history. Since then, over the centuries, Jerusalem had almost always been under the control of great empires such as the Byzantine, the Ottoman, and the British empires, and it was only after the war that it returned to be fully controlled by the Jewish state.

Because of the war, the 'Palestinians' fled their homes. As a result, the number of refugees in Jordan, and other neighbouring countries (especially Lebanon) increased. The conflict created 350 000 refugees, who were rejected by some neighbouring Arab states. Such refugees have constantly attacked the Israeli state in isolation from Transjordan, the Gaza Strip and even south Lebanon.

With the Israelis controlling the eastern shore of the Suez Canal, the naval route remained closed from 1967 until 1975. The fifteen ships that crossed the channel when the war broke out were stranded on the Great Bitter Lake and Lake Timsah.

Consequences

Syria lost the Golan Heights; Egypt lost the Gaza strip that it had occupied since 1948 and the area between the Sinai Peninsula and the Suez Canal. Although Israel hoped to negotiate a peace treaty, the Arab countries that gathered at the Khartoum conference, vehemently opposed any peace offerings.

However, the great powers and the UN proposed a compromise, Resolution 242: it established Israel's withdrawal from the occupied territories and the cessation of terrorist activities by the Palestinians. Israel adhered to it reluctantly, followed by Nasser and King Hussein of Jordan, while the Palestinians who had the support of Syria refused it, continuing their terrorist aggression towards Israel, which continues to this day.[75]

The War on Terror.

The War on Terror, also known as the Global War on Terrorism and U.S. War on Terror, is an international military campaign launched by the United States government after the 11 September 2001 attacks on the World Trade Centre in New York. The targets of the campaign are primarily Sunni Islamic fundamentalist armed groups located throughout the Muslim world, with the most prominent groups being Al-Qaeda, the Islamic State, the Taliban, Tehrik-i-Taliban Pakistan, and the various franchise groups of the former two organizations. The naming of the campaign uses a metaphor of war to refer to a variety of actions that do not constitute a specific war as traditionally defined. U.S. President George W. Bush first used the term "war on terrorism" on 16 September 2001, and then "war on terror" a few days later in a formal speech to Congress. In the latter speech, George Bush stated, *"Our enemy is a radical network of terrorists and every government that supports them"*. The term was originally used with a particular focus on countries associated with al-Qaeda. The term was immediately criticised by such people as Richard B. Myers, chairman of the Joint Chiefs of Staff, and more nuanced terms subsequently came to be used by the Bush administration to publicly define the international campaign led by the U.S. While it was never used as a formal designation of U.S. operations in internal government documentation, a Global War on Terrorism Service Medal was issued.

U.S. President Barack Obama announced on 23 May 2013 CE that the Global War on Terror was over, saying the military and intelligence agencies will not wage war against a tactic but will instead focus on a specific group of networks determined to destroy the U.S. On 28 December 2014 CE, the Obama administration announced the end of the combat role of the U.S.-led mission in Afghanistan. However, the U.S. continued to play a major role in the War in Afghanistan, and in 2017 CE, U.S. President Donald Trump expanded the American military presence in Afghanistan. The rise of the Islamic State of Iraq and the Levant (ISIL) led to the global Operation Inherent Resolve, and an international campaign to destroy ISIL.

According to a 2020 CE study conducted under the auspices of the Watson Institute for International and Public Affairs, the several wars initiated by the United States in its war against terror have caused the displacement, conservatively calculated, of 37 million people.

Criticism of the war on terror focused on its morality, efficiency, and cost; some, including President Barack Obama, objected to the phrase itself as a misnomer. The notion of a 'war' against 'terrorism' has proven contentious, with critics charging that it has been exploited by participating governments to pursue long-standing policy/military objectives, reduce civil liberties, and infringe upon human rights. Critics also assert that the term 'war' is not appropriate in this context (much like the term 'War on Drugs') since terror is not an identifiable enemy and it is unlikely that international terrorism can be brought to an end by military means. [76] [77] [78]

Section 2

The Middle East Today

CHAPTER 7:
RECENT ISSUES

Al Qaeda

During the 1979-1989 CE Soviet-Afghan War in Afghanistan, in which the Soviet Union gave support to the communist Afghan government, Muslim insurgents, known as the mujahideen, rallied to fight a jihad (or holy war) against the invaders. Among them was a Saudi Arabian, the 17th child (of 52) of a millionaire construction magnate, named Osama bin Laden, who provided the mujahideen with money, weapons and fighters.

Along with Abdullah Azzam, a Palestinian Sunni Islamic scholar, preacher and mentor of bin Laden, the men began to grow a large financial network, and when the Soviets withdrew from Afghanistan in 1989 CE, al-Qaeda was created to take on future holy wars. For Bin Laden, that was a fight he wanted to take globally.

Azzam, conversely, wanted to focus efforts on turning Afghanistan into an Islamist government. When he was assassinated in a car bombing in Pakistan in 1989 CE, bin Laden was left as the group's leader.

The al-Qaeda Network

Exiled by the Saudi regime, and later stripped of his citizenship in 1994 CE, bin Laden left Afghanistan and set up operations in Sudan, with the United States in his sights as enemy No. 1.

Al Qaeda took credit for the attack on two Black Hawk helicopters during the Battle of Mogadishu in Somalia in 1993 CE, as well as the World Trade Centre Bombing in New York in 1993 CE, and a car bombing in 1995 CE that destroyed a U.S.-leased military building in Saudi Arabia. In 1998 CE the group claimed responsibility for attacks on U.S. embassies in Kenya and Tanzania and, in 2000 CE, for the suicide bombings against the U.S.S. Cole in Yemen, in which 17 American sailors were killed, and 39 injured.

Expelled from Sudan in 1996 CE, bin Laden returned to Afghanistan under protection of the Taliban, where he provided military training to thousands of Muslim insurgents. In 1996 CE, he announced a *fatwa* against the United States, '*Declaration of War Against the Americans Occupying the Land of the Two Holy Places*', with a second declaration of *fatwa* issued in 1998 CE, citing protests against the United States, Israel and other allies.

'*The U.S. today, as a result of the arrogant atmosphere, has set a double standard, calling whoever goes against its injustice a terrorist*', bin Laden said in a 1997 CE interview with CNN, the U.S. cable news network. '*It wants to occupy our countries, steal our resources, impose on us agents to rule us, and then wants us to agree to all this*'.

According to the Council on Foreign Relations, the terrorist network's violent opposition of the United States stemmed from its support of 'infidel' governments, including those of Israel, Saudi Arabia and Egypt, along with the UN and America's involvement in the 1991 CE Persian Gulf War and in Somalia's 1992 – 1993 CE Operation Restore Hope mission.

'*In particular, al-Qaeda opposed the continued presence of American military forces in Saudi Arabia (and elsewhere on the Saudi Arabian Peninsula) following the Gulf War*', the Council reports, adding that '*al-Qaeda opposed the United States Government because of the arrest, conviction and imprisonment of persons be-*

longing to al-Qaeda or its affiliated terrorist groups or those with whom it worked. For these and other reasons, Bin Laden declared a jihad, or holy war, against the United States, which he has carried out through al-Qaeda and its affiliated organizations'.

The U.S. Led War on Terror

After 11 September 2011 CE, when four passenger airplanes were hijacked by al-Qaeda terrorists, resulting in the mass murder of 2 977 victims in New York, Washington, D.C., and Somerset County, Pennsylvania, Bin Laden was named as the orchestrator and prime suspect.

The attacks led to the U.S. War in Afghanistan, a.k.a. Operation Enduring Freedom, launched on 7 October 2001 CE, driving bin Laden's protector, the Taliban, from power, although the war continued. Bin Laden was forced into hiding; he had an FBI-issued $25 million bounty on his head. Bin Laden evaded authorities until 2 May 2011 CE, when a covert operation by U.S. Navy SEALs, shot and killed the terrorist leader at a private compound in Abbottabad, Pakistan.[79]

The Arab Spring

The Arab Spring was a series of anti-government protests, up-risings, and armed rebellions that spread across much of the Arab world in the early 2010s. It began in response to oppressive regimes and a low standard of living, starting with protests in Tunisia. From Tunisia, the protests then spread to five other countries: Libya, Egypt, Yemen, Syria, and Bahrain, where either the ruler was deposed (Zine El Abidine Ben Ali, Muammar Qaddafi, Hosni Mubarak, and Ali Abdullah Saleh) or major uprisings and social violence occurred including riots, civil wars, or insurgencies. Sustained street demonstrations took place in Morocco, Iraq, Algeria, Iran, Lebanon, Jordan, Kuwait, Oman, and Sudan. Minor protests took place in Djibouti, Mauritania, Palestine, Saudi Arabia, and the Moroccan-occupied Western Sahara. A major slogan of the demonstrators in the Arab world is *ash-sha'b yurīd isqāṭ an-niẓām!* (*'the people want to bring down the regime'*).

The importance of external factors versus internal factors to the protests' spread and success is contested. Social media is one-way governments try to inhibit protests. In many countries, governments shut down certain sites or blocked Internet service entirely, especially in the times preceding a major rally. Governments also accused content creators, such as Facebook, of unrelated crimes or shutting down communication on specific sites or groups. In the news, social media has been heralded as the driving force behind the swift spread of revolution throughout the world, as new protests appear in response to success stories shared from those taking place in other countries.

The wave of initial revolutions and protests faded by mid-2012, as many Arab Spring demonstrations met with violent responses from authorities, as well as from pro-government militias, counterdemonstrators, and militaries. These attacks were answered with violence from protesters in some cases. Large-scale conflicts resulted:

- The Syrian Civil War.
- The rise of ISIL.
- Insurgency in Iraq and the following civil war.
- The Egyptian Crisis, coup, and subsequent unrest and insurgency.
- The Libyan Civil War.
- Yemeni Crisis and following civil war.

Regimes that lacked major oil wealth and hereditary succession arrangements were more likely to undergo regime change.

A power struggle continued after the immediate response to

the Arab Spring. While leadership changed and regimes were held accountable, power vacuums opened across the Arab world. Ultimately, it resulted in a contentious battle between a consolidation of power by religious elites and the growing support for democracy in many Muslim-majority states. The early hopes that these popular movements would end corruption, increase political participation, and bring about greater economic equity quickly collapsed in the wake of the counter-revolutionary moves by foreign state actors in Yemen, the regional and international military interventions in Bahrain and Yemen, and the destructive civil wars in Syria, Iraq, Libya, and Yemen.

Some have referred to the succeeding and still ongoing conflicts as the Arab Winter. As of May 2018, only the uprising in Tunisia has resulted in a transition to constitutional democratic governance. Recent uprisings in Sudan and Algeria show that the conditions that started the Arab Spring have not faded and political movements against authoritarianism and exploitation are still occurring. In 2019, multiple uprisings and protest movements in Algeria, Sudan, Iraq, Lebanon, and Egypt have been seen as a continuation of the Arab Spring.

In 2020, multiple conflicts are still continuing that might be seen as a result of the Arab Spring. The Syrian Civil War has caused massive political instability and economic hardship in Syria, with the Syrian currency plunging to new lows. In Libya, a major civil war is ongoing, with Western powers and Russia sending in proxy fighters. In Yemen, a civil war continues to affect the country. In Lebanon, a major banking crisis is threatening that country's economy as well as that of neighbouring Syria.[80]

ISIL

The history of the Islamic State of Iraq and the Levant (ISIL) began with the group's foundation in 1999 CE by Jordanian Salafi jihadist Abu Musab al-Zarqawi under the name *Jamā'at al-Tawḥīd wa-al-Jihād* (translated as: *'The Organisation of Monotheism and Jihad'*). In a letter published by the U.S. State Department in February 2004 CE, Zarqawi wrote that jihadists should use bombings to start an open sectarian war in Iraq so that Sunnis from other countries would mobilize against the assassinations carried out by Shias, specifically the Badr Organisation, against Ba'athists and Sunnis. The Islamic State would eventually grow to control territory with a population of millions.

U.S. Colonel Derek Harvey told Reuters that, *"the U.S. military detained Badr assassination teams possessing target lists of Sunni officers and pilots in 2003 and 2004 but did not hold them"*. Harvey said his superiors told him that, *"this stuff had to play itself out"*; implying that revenge attacks by returning Shiite groups were to be expected. Jerry Burke, a U.S. adviser to the Iraqi Interior Ministry, said that in 2005 CE a plan from him and several colleagues to surveill and stop suspected Badr Brigade death squads in the special police forces was rejected when it got to an American Flag (General) Officer.

Following the 2003 CE invasion of Iraq by Western forces, al-Zarqawi and *Jama'at al-Tawhid wal-Jihad* achieved notoriety in the early stages of the Iraqi insurgency for their suicide attacks on Shia mosques, civilians, Iraqi government institutions and Italian soldiers of the U.S.-led 'Multi-National Force'.

In October 2004 CE, when al-Zarqawi swore loyalty to Osama bin Laden and al-Qaeda, he renamed the group *Tanzīm Qā'idat al-Jihād fī Bilād al-Rāfidayn* (translated as: *'The Organisation of Jihad's Base in Mesopotamia'*), commonly known as al-Qaeda in Iraq (AQI). Although the group never called itself *al-Qaeda in Iraq*, this remained its informal name for many years. Attacks by the group on civilians, Iraqi government forces, foreign diplomats and soldiers, and American convoys continued with roughly the same intensity. In a letter to al-Zarqawi in July 2005 CE, al-Qaeda's then deputy leader Ayman al-Zawahiri outlined a four-stage plan to expand the Iraq War. The plan included expelling U.S forces from Iraq, establishing an Islamic authority as a caliphate, spreading the conflict to Iraq's secular neighbours, and clashing with Israel, which the letter said, *'[...] was established only to challenge any new Islamic entity'.*

In January 2006 CE, AQI joined with several smaller Iraqi Sunni insurgent groups under an umbrella organisation called the Mujahideen Shura Council (MSC). The merger was an attempt to give the group a more Iraqi flavour, and perhaps to distance al-Qaeda from some of al-Zarqawi's tactical errors, such as the 2005 CE bombings by AQI of three hotels in Amman. On 7 June 2006 CE, a U.S airstrike killed al-Zarqawi, who was succeeded as leader of the group by the Egyptian militant Abu Ayyub al-Masri.

On 12 October 2006 CE, MSC united with three smaller groups and six Sunni tribes to form the Mutayibeen Coalition, pledging *'To rid Sunnis from the oppression of the rejectionists (Shi'ite Muslims) and the crusader occupiers ... to restore rights even at the price of our own lives ... to make Allah's word supreme in the world, and to restore the glory of Islam'.* A day later, MSC declared the establishment of the Islamic State of Iraq (ISI), comprising Iraq's six mostly Sunni Arab governorates, with Abu Omar al-Baghdadi its emir and al-Masri Minister of War within ISI's ten-member cabinet.

According to a study compiled by U.S. intelligence agencies in early 2007 CE, ISI planned to seize power in the central and western areas of Iraq and turn it into a Sunni caliphate. The group improved in strength and at its height enjoyed a significant presence in the Iraqi governorates of Al Anbar, Diyala and Baghdad, claiming Baqubah as a capital city.

The Iraq War troop surge of 2007 CE supplied the U.S. military with more manpower for operations, and dozens of high-level AQI members being captured or killed. Between July and October 2007 CE, al-Qaeda in Iraq was reported to have lost its secure military bases in Al Anbar province and the Baghdad area. During 2008 CE, a series of U.S. and Iraqi offensives managed to drive out AQI-aligned insurgents from their former safe havens, such as the Diyala and Al Anbar governorates, to the area of the northern city of Mosul.

By 2008 CE, the ISI was describing itself as being in a state of 'extraordinary crisis'. Its violent attempts to govern territory led to a backlash from Sunni Arab Iraqis and other insurgent groups and a temporary decline in the group, which was attributable to a number of factors, notably the Anbar Awakening.

In late 2009 CE, the commander of U.S. forces in Iraq, General Ray Odierno, stated that ISI *'has transformed significantly in the last two years. What once was dominated by foreign individuals has now become more and more dominated by Iraqi citizens.* On 18 April 2010 CE, ISI's two top leaders, al-Masri and Omar al-Baghdadi, were killed in a joint U.S-Iraqi raid near Tikrit. In a press conference in June 2010 CE, General Odierno reported that 80% of ISI's top 42 leaders, including recruiters and financiers, had been killed or captured, with only eight remaining at large. He said that they had been cut off from al-Qaeda's leadership in Pakistan.

On 16 May 2010 CE, Abu Bakr al-Baghdadi was appointed the new leader of ISI. Al-Baghdadi replenished the group's leadership by appointing former Iraqi military and Intelligence Service officers who had served during Saddam Hussein's rule. These men, nearly all of whom had spent time imprisoned by the U.S. military at Camp Bucca, came to make up about one third of Baghdadi's top 25 commanders, including Abu Abdulrahman al-Bilawi, Abu Ayman al-Iraqi, and Abu Muslim al-Turkmani. One of them, a former colonel called Samir al-Khlifawi, also known as Haji Bakr, became the overall military commander in charge of overseeing the group's operations. Al-Khlifawi was instrumental in doing the groundwork that led to the growth of ISIL.

In July 2012 CE, al-Baghdadi released an audio statement online announcing that the group was returning to former strongholds from which U.S. troops and the Sons of Iraq had driven them in 2007 and 2008. He declared the start of a new offensive in Iraq called *Breaking the Walls*, aimed at freeing members of the group held in Iraqi prisons. Violence in Iraq had begun to escalate in June 2012 CE, primarily with AQI's car bomb attacks, and by July 2013 CE, monthly fatalities exceeded 1 000.

In March 2011 CE, protests began in Syria against the Syrian government of Bashar al-Assad. In the following months, violence between demonstrators and security forces led to a gradual militarisation of the conflict. In August 2011 CE, following the outbreak of the Syrian Civil War, al-Baghdadi began sending Syrian and Iraqi ISI members experienced in guerrilla warfare across the border into Syria to establish an organisation there. Under the name *Jabhat an-Nuṣrah li-Ahli ash-Shām* (or al-Nusra Front), it established a large presence in Sunni-majority Raqqa, Idlib, Deir ez-Zor, and Aleppo provinces. Led by a Syrian known as Abu Muhammad al-Julani, this group began to recruit fighters and establish cells throughout the country.

On 23 January 2012 CE, the Syrian group called itself *Jabhat al-Nusra li Ahl as-Sham*, more commonly known as the al-Nusra Front. Al-Nusra grew rapidly into a capable fighting force, with popular support among Syrians opposed to the Assad government.

On 8 April 2013 CE, al-Baghdadi released an audio statement in which he announced that the al-Nusra Front had been established, financed, and supported by ISI, and that the two groups were merging under the name Islamic State of Iraq and al-

Sham (ISIL, Al-Sham also translates as the Levant). However, Abu Mohammad al-Julani and Ayman al-Zawahiri, the leaders of al-Nusra and al-Qaeda respectively, rejected the merger. Al-Julani issued a statement denying the merger and complaining that neither he nor anyone else in al-Nusra's leadership had been consulted about it. In June 2013 CE, Al Jazeera (the Qatari News Agency) reported that it had obtained a letter written by al-Qaeda's leader Ayman al-Zawahiri, addressed to both leaders, in which he ruled against the merger, and appointed an emissary to oversee relations between them to put an end to tensions. That same month, al-Baghdadi released an audio message rejecting al-Zawahiri's ruling and declaring that the merger was going ahead.

Meanwhile, the ISIL campaign to free its imprisoned members culminated in simultaneous raids on Taji and Abu Ghraib prisons in July 2013 CE, freeing more than 500 prisoners, many of them veterans of the Iraqi insurgency. In October 2013 CE, al-Zawahiri ordered the disbanding of ISIL, putting al-Nusra Front in charge of jihadist efforts in Syria, but al-Baghdadi rejected al-Zawahiri's order, and his group continued to operate in Syria. In February 2014 CE, after an eight-month power struggle, al-Qaeda publicly disavowed any relations with ISIL.

According to some there are significant differences between al-Nusra Front and ISIL. While al-Nusra actively calls for the overthrow of the Assad government, ISIL tends to be more focused on establishing its own rule on conquered territory. ISIL is far more ruthless in building an Islamic state, carrying out sectarian attacks and imposing Sharia law immediately. While al-Nusra has a large contingent of foreign fighters, it is seen as a home-grown group by many Syrians; by contrast, ISIL fighters have been described as foreign occupiers by many Syrian refugees. Foreign fighters in Syria include Russian-speaking jihadists who were part of Jaish al-Muhajireen wal-Ansar (JMA). In November 2013 CE, Abu Omar al-

Shishani, leader of the Jaish al-Muhajireen wal-Ansar (JMA), swore an oath of allegiance to al-Baghdadi; the group then split between those who followed al-Shishani in joining ISIL and those who continued to operate independently in the JMA under new leadership.

In January 2014 CE, rebels affiliated with the Islamic Front and the U.S-trained Free Syrian Army launched an offensive against ISIL militants in and around the city of Aleppo, following months of tensions over ISIL's behaviour, which included the seizure of property and weapons from rebel groups, and the arrests and killings of activists. Months of clashes ensued, causing thousands of casualties, with ISIL withdrawing its forces from Idlib and Latakia provinces and redeploying them to reinforce its strongholds in Raqqa and Aleppo. It also against all other opposition forces active in the eastern province of Deir ez-Zor, on the border with Iraq. By June 2014 CE, ISIL had largely defeated its rivals in the province, with many who had not been killed or driven away pledging allegiance to it.

In Iraq, ISIL was able to capture most of Fallujah in January 2014 CE, and in June 2014 CE was able to seize control of Mosul.

After an eight-month power struggle, al-Qaeda cut all ties with ISIL by February 2014 CE, citing its failure to consult and "notorious intransigence".

In early 2014 CE, ISIL drove Iraqi government forces out of key cities in its Anbar campaign, which was followed by the capture of Mosul and the Sinjar massacre. The loss of control almost caused a collapse of the Iraqi government and prompted a renewal of U.S. military action in Iraq. In Syria, ISIL has conducted ground attacks on both the Syrian Arab Army and rebel factions.

On 29 June 2014 CE, ISIL proclaimed itself to be a worldwide caliphate. Abu Bakr al-Baghdadi, known by his supporters as Amir al-Mu'minin, Caliph Ibrahim – was named its caliph, and the group renamed itself *ad-Dawlah al-Islāmiyah ('Islamic State' (IS))*. As a 'Caliphate', it claimed religious, political and military authority over all Muslims worldwide. The concept of it being a caliphate and the name 'Islamic State' have been rejected by governments and Muslim leaders worldwide.

In June and July 2014 CE, Jordan and Saudi Arabia moved at least 30,000 troops to their borders with Iraq, after the Iraqi government lost control of (or withdrew from) strategic crossing points that were captured by either ISIL or tribes that supported it. There was speculation that Iraqi Prime Minister- Nouri al-Maliki had ordered a withdrawal of troops from the Iraq–Saudi crossings in order 'to increase pressure on Saudi Arabia and bring the threat of ISIS over-running its borders as well'.

In July 2014 CE, ISIL recruited more than 6,300 fighters, according to the Syrian Observatory for Human Rights, some of whom were thought to have previously fought for the Free Syrian Army. On 23 July 2014 CE, Abu Sayyaf leader Isnilon Totoni Hapilon and some masked men swore loyalty to al-Baghdadi in a video, giving ISIL a presence in the Philippines. In September 2014 CE, the group began kidnapping people for ransom.

In 2016 CE, according to the daily, La Stampa, officials from Europol conducted an investigation into the trafficking of fake documents for ISIL. They have identified fake Syrian passports in the refugee camps in Greece that were destined to supposed members of ISIL, in order to avoid Greek government controls and make their way to other parts of Europe. Also, the chief of Europol said that a new task force of 200 counter terrorism officers will be deployed to the Greek islands alongside Greek border guards in order to help Greece thwart a 'strategic' level campaign by Islamic State to infiltrate terrorists into Europe.

In early May 2019 CE, after almost 5 years since his last public appearance in the summer of 2014 CE, al-Baghdadi appeared in a video declaring his organisation's new geographical ambitions. After the loss of the territories it had once occupied in the Levant and the crumbling of the 'Caliphate' project, the leader of the group boasted in his speech of 'new oaths of allegiance extended to him from jihadis in Mali, Burkina Faso, Afghanistan, and Sri Lanka' as well as in Turkey. According to Syrian-American journalist Hassan Hassan, in a comment in *'Foreign Policy'* magazine, *"Baghdadi's video marks the failure of the U.S.-led coalition to capture Baghdadi and dismantle his organization. It demonstrates the health of both Baghdadi and his organization, refuting recent rumours that he was ailing, and allows them to boast about a major terrorist attack, their expansion to new places, and the recruitment of new members"*.

On 3 August 2014 CE, ISIL captured the cities of Zumar, Sinjar and Wana in northern Iraq. Thousands of Yazidis fled up Mount Sinjar, fearful of the approaching hostile ISIL militants. The stranded Yazidis' need for food and water, the threat of genocide to them and to others announced by ISIL, along with the desire to protect U.S. citizens in Iraq and support the Iraqi government in its fight against ISIL, were all reasons given for the 2014 CE American intervention in Iraq, which began on 7 August. A U.S. aerial bombing campaign began the following day.

At the end of October 2014 CE, 800 militants gained partial control of the Libyan city of Derna and pledged their allegiance to Abu Bakr al-Baghdadi, thus making Derna the first city outside Syria and Iraq to be a part of the 'Islamic State Caliphate'. On 10 November 2014 CE, a major faction of the Egyptian militant group Ansar Bait al-Maqdis also pledged its allegiance to ISIL. In mid-January 2015 CE, a Yemeni official said that ISIL had 'dozens' of members in Yemen, and that they were coming into direct competition with al-Qaeda in the Arabian Peninsula because of their recruitment drive. The same month, Afghan officials confirmed that ISIL had a military presence in Afghanistan. However, by February 2015 CE, 65 of the militants were either captured or killed by the Taliban, and ISIL's top Afghan recruiter, Mullah Abdul Rauf, was killed in a U.S. drone strike.

In early February 2015 CE, ISIL militants in Libya managed to capture part of the countryside to the west of Sabha, and later, an area encompassing the cities of Sirte, Nofolia, and a military base to the south of both cities. By March, ISIL had captured additional territory, including a city to the west of Derna, additional areas near Sirte, a stretch of land in southern Libya, some areas around Benghazi, and an area to the east of Tripoli.

On 7 March 2015 CE, Boko Haram swore formal allegiance to ISIL, giving ISIL an official presence in Nigeria, Niger, Chad and Cameroon. On 13 March 2015 CE, a group of militants from the Islamic Movement of Uzbekistan swore allegiance to IS-IL; the group released another video on 31 July 2015 CE showing its spiritual leader also pledging allegiance. In June 2015 CE, the U.S. Deputy Secretary of State announced that ISIL had lost more than 10,000 members in airstrikes over the preceding nine months.

Since 2015 CE, ISIL lost territory in Iraq and Syria, including Tikrit in March and April 2015 CE, Baiji in October, Sinjar in November 2015 CE, Ramadi in December 2015 CE, Fallujah in June 2016 CE and Palmyra in March 2017 CE, the latter by a Russia-Syria-Iran-Iraq coalition.

On 10 July 2017 CE, Iraqi Prime Minister Abadi formally declared a local Iraqi victory over ISIL in the recent Iraqi army expulsion of ISIL from the city of Mosul. Since the fall of ISIL in Mosul, the overall extent of ISIL held territory in both Syria and Iraq has significantly diminished. On 17 October 2017 CE, ISIL lost control of Raqqa in the second battle of Raqqa. On 3 November, Deir ez-Zor, ISIL's last major city in Syria, was recaptured, and Rawa, the last town held by ISIL in Iraq, was captured on 17 November.

On 21 November 2017 CE, Iranian president Hassan Rouhani declared victory over ISIL. Qasem Soleimani, senior military officer of the Guardians of the Islamic Revolution, wrote to Iran's supreme leader Ali Khamenei that ISIL had been defeated. Vladimir Putin, President of Russia, declared victory over ISIL in Syria as well. Iraqi prime minister, Haider al-Abadi, also announced the military defeat of ISIL in Iraq.

On 23 November 2018 CE, Britain's Chief of the General Staff General Mark Carleton-Smith said that the *"physical manifestation of the Islamist threat has diminished with the complete destruction of the geography of the so-called Caliphate."*

On 19 December 2018 CE, U.S. president Donald Trump declared ISIL to have been defeated. The UK's junior Defence Minister Tobias Ellwood said that he strongly disagreed with Trump that ISIL had been defeated. German Foreign Minister- Heiko Maas said that IS has been pushed back but the threat is not yet over. There is a danger that the consequences of Trump's Syria withdrawal will damage the fight against IS and jeopardise the successes already achieved. The U.S.-backed *Syrian Democratic Forces* declared military victory over ISIL on 23 March 2019 CE following the Battle of Baghuz Fawqani, although the group maintains a scattered presence and sleeper cells across Syria and Iraq.

Beginning primarily in 2017 CE, as the Islamic State lost more swathes of territory and lost control over major settlements and cities, the group increasingly resorted to more terror bombings and insurgency operations, using its scattered underground networks of sleeper cells across regions in the Middle East and various offshoots and adherents. The collapse of its final Middle Eastern territories in 2019 CE after the Battle of Baghuz Fawqani propelled the group into full insurgency phase in the regions it once controlled, while retaining influence via propaganda efforts and in remote hideouts, such as in the Syrian Desert.

In July 2019 CE, UN analysts on the Security Council Counter-Terrorism Committee warned al-Baghdadi was plotting a comeback from Iraq. He could launch international terrorist attacks before the end of the year in European nations. By 7 October 2019 CE, it was thought that ISIL could re-emerge with the withdrawal of American troops from the region.

On 27 October 2019 CE, al-Baghdadi was targeted by U.S. military and died after he detonated a suicide vest in Barisha, Idlib, Northwest Syria. Trump confirmed in a televised announcement from the White House later that day that al-Baghdadi had died during a raid by U.S. special forces in Idlib. (This is the formal version of events.)

In September 2019 CE, a statement attributed to ISIL's propaganda arm, the Amaq news agency, claimed that Abdullah Qardash was named as al-Baghdadi's successor. Analysts dismissed this statement as a fabrication, and relatives were reported as saying that Qardash died in 2017 CE. Terrorist analysts noted that the alleged statement used a different font when compared to other statements and it was never distributed on Amaq or ISIL channels.

On 29 October 2019 CE, Trump stated on social media that al-Baghdadi's number one replacement had been killed by American forces, adding: *"Most likely would have taken the top spot - now he is also dead"*. While Trump did not specify a name, a U.S. official later confirmed that Trump was referring ISIL spokesman and senior leader Abul-Hasan al-Muhajir, who was killed in a U.S. airstrike in Syria two days earlier. Less than a week after the death of Abu Bakr al-Baghdadi on 31 October, ISIL named Abu Ibrahim al Hashimi al-Qurayshi as Baghdadi's successor, indicating that the group still considers itself a caliphate despite having lost all of its territory in Iraq and Syria. Two other individuals close to Baghdadi and believed to have been present in his last video appearance, the Saudi Abu Saleh al-Juzrawi and the Tunisian Abu Othman al-Tunsi, were also named as possible candidates to succeed Abu Bakr al-Baghdadi. In April 2021 CE Russian forces killed dozens of Islamic State militants in a series of air strikes following the Islamic State's killing of two Russian pilots.

ISIL claimed responsibility for a number of high-profile terrorist attacks outside Iraq and Syria, including a mass shooting at a Tunisian tourist resort (38 European tourists killed), the Suruç bombing in Turkey (33 leftist and pro-Kurdish activists killed), the Tunisian National Museum attack (24 foreign tourists and Tunisians killed), the Sana'a mosque bombings (142 Shia civilians killed), the crash of Metrojet Flight 9268 (224 killed, mostly Russian tourists), the bombings in Ankara (102 pro-Kurdish and leftist activists killed), the bombings in Beirut (43 Shia civilians killed), the November 2015 Paris attacks (130 civilians killed), the killing of Jaafar Mohammed Saad, the Governor of Aden, the January 2016 CE Istanbul bombing (11 foreign tourists killed), the 2016 Brussels bombings (32 civilians killed), the 2016 Atatürk Airport attack (48 foreign and Turkish civilians killed), the 2016 CE Nice truck attack (86 civilians killed), the July 2016 CE Kabul bombing (at least 80 civilians killed, mostly Shia Hazaras), the 2016 CE Berlin truck attack (12 civilians killed), the 2017 CE Istanbul nightclub shooting (39 foreigners and Turks killed), the 2017 CE Saint Petersburg Metro bombing (15 civilians killed), the 2017 CE Manchester Arena bombing (22 civilians killed), the 2017 CE Catalonia attacks (16 civilians killed), the 2017 CE Tehran attacks (18 civilians killed), 13 July 2018 CE Pakistan bombings (at least 131 killed).

The Saudi Arabian government reported that in one relatively short period, the first eight months of 2016 CE, there were 25 attacks in the kingdom by ISIL.

On 30 August 2016 CE, a survey conducted by the Associated Press found that around 72 mass graves have been discovered in areas that have been liberated from ISIL control. In total, these mass graves contain the bodies of approximately 15,000 people killed by ISIL. The report stated that the mass graves were evidence of genocides conducted by ISIL in the region, including the genocide of Yazidis. Seventeen graves were discovered in Syria, with the rest being found in Iraq. At least 16 of the graves in Iraq contained remains that were not counted, as they are located in dangerous conflict zones. Instead, the number of dead in these graves has been estimated.

On 6 November 2018 CE, a United Nations report revealed over 200 mass graves of thousands of ISIL's victims were discovered. The grave sites, which may contain up to 12,000 bodies, were found in the northern and western Iraqi provinces of Nineveh, Kirkuk, Salah al-Din and Anbar.

For Sunnis ISIL has been a disaster. It could have been so much different. Had the leadership been less religiously extreme, more tolerant to those it invaded, more pragmatic in dealing with other countries and other related groups such as al-Qaeda, it could have been a huge success. It was financed, at least in part, by wealthy Gulf State individuals and, according to some, Governments too. For Shias ISIL has been a disaster too. The brutality with which Shias were treated was on a par and often exceeded the extremes of the Taliban in Afghanistan. For Islam it was a disaster because Islam means submission to God not to some gang. For the rest of the world it has also been a disaster in terms of stoking Islamic terrorism and conflict everywhere from the Philippines to the Sahel. The 'state' is not dead, it is not defeated, it is still there being reformed. [81]

The Abraham Accords.

The Abraham Accords are a joint statement between Israel, the United Arab Emirates, and the U.S., reached on 13 August 2020 CE. Subsequently, the term was used to refer collectively to agreements between Israel and the United Arab Emirates (the Israel–United Arab Emirates normalization agreement) and Bahrain, respectively (the Bahrain–Israel normalization agreement). Note: Bahrain is unlikely to have signed these without Saudi Arabia's prior knowledge.

The statement marked the first public normalization of relations between an Arab country and Israel since that of Egypt in 1979 and Jordan in 1994. The original Abraham Accords were signed by the Emirati Foreign Minister Abdullah bin Zayed Al Nahyan, the Bahraini Foreign Minister Abdullatif bin Rashid Al Zayani, Israeli Prime Minister Benjamin Netanyahu, and U.S. President Donald Trump on 15 September 2020 CE, at the South Lawn of the White House in Washington, D.C. The Accords were negotiated by Jared Kushner and Avi Berkowitz.

The agreement with the UAE was officially titled the '*Abraham Accords Peace Agreement: Treaty of Peace, Diplomatic Relations and Full Normalization Between the United Arab Emirates and the State of Israel*'. The agreement between Bahrain and Israel was officially titled the '*Abraham Accords: Declaration of Peace, Co-operation, and Constructive Diplomatic and Friendly Relations*', and was announced by the U.S. on 11 September 2020 CE.

The Accords are named after Abraham to emphasize the shared origin of belief between Judaism and Islam, both of which are Abrahamic religions that strictly espouse the monotheistic worship of the God of Abraham. (See Chapter 4).

The signing of the Abraham Accords between Israel, the UAE and Bahrain was heralded as a historic breakthrough promoting economic, technological, scientific and cultural ties between former enemies, building a strong coalition to confront Iran and debunking the conventional wisdom that peace between Israel and her Arab neighbours would only come after the Palestinian conflict with Israel was resolved.

The Abraham Accords may also weaken Beijing's considerable influence in the region, especially in Israel.

Chinese President Xi Jinping envisions a future in which China replaces the U.S. as the dominant world power. Beijing's Belt and Road Initiative (BRI), a $1 trillion program to invest in and acquire infrastructure projects in more than 100 countries around the world, and the 'Made in China 2025' initiative to make the country the undisputed leader in global hi-tech, are both designed to further this ambition. Note: In the Middle East all countries have agreed that China is not a tormentor of its Muslim minorities.

China is Israel's second-largest trading partner and source of foreign investment after the U.S. Sino-Israeli trade in 2018 CE was over $15 billion, more than 40 times greater than 23 years earlier. Chinese investment in Israeli hi-tech doubled to $1 billion from 2014 CE to 2016 CE. Chinese venture capital investments in Israeli start-ups more than quadrupled from 2013 CE to 2018 CE.

China's investments are strategic, focused on artificial intelligence, biotechnology, robotics, machine learning, quantum and edge computing, and big data — technologies that are essential to China's military modernization efforts. In 2017 CE, President Xi and Israeli Prime Minister Benjamin Netanyahu announced the Innovative Comprehensive Partnership to foster cooperation and exchanges of technological personnel. With Beijing accounting for 10%-15% of Israel's economy, it holds considerable leverage over the Jewish state.

The Trump administration warned Israel about allowing China's involvement in critical projects such as the Haifa and Ashdod ports and Tel Aviv's subway system, while also raising concerns about the danger of Chinese espionage and theft of technical expertise. As a result, the Israeli government rejected China's bid to build the country's largest desalination plant and is expected to decline Huawei's bid on a 5G network.

Then-Secretary of State Mike Pompeo said, *"We don't want the Chinese Communist Party to have access to Israeli infrastructure,*

Israeli communication networks, things that endanger the Israeli people and the ability of the U.S. to cooperate with Israel".

The U.S. shares a vast quantity of sensitive information with Israel and is rightly concerned with Chinese espionage and intellectual property theft. Israeli security experts share this fear, especially now that Beijing plans to invest hundreds of billions in infrastructure projects in Iran, Israel's mortal enemy, and also coordinate on intelligence and weapons development with Tehran.

The Abraham Accords give Israelis new options to reduce their dependency on China.

The world's fourth largest port operator, UAE-based DP World together with Israel's Dover Tower are preparing a joint bid to operate the important Port of Haifa, exclusive of the new container terminal operated by the Shanghai International Port Group.

It is estimated that $1 billion in investments between Israel and the UAE were made in the last two months of 2020 CE. In October, the Trump administration, Israel and the UAE announced the creation of the Abraham Fund which is planning to invest as much as $3 billion in various private sector projects. The fund is already financing an Israeli company constructing an oil pipeline from the UAE to Europe.

The UAE's Masdar, wholly owned by the Mubadala Investment Fund, one of the largest in the world, recently announced its first investment in Israeli renewable energy. Although Saudi Arabia has not as yet joined the Accords, its Crown Prince views Israeli technologies as useful for the economic transformation of his country.

Previously, Middle Eastern countries traded heavily with China, but very little among themselves. The Abraham Accords will help to reverse this imbalance, with Israel and the UAE, among the region's top three sources and destinations for foreign investment (Saudi Arabia being the third) offering each other an alternative to Chinese capital.

Asked whether discouraging Israel from relying on Chinese investments was a consideration in the Abraham Fund's founding, a State Department source said, *'Reducing dependence on the Chinese Communist Party is a good thing'.*

According to U.S. CENTCOM commander Gen. Kenneth F. McKenzie Jr., the Abraham Accords will most likely facilitate a long-term U.S. ambition — *'a collective approach to security'* in which the countries in the region can increasingly ensure their own security and stability. This would allow the U.S. to shift forces to other theatres while preserving its regional influence. An America perpetually bogged down in the Middle East works to China's advantage.

It is not yet clear if the Biden administration recognizes the important opportunities the Abraham Accords offer to thwart China's Middle East initiative. Hopefully, it will understand the strategic value of the Israel-Sunni alliance. This is so far unknown.

The reinstatement of a 10% aluminium tariff on imports from the UAE, one of the largest aluminium producers in the world, and the U.S. suspension and 'review' of the previously approved sale of F-35 aircraft to the Emiratis are guaranteed to raise concerns about the reliability of any alliance with America.

The U.S. refusing to support offensive operations in Yemen where the UAE is part of the Saudi-led coalition fighting the Iran-backed Houthis, the revoking of the Houthis' terrorist designation, along with the pause of a Saudi Arabia munitions sale, and mixed messages on the Iran nuclear deal, all endanger the agreement.

The Biden administration may need to build on the opportunities to strengthen and expand the Israel-Sunni alliance —

Morocco and Sudan have recently joined the Accords and Saudi Arabia is likely to join soon (although by mid-2021 this was by no means certain) — and use the strategic gains from the Abraham Accords to check the power of China and Iran in this critically important region.

Peace between Israel and her Arab neighbours is a win-win, both for the U.S. and for the Middle East.

Israel and Palestine

Issues between Israel and Palestine are also covered elsewhere in this book. However, it is worth summarising the current situation.

In May 2021 CE fears of a full-scale war grew as Israel continued its relentless airstrikes on Gaza, while Palestinian militants fire rockets into Tel Aviv. The latest outbreak of violence has been the heaviest between the two sides since 2014 CE. Clashes began after more than 300 people were injured after Israeli police stormed into East Jerusalem's al-Aqsa mosque during the holy month of Ramadan.

Officers fired tear gas, rubber coated bullets and stun grenades, claiming they were trying to *'restore order'* following the *'rioting of thousands of worshippers'* after evening prayers. Tensions have been mounting for weeks over a now-delayed Israeli court ruling on whether dozens of Palestinians could be evicted from the Old City's Sheikh Jarrah neighbourhood to make way for Jewish settlers. Airstrikes have reportedly killed 43 people in Gaza, inducing 13 children, while six people have been killed in Israel.

But this is just one of many rounds of bloodshed in a decades-long dispute over land and self-determination.

Violence between both sides relates to Israel's half-century military occupation of Palestine and its expansion of Jewish settlements on Palestinian land. Many countries agree that these settlements are illegal, but Israel denies this and encourages settlers to move to the West Bank with economic perks, including tax exemptions. Palestine wants to be an independent state with East Jerusalem as its capital, which is currently occupied. But Israel views the whole city as its capital, with only the U.S. and a handful of other countries recognising this claim. There have been numerous attempts to negotiate peace and a two-state solution, but the boundary between the two countries is still in dispute. Palestinians have proposed 1967 CE borders, referring to armistice lines from before the Six Day War, when Israel captured the Gaza Strip from Egypt, the West Bank and East Jerusalem from Jordan and expanded its territory beyond the borders agreed upon in 1949 CE. However, Israel has rejected this proposal in the past as unrealistic and indefensible. The chances of reaching a solution look increasingly remote, after decades of on-off violence between both sides.

Israelis celebrate Jerusalem Day on 7 June, marking the Israelis gaining control of the Old City following the 1967 CE Six Day War

After World War I Britain took control of the area known as Palestine after defeating the Ottoman Empire. The land was inhabited by an Arab majority and a Jewish minority, and for a while both groups coexisted in relative peace. But tensions mounted when Britain took on the task of establishing a 'national home' for the Jewish people, issued through the Balfour Declaration in 1917 CE. Both the Arabs and the Jews claim the region as their ancestral home, and as more Jews arrived between the 1920s CE and 1940s CE, violence between both groups and British rule grew. In 1947 CE the UN voted for Palestine to be split into two states, one for the Jews and one for the Arabs, with Jerusalem as an international city. Jewish leaders accepted the proposal but it was rejected by the Arabs and never materialised. In 1948 CE British rulers left and Jewish leaders declared the state of Israel, which led to neighbouring Arab countries launching an attack the following day.

Around 700 000 Palestinian (i.e. Ex Jordan West Bank and Ex Egyptian Sinai) Arabs fled or were forced out of their homes and became refugees, and by the time the war was over in 1949 CE, Israel controlled most of the territory.

Tensions between Israel and its Arab neighbours remained and led to a short but bloody conflict with Egypt, Syria and Jordan. Israel seized the Sinai Peninsula and the Gaza Strip from Egypt, the West Bank and East Jerusalem from Jordan, and the Golan Heights from Syria. The UN brokered a ceasefire, bringing the Six Day War to an end, but it significantly altered the map of the region and is still the source of political tension. As a result, most Palestinian refugees and their descendants live in Gaza and the Israeli-occupied West Bank, along with neighbouring Jordan, Syria and Lebanon. They are not allowed to return to their homes in Israel as it says this would threaten its existence as a Jewish state. The Palestinian Liberation Organisation came into existence, supported by the USSR's KGB, as a direct consequence – with the word Palestine in its modern iteration being a creation of this organisation covering the refugees from Jordan and Egyptian conquered territory.

Palestinian militants have been launching rockets from the Gaza Strip into the southern Israeli city of Ashkelon. In 2005 Israel completed its withdrawal of the Gaza strip, although it is still considered by the UN to be occupied. It is surrounded by a barrier and Israeli forces tightly control what comes in and out in an attempt to stop weapons reaching Hamas, the Islamist militant group that governs the strip. Since its founding in 1987, Hamas have terrorised Israeli civilians with suicide bombings and rocket attacks. The Hamas charter long called for the complete destruction of Israel, and the group's extremism and dogmatism is often seen as a hindrance to long-term peace in region. However, its charter was revised in 2017 CE, accepting a Palestine based on 1967 CE borders – rather than the entire territory – although it still doesn't recognise the legitimacy of Israel.

Israel says its occupation of Gaza and the West Bank is necessary to protect itself from terrorism, but Palestinians say they are suffering as a result. For more than 25 years, the international community have tried, and failed, to reach some kind of solution. The most recent peace plan, prepared under Donald Trump's presidency, was hailed as the *"deal of the century"* by Israeli Prime Minister Benjamin Netanyahu. But Palestinian leaders were united in their rejection of the proposal, which would have put Jerusalem under complete Israeli control. Palestine would have been offered a capital on the outskirts of the city currently behind the Israeli barrier. The plan also denied the right of return of Palestinian refugees into lands they were forced to flee and said Israel would maintain security responsibility for the future state of Palestine, which would have to be demilitarised.[82]

The Chinese Expansion.

While the world is engaged in an ongoing discussion about the ramifications of the trade war between Washington and Beijing, the economies of the Middle East are shifting away from their longstanding ties with the U.S. toward economically powerful China — a move that may have long-term implications for the economic and political dynamics of the region. An example would be the recent agreement to let Huawei into Saudi Aramco premises; this would not have been countenanced five years ago.

There is no doubt that the relationship between the countries of the Middle East and North Africa (MENA) and China has taken a significant turn in the 21st century. China's rapid economic growth necessitated an aggressive approach in pursuit of much-needed natural resources. The Middle East region was largely excluded from China's pivot toward Asia and Africa, and it was not until the Arab Spring in 2011 CE that China adopted a more engaged policy toward the key countries in the region. It was during this period, for example, that China embarked on the evacuation of its 40 000 citizens trapped in the civil conflict in Libya. This action was symbolic of the more active Chinese presence that followed in the region.

For their part, many Middle East and North Africa countries, now faced with the ramifications of the Arab Spring, such as political and economic instability, as well as slow growth due to falling oil prices, combined with a policy of disengagement by the U.S. from the region, welcomed China and its financing models with open arms.

China's new approach toward the Middle East and North Africa region can be attributed to the following factors:

- China's energy needs, national security interests, and economic growth goals require the uninterrupted flow of oil and gas from the region. This is particularly important given China's strained relationship with the U.S., which is destined to escalate in the coming years.

- China embraces the notion that economic development is a key source of stability in the region, and stability is a top priority for its government. The unrest that came with the Arab Spring, and the positive reaction from around the world, caught the attention of the Chinese leadership.

- The nexus of U.S.-China-Middle East relationships and how each of those bilateral relationships influences standing with the third party. This includes:

  - The significant shift by the administration of former President Barack Obama, which continues under President Donald Trump, to disengage from the region left a lot of room to be filled by other players, including China.

  - The 2008 financial crisis shifted the focus of Middle East economies toward China to seek investment and trade as the U.S. went through a recession that China largely avoided.

- U.S. domestic policies that were viewed as discriminatory against some Middle East countries shifted the focus of many regional investors to destinations other than the U.S.

- The trade tensions between China and the U.S. provided the impetus for increased Chinese economic involvement in the region through loans, investments, and trade.

- President Xi Jinping's activism in terms of expanding China's footprint in the region through the launch of the Belt and Road Initiative (BRI) in 2013 CE, which was later added to the Chinese constitution. Xi visited the region twice in 2016 CE and 2018 CE, the latter his first foreign visit in his second term; and China elevated the level of partnership with Egypt, Iran, Saudi Arabia, and the UAE to a comprehensive strategic one.

This more engaged involvement was reciprocated by similar high-level visits by leaders from the region to China. Many Middle Eastern leaders have visited Beijing more than once over the past five years. Egyptian President Abdel-Fattah el-Sisi has visited at least six times since taking office in 2014 CE. Each visit involved the signing of a number of economic agreements, many of them large in scale, as the leaders attempted to solidify the political relationship in order to expand their economic ties.

In addition, many countries in the region have aligned their sustainable development strategies with China's BRI in order to get better access to financing for their clean energy projects. Sustainability promises to be one of the big economic drivers as well as a political necessity, given the health and other consequences involved, for the region, especially as countries seek alternative sources of energy to oil. China, and not the U.S., is emerging as a leader in this field, and is actively seeking to promote green development in the Middle East area.

As a result of this increased engagement, China has become the largest investor in the region, and the most sought after. In 2018 CE, China committed $20 billion in loans for reconstruction in the Arab world, as well as $3 billion in loans for the banking sector. Furthermore, and through a wide range of financing vehicles, China has provided a mixture of concessional, preferred, and commercial loans, as well as currency swaps, to support central banks and fund infrastructure megaprojects that use Chinese companies (mainly state-owned) and Chinese labour. These mechanisms do not entail any political requirements, but often involve strict conditions on the use of Chinese materials and labour. E.g., China – financed infrastructure projects in Kuwait are all Chinese crewed.

There has also been a boom in trade between the two sides, which has multiplied to reach almost $245 billion. In addition, the Middle East region is witnessing a growing presence from Chinese private sector companies, especially technology firms. For example, five of the top 10 e-commerce companies in the region are from China. They are drawn by the growing size of the Middle East e-commerce market, which is expected to reach $49 billion by 2021 CE.

Chinese tourism is also growing in the region. While Chinese outbound tourism increased from 98 million people in 2013 CE to 154 million in 2018 CE, the percentage of total outbound Chinese tourists going to Gulf Cooperation Council countries rose from 1.3 percent in 2012 CE to 1.9 percent in 2018 CE. Egypt, for example, received 450 000 Chinese tourists in 2018 CE, up from 135 000 in 2015 CE.

This trend of strengthening China-Middle East relations is expected to continue, especially as the BRI expands in the region. China has much of what the region needs, whether through its private sector in technology-related fields, state-owned conglomerates in infrastructure and construction, or state-sponsored financing vehicles such as the Export-Import Bank of China, the Silk Road Fund, and its banks.

This formula provides an easy fix for many of the region's developmental challenges, but it does not come without attendant potential conundrums for China. It remains to be seen how the U.S. will be able to balance the increasing influence of China in the region, and how China will leverage its growing presence to advance its interests vis-à-vis the U.S. and the West. As China's presence grows, it will become increasingly difficult to avoid being dragged into the political dilemmas of the region.

Sovereign Wealth Funds

A sovereign wealth fund (SWF) is a state-owned investment fund composed of financial assets such as stocks, bonds, property, precious metals, or other financial instruments. Sovereign wealth funds invest globally. Most SWFs are funded by foreign exchange assets.
Some sovereign wealth funds may be held by a central bank, which accumulates the funds in the course of its management of a nation's banking system; this type of fund is usually of major economic and fiscal importance. Other sovereign wealth funds are simply the state savings that are invested by various entities for the purposes of investment return, and that may not have a significant role in fiscal management.

The accumulated funds may have their origin in, or may represent, foreign currency deposits, gold, special drawing rights (SDRs) and International Monetary Fund (IMF) reserve positions held by central banks and monetary authorities, along with other national assets such as pension investments, oil funds, or other industrial and financial holdings. These are assets of the sovereign nations that are typically held in domestic and different reserve currencies (such as the dollar, euro, pound, and yen). Such investment management entities may be set up as official investment companies, state pension funds, or sovereign oil funds, among others.

There have been attempts to distinguish funds held by sovereign entities from foreign exchange reserves held by central banks. Sovereign wealth funds can be characterized as *'maximizing long-term return'*, with foreign exchange reserves serving short-term *'currency stabilization'*, and *'liquidity management'*. Many central banks in recent years possess reserves massively in excess of needs for liquidity or foreign exchange management. Moreover, it is widely believed most have diversified hugely into assets other than short-term, highly liquid monetary ones, though almost no data is publicly available to back up this assertion. Some central banks have even begun buying equities, or derivatives of differing ilk (even if fairly safe ones, like overnight interest rate swaps).

Some countries may have more than one SWF.

(See also the list of largest sovereign wealth funds as shown in Table 7-1.)

Table 7-1: Sovereign Wealth Funds The Top 40

Rank	Country	Funds	Assets (U.S $Billion)	Origin
1	China	CADF / CIC / NSSF / SAFE	1,189.4	Non-commodity
2	United Arab Emirates	ADIA / ADIC / EIA / ICD / IPIC / MDC / RIA	816.6	Oil
3	Norway	GPF	715.9	Oil
4	Saudi Arabia	PIF / SAMA	538.1	Oil
5	Singapore	GIC / TH	405	Non-commodity
6	Hong Kong	HKMA	298.7	Non-commodity
7	Kuwait	KIA	296	Oil

8	Russia	RNWF	175.5	Oil
9	Qatar	QIA	115	Oil
10	United States	APF / NMSIOT / PWMTF / PSF / ATF / NDLF	93.4	Oil & Gas / Non-commodity / Minerals / Public Lands
11	Australia	AFF / WAFF	83.3	Non-commodity
12	Libya	LIA	65	Oil
13	Kazakhstan	KNF	61.8	Oil
14	Algeria	RRF	56.7	Oil
15	South Korea	KIC	56.6	Non-commodity
16	Iran	NDFI	42	Oil
17	Malaysia	KN	39.1	Non-commodity
18	Azerbaijan	SOF	32.7	Oil
19	Brunei	BIA	30	Oil
20	France	SIF	25.5	Non-commodity
21	Chile	SESF / PRF	20.9	Copper/ Non-commodity
22	Ireland	NPRF	19.4	Non-commodity
23	New Zealand	NZSF	16.6	Non-commodity
24	Canada	AHSTF	16.4	Oil
25	Brazil	SFB	11.3	Non-commodity
26	East Timor	TLPF	11.1	Gas / Oil
27	Bahrain	MHC	9.1	Oil
28	Oman	OIF / SGRF	8.2	Gas / Oil
29	Peru	FSF	7.1	Non-commodity
30	Botswana	PF	6.9	Diamonds / Minerals
31	Mexico	ORSFM	6	Oil
32	Angola	FSA	5	Oil
33	Trinidad and Tobago	HSF	2.9	Oil
34	Italy	ISF	1.4	Non-commodity
35	Nigeria	NSIA	1	Oil
36	Palestinian territories	PIF	0.8	Non-commodity
36	Venezuela	FEM	0.8	Oil
37	Vietnam	SCIC	0.5	Non-commodity
38	Kiribati	RERF	0.4	Phosphates
38	Gabon	GSWF	0.4	Oil
39	Indonesia	GIU	0.3	Non-commodity
39	Mauritania	NFHR	0.3	Gas / Oil
39	Panama	FAP	0.3	Non-commodity
40	Equatorial Guinea	FFG	0.08	Oil

This table is not important for the sums listed, these are always out of date, but for the relative importance of different states' funds. Middle East funds are nearly all in the Top 20.

Think tanks such as the World Pensions Council (WPC) have argued that the extended investment horizon of sovereign wealth funds allows them to act as long-term investors in less liquid assets such as unlisted companies, commodities, real estate and infrastructure assets, a trend likely to develop further as banks and insurance companies decrease their exposure to these asset classes in the context of the Basel 2/3 and Solvency 2/3 regulatory constraints.

There are several reasons why the growth of sovereign wealth funds is attracting close attention:

- As this asset pool continues to expand in size and importance, so does its potential impact on various asset markets.

- Some countries worry that foreign investment by SWFs raises national security concerns because the purpose of the investment might be to secure control of strategically important industries for political rather than financial gain. These concerns have led the European Union (EU) to reconsider whether to allow its members to use 'golden shares' to block certain foreign acquisitions. This strategy has largely been excluded as a viable option by the EU, for fear it would give rise to a resurgence in international protectionism. In the United States, these concerns are addressed by the Exon–Florio Amendment to the Omnibus Trade and Competitiveness Act of 1988 CE, Pub. L. No. 100-418, § 5021, 102 Stat. 1107, 1426 (codified as amended at 50 U.S.C. app. § 2170 (2000)), as administered by the Committee on Foreign Investment in the United States (CFIU.S). (Since amended).

• Their inadequate transparency is a concern for investors and regulators: for example, size and source of funds, investment goals, internal checks and balances, disclosure of relationships, and holdings in private equity funds. Many of these concerns have been addressed by the IMF and its Santiago Principles, which set out common standards regarding transparency, independence, and governance.

• SWFs are not nearly as homogeneous as central banks or public pension funds.

The governments of SWF's commit to follow certain rules:

• Accumulation rule (what portion of revenue can be spent/saved);

• Withdraw rule (when the Government can withdraw from the fund);

• Investment (where revenue can be invested in foreign or domestic assets).

Sovereign wealth funds are estimated to manage close to $10 trillion of assets, twice as much as the hedge fund industry. According to popular belief, these funds can invest for the long term without the baggage of liabilities and short-term constraints that impede other institutional investors. Research organised by the Edhec-Risk Institute and Deutsche Bank has suggested otherwise, and a survey conducted in 2011 CE confirms this view.

A paper published in 2010 CE put forward a model to optimise the investment and risk management practices of sovereign wealth funds, drawing on the liability-driven investing paradigm developed in the pension fund industry. The model suggests the investment strategy of a sovereign wealth fund should involve dynamic allocation to three main building blocks: a performance-seeking portfolio using optimal diversification to reap the highest possible risk-adjusted rewards;

a liability-hedging portfolio protecting the fund against risks undermining its ability to perform its specific mission (e.g., protect the real value of savings for future generations); and a portfolio hedging the fluctuations in the endowment stream that aims to reduce the fund's dependence on the main sources of wealth of the country.

The third block is a distinguishing feature of sovereign investment. Like the previous block, it is customised to the specificities of each fund, but in general, assets that benefit from rising oil prices would be natural candidates for inclusion in the endowment-hedging portfolio of foreign reserve funds whose economies are vulnerable to oil price appreciation, while the reverse would be expected for oil funds.

These academic findings contradict the widespread view of sovereign wealth funds as relatively free agents, so the Edhec-Risk Institute asked sovereign investment practitioners about their perceived constraints and liabilities and the theoretical and practical appeal of dynamic asset-liability management. Conducted over 2011, the survey generated 27 responses from senior executives and investment officers working for 24 sovereign investment vehicles and central banks around the world.

A large majority (89 %) of the respondents agree that sovereign wealth funds are subject to implicit short-term constraints such as maximum drawdown and minimum performance due to peer comparison, loss aversion or sponsor risk. Just as many respondents (92 %) think implicit liabilities, such as the future use of the wealth, should be taken into account.

Responses also offer a strong rebuttal of the purported irrelevance of asset-liability management for sovereign investors. Seventy % of the respondents agree that extending the liability-driven investing paradigm to sovereign wealth management provides a better understanding of optimal investment policy and risk management practices; the remaining 30 %

neither agree nor disagree. The majority of respondents (63 % in agreement vs. 22 % in disagreement) also recognise the need to hedge fluctuations in endowment flows.

Finally, a majority (55 % in agreement vs 23 %) endorse the particular approach put forward by the Edhec-Risk Institute. The concerns of the minority point to the need for further applied research and education aimed at illustrating how the approach can be tailored to a particular fund's policy and its specific governance model.

With respect to policy, it is important to underline that the structure of the endowment- and liability-hedging portfolios, as well as the dynamic allocation between the three blocks, would reflect the objectives and the constraints of each individual fund.

These results provide practical vindication of the asset-liability management analysis of sovereign investment; as the majority of sovereign investment managers surveyed lament the lack of genuinely dedicated solutions for asset-liability and risk management, opportunities exist for investment banks, asset managers and consultants to better serve these increasingly important investors.

Jonsson (2007) gives another perspective in his essay on the use of Sovereign Wealth Funds in Asymmetric Warfare.

'Liberal democracy, led by the United States may have emerged triumphant from the struggles of the 20th century. But the rise of the non-democratic powers of Russia, China and the Islamist states utilizing the combined power of control of energy resources and the growth of Sovereign Wealth Funds (SWF) leaves the liberal democracy's ultimate victory and future dominance in doubt. Overseas investments by Sovereign Wealth Funds have always had the potential to cause alarm in the destination countries. Because they are driven by governments of the totalitarian and Authoritarian Great Powers, they compel countries to take immediate attention

How powerful Sovereign Wealth Funds decide to invest their vast armoury of cash will play a pivotal role in reshaping financial markets in the next decade. These funds are going to have the ability to buy any global company, to create panic in markets if they move too precipitously, even to dwarf the political clout of international financial institutions. They can no longer be ignored. The Sovereign Wealth Funds are potentially a powerful tool of asymmetric warfare like none witnessed before.

The Leftist/Marxist – Islamist Alliance is using its propaganda machine to convince us that Investment funds run by authoritarian governments sound scary. They are not. So trumpets The Economist print edition of July 26, 2007. On the other hand go for a walk in Chelsea, an expensive bit of London, and you may stroll by the Coldstream Guards' barracks, now the property of the government of Qatar; a branch of the venerable Barclays bank, soon to be part-owned by the People's Republic of China; and then buy a picnic at Sainsbury's, Britain's oldest supermarket, which the Anglophile Qataris are trying to buy too. What goes for Chelsea may soon be true for neighbourhoods in open economies all over the world: governments are on a shopping spree.

In considering the role of Sovereign Wealth Funds it is imperative to consider the difference between state vs. private ownership. However, in some cases the difference is blurred because in some cases the state influence, political motives and ideology override the fund ownership as in the case of funds from Islamist countries.

In much of Europe and emerging markets, it took decades for many economies to be free from the controls of state-owned enterprises (SOEs). Are we now seeing the return of state ownership in the infrastructures and large industries, not by the local governments, but by foreign states? In any case, there should be more discussions and studies on whether SWFs are really returning our Western economies to the former days of state-owned enterprises, but to an even worse case that of foreign state-owned entities. Beware, Wakeup, a foreign state entity – be it either from an Authoritarian

Islamist state or Russia or China – they may be the new owner of your newspaper, radio station, electric utility, and even your most sensitive supplier of war material. The rapid growth of Sovereign Wealth Funds poses risks beyond that of national security. There are worries over competence within some funds; concerns that their scale and ability to affect asset prices could lead to market volatility; and suspicion that they could help countries preserve a favourable currency regime. If decisions are swayed by political considerations, they could also undermine market discipline that matches rewards to sound corporate governance. The ownership may also have a devastating impact on employment practices and human rights. Big and powerful they are coming to company near you or one you work for.'

Although a somewhat strident piece there is some resonance in Jonsson's comments with remarks made earlier in this book. A free and open market and vast Sovereign Wealth viewing UK assets as relatively risk free may be more of a problem than at first appeared. It is not just a UK problem; but the UK is particularly vulnerable because of the openness of the market there.[83]

CHAPTER 8: THE NORTHWEST OF AFRICA

Libya

Libya is a country in North Africa bordered by the Mediterranean Sea to the north, Egypt to the east, Sudan to the southeast, Chad to the south, Niger to the southwest, Algeria to the west and Tunisia to the northwest. It is a sovereign state and a member of the United Nations. It is divided into three historical regions: Tripolitania, Fezzan, and Cyrenaica. With an area of almost 1.8 million sq.km it is the 4th largest country in Africa and the 16th largest in the world. Libya has the 10th largest oil reserves of any country in the world. The largest city and capital, Tripoli, is located in western Libya and contains half the population.

General Geography and Topography

Libya has a fertile and Mediterranean littoral strip behind which, to the south, is the Sahara. In the far south, and in land disputed with Chad, the topography is more Sahel like.

Climate

Apart from the littoral strip the climate is arid.

Soils

Apart from the littoral strip soils are generally very poor.

Mineral Natural Resources

Oil and natural gas plus gypsum are the main mineral natural resources.

Food, Agriculture, Flora and Fauna

Libya is no longer self-sufficient in food and is trying to rectify this by quadrupling grain production from around 200 000 tonnes of grain to 800 000 tonnes. This is difficult in the current situation, and with an agrarian population that has declined. Libya was a leader in pivot irrigation, the greening of the desert using modern irrigation techniques, but this is costly. The desert, the Sahara, south of the fertile littoral strip is arid and not independently fertile. Further south towards the borders of Chad and Niger a more Sahel type region is encountered; but this too is more arid than the Niger and Chad lands.

The littoral strip contains a range of herbs, fruits and grasses. There is some livestock farming. Under Ghaddafi large beef and milk herds were run in the desert – but these have now largely disappeared. Wild fauna is basically small mammals and birds concentrated along the littoral strip with a decreasing fauna population inland of oryx, camel, African buffalo. As in many parts of North Africa large mammals such as lions, cheetah and elephant have largely disappeared. The country is an important bird migration route and stop off for transits from Africa to Europe.

Population

The current population is around 6.5 million (2020 CE) up from just over 1.5 million in 1964. This population is concentrated within the littoral strip close to the Mediterranean and in the cities. 80% plus of the population is urban; and as elsewhere over 30% are under 20. However, this is a population considerably smaller than the countries that surround; thus, Libya is often a target of those seeking to expand.

Historically, Libya was home to the Berbers but today it is

mostly Arab. For a time, Italians made up nearly 20% of the population, in the early first half of the 20th century. They left over time. Italians perpetrated many killings of Libyans in the 20th century.

Today Libya has a large transit population and is a key route of illegal migration from the Sahel and West Africa to Europe.

Politics

At the end of World War I Italy, having liberated the area from the Ottomans in 1911 CE, created first three then two Italian provinces (colonies) until 1934 CE when it was united into one country under Italian colonial rule. During the second world war and consequent to the defeat of the Axis powers Libya was divided into French and British zones. Post – war the Italian control was effectively ended in 1947 CE.

After World War II Libya was granted full independence in 1951 CE, as a Kingdom. The reign of King Idris continued until 1969 CE when a 'bloodless coup' brought the Army Colonel, Muammar Qaddafi, to power. Qaddafi revolutionised Libya on the back of oil resources and by the end of his tenure the Libyans were the wealthiest individuals in the Arab world. They were also equal, men and women, as Libya had effectively become an 'equal' Islamic socialist dictator republic. Qaddafi supported many non-mainstream political groups, from the IRA through Idi Amin's war with Tanzania through Australian trade unions to the Palestinian Liberation Organisation. He fought wars with Chad and was a constant enemy of the UK, France (whose quasi -colonial control of former French Africa he challenged) and the U.S.A.

In 2011 CE the Arab Spring saw the start of the Libyan Civil War and the end of the Qaddafi regime, he was killed. The country then basically split into several fiefdoms before two groups, one based in Tripoli, the other in Tobruk, split Libya in two. The split was reunited in 2015 CE before degenerating into the second Libyan civil war which continued until the signing of a peace treaty in October 2020 CE.

Many different players were involved in the 'mess' that was Libya after 2011 CE, from the UAE to ISIS. 96% of Libya is Sunni Muslim. The key was, as ever, oil. However, increasingly important was the region south of Libya and Niger. The route to Europe for illegal migrants came up through Niger through Libya to Europe. This route was in the hands of organised crime and, to a large extent, ISIS. It is a continuing problem that both Libya and, particularly, Italy are trying to resolve.

As this is written there is a Government of National Unity (2021).

Language

Libya uses Modern Standard Arabic.

Religion

Libya is predominantly a Sunni religious country. Under Qaddafi there was effective separation between state and religion.

Economy (Snapshot) – Note in each of these snapshots the UK is used as a reference.

Libya's economy is 95% based on oil.

- GDP: $40.951 billion (nominal, 2018 CE est.); $74.719 billion (PPP, 2018 CE est.) (UK: GDP: $2.64 trillion (nominal, 2020 CE est.); $2.98 trillion (PPP, 2020 CE).

- GDP per capita: $6 288 (nominal, 2018 CE est.); $11 473 (PPP, 2018 CE est.).

- Labour Force: 2 553 671 (2019 CE); 38.7% employment rate (2012 CE).

- Labour Force by occupation: Agriculture: 17%; Industry: 23%; Services: 59% (2004 CE).

- Main export partners: Italy 19%; Spain 12.5%; France 11%; Egypt 8.6%; Germany 8.6%; China 8.3%; U.S 4.9%;

UK 4.6%; Netherlands 4.5% (2017 CE).

Egypt

Egypt is a country that as a defined geographical unit has survived for a longer period of time than any other state unit in the world, except perhaps China. It has an area of 1 010 408 sq.km. it is the 29th largest country in the world. Egypt is a Mediterranean country in northeast Africa. It is bounded to the north by the Mediterranean and beyond that by Greece, Turkey, and Cyprus. To the west is Libya. To the south is Sudan. To the east, across the Red Sea, is Saudi Arabia and to the north and northeast, beyond the Gulf of Aqaba, is the Gaza Strip and Jordan. The capital is Cairo, most of the population is urban and crammed into the northern Nile valley.

General Geography and Topography

The defining geographical feature of Egypt is the Nile River. This was, until the discovery of natural gas, also the key national resource. It provides water and food. Beyond the reach of the Nile irrigation systems the country is largely desert apart from a littoral strip close to the Mediterranean. The construction of the Aswan Dam basically stopped the annual floods, with a consequent and deleterious effect on soils.

Climate

The climate has historically been arid. It is unusually hot and sunny with almost no rainfall except along a narrow littoral strip. However, as with many parts of the world the climate has changed somewhat; with more rainfall than is usual in recent years. There is a potential threat from rising sea levels which, if realised, would create a significant number of refugees along the littoral strip where most of the population live. Egypt does not have the most human friendly environment.

Soils

Soils are largely desert soils. The exceptions are the Mediterranean littoral and the Nile. Here soils are better with often superb alluvial based soils adjoining the Nile. However, in recent decades increased population pressure has led to deterioration and relatively poor management. There has been a drop in the quality of Nile water from upstream, less flooding, more salinity and pollution as well as less suspended solids for soil. This has had an impact on production.

Minerals and Natural Resources

Until the discovery of natural gas offshore Egypt, from drilling in the Mediterranean, Egypt had started to run out of domestically produced hydrocarbons. After recent discoveries of huge natural gas deposits offshore in the Mediterranean and further oil and gas in the western desert Egypt will remain self-sufficient in these resources for the foreseeable future.

Despite the Nile there is extreme pressure on water resources; and with more dams due either completion or building south of Egypt this position is likely to deteriorate rather than improve.

Food, Agriculture, Flora and Fauna

The major Egyptian crops are:

- Rice: it is one the major cereals cultivated in the country. It is the second most exported crop after cotton. The country's production in 2014 CE was 4.53 million metric tonnes. Egypt is the biggest producer of rice in Africa.

- Cotton: it is the major fibre crop cultivated in the country and the most exported crop. In 2014 CE, the production was 525 000 bales of 480 lb (220 Kg)., an increase of 20.69% compared to 2013 CE after two years of decline. The country is the second producer in Africa after Mali.

- Corn: With nearly 6 million metric tons produced in 2014 CE and a 2.76% growth compared to 2013 CE, it is one of the major crops cultivated in the country. The country is the eighth largest consumer in the world and the fifth largest importer and the third producer in Africa after Nigeria and South Africa.

- Wheat: The country is the major producer of wheat in Africa, with 8.3 million tonnes in 2014 CE. Egypt is also the second largest importer in the world.

- Sugar cane: it is the main sugar crop with 90% of the yield used for sugar extraction.

- Forage crops: Egyptian clover is the main produced forage crop in the Nile valley.

- The other major crops cultivated in Egypt are fruits, vegetables, and beans.

Livestock production is an essential element of Egypt's agricultural sector. The population has increased steadily between 2000 CE and 2009 CE, the number of cattle heads went from 3.53 to 5 million, buffaloes from 3.38 to 4 million, goats from 3.43 to 4.55 million and sheep from 4.47 to 5.50 million, camels, however, have declined from 141 000 to 110 000 head.

Egypt is the world's second largest producer of table olives and produced around 450 000 tons in 2018/19 CE of which around 100 000 tons were exported. Grape exports recorded $213 million, topping the list of the top 20 foodstuffs of the Egyptian non-petroleum exports during June 2018 CE. Egypt is also the world's second largest producer of figs, 189 339 tons in 2018 CE.

There is a large commercial fish farming sector, based on Tilapia.

Large mammals are generally absent with no elephants, cheetahs, leopards, lions and few wild ruminants. Smaller animals such as snakes, rodents are common and relatively diverse. Insects are diverse as are fungi and algae; with many new species being discovered.

Population

The population of Egypt is around 100 million. This population is highly urbanised around Cairo and Alexandria. The population was estimated at less than 3 million when Napoleon invaded the country, and 10 million at the turn of the 19th and 20th centuries. A population explosion occurred between 1970 and 2000 following advances in healthcare. 99% of the population is ethnic Egyptian. 60% of the country is aged under 30.

Politics

Modern Egypt dates back to 1922 CE, when it gained independence from Britain as a monarchy. The monarchy was overthrown in 1952 CE in an army coup one of whose leaders was Nasser, who went on to rule from 1958 CE to 1970 CE. As a republic it joined with Syria in 1958 CE, but this union was dissolved in 1961 CE. The Nasser period is generally regarded as a positive and culturally successful period. However, in the last quarter of the century things declined somewhat under Sadat. In 1978 CE, Egypt signed the Camp David Accords officially withdrawing from the Gaza Strip and recognising Israel. Mubarak ruled from 1981 CE to 2011 CE in an authoritarian regime. The Arab Spring brought him down to be eventually replaced by Sisi who has ruled since 2014 CE. The country continues to face challenges. Most of the country is Sunni Muslim, it is the largest Muslim country in the Middle East. There is a large Egyptian diaspora particularly in the GCC. The country has relied heavily on Saudi Arabian financial support from time to time. It is important to note that many Palestinians were originally Egyptians.

Language

Egypt's language is Modern Standard Arabic.

Religion

The overwhelming majority of Egypt's population is Sunni Muslim (85% plus) with much of the remaining being Coptic Christian.

Economy (Snapshot)

- GDP: $362 billion (nominal, 2020 CE); $1.502 trillion (PPP 2020 CE (UK: GDP: $2.64 trillion (nominal, 2020 CE est.); $2.98 trillion (PPP 2020 CE).

- GDP by sector: Agriculture: 11.7%; Industry: 34.3%; Services: 54%; (2017 CE est.).

- Labour force: 31 964 260 (2019 CE); 39.7% employment rate (2017 CE).

- Labour force by occupation: Agriculture: 25.8%; Industry: 25.1%; Services: 49.1% (2015 CE est.).

- Main export partners: United Arab Emirates 10.9%; Italy 10%; United States 7.4%; United Kingdom 5.7%; Turkey 4.4%; Germany 4.3%.

Sudan

Sudan is situated in the northeast of Africa. It is bounded to the north by Egypt, to the south by South Sudan, which was an integral part until 2011 CE. To the northeast is the Red Sea, to the east is Eritrea and to the southeast Ethiopia. To the northwest is Libya, to the west Chad and to the southwest the Central African Republic. It is another huge country comprising 1,886,068 sq.km. It is the third largest country in Africa. Its capital is Khartoum.

General Geography and Topography

Sudan is generally flat plain, with mountains in the west and hills next to the Red Sea. The Blue and White Niles meet at Khartoum, the capital. From here the Nile flows northwards to Egypt. The Blue Nile is nearly 800km long in Sudan and is joined by the Dinder and Rahad Rivers. This is the defining feature of the country. The White Nile has no significant tributaries.

Both major rivers have dams including Lake Nubia on the Sudanese - Egyptian border.

Climate

In Sudan the amount of rainfall increases towards the south. The central and the northern part have extremely dry, desert areas such as the Nubian Desert to the northeast and the Bayuda Desert to the east; in the south, there are steppe grasslands and tropical savanna. Sudan's rainy season lasts for about four months (June to September) in the north, and up to six months (May to October) in the south. In recent years this has varied.

Soils

In Sudan most northern soils are desert soils, with a significant desertification problem. Steppe soils then graduate to the more fertile tropical savannah. Soil erosion, soil desiccation and uncontrolled agricultural expansion are problems. The Nile supports much of agriculture, and cash crops, but suffers from poor management.

Minerals and Natural Resources

The main resources of Sudan are: petroleum (extensive petroleum exploration in Sudan started in the mid-1970s CE, and this resulted in the discoveries of oil in the Upper Nile region); gold; the Nile River. chromium ore and iron ore.

Outside the Nile valley water is scarce.

Food, Agriculture, Flora and Fauna

Sudan's main crops include cotton, peanuts (groundnuts), sesame, gum arabic, sorghum, and sugarcane. The main subsistence crops are sorghum and millet, with smaller amounts of wheat, corn, and barley.

The nation's wildlife is threatened by poaching. As of 2001 CE, twenty-one mammal species and nine bird species are endangered, as well as two species of plants.

Population

The population is 45 million and the major religion is Islam; although following various peace agreements over the last decade Sudan is officially a secular state. However, the majority is Sunni Muslim. The population is 7 times bigger than it was in 1956 CE and over 30 % of the population is under 20 years old.

Politics

Sudan was governed by the British from 1898 CE to independence in 1956 CE. There followed many years of political instability centred, mostly, on disagreements between the Islamic north and the Christian and animist south. This led to the independence of South Sudan in 2011 CE.

Sudan had two strong dictators, Nimeiry 1969 – 1985 CE. and then Al-Bashir from 1989 to 2019 CE when he was deposed in a coup. The coup led to further disagreements until a transitional government led by Hamdok brought peace and some stability. He appointed a woman, Christian, foreign minister. He was heavily supported by the Saudi and UAE Governments.

More recently there have been tensions between Sudan and Ethiopia following the latter's military expeditions into Sudan in parallel to the Tigray conflict. These have been condemned by both Sudan and Egypt.

Language

The main language in Sudan is Arabic, but not always Modern Standard Arabic. The official written languages are Modern Written Arabic and English.

There are a variety of African languages.

Religion

Around 90% of Sudan's population is Sunni Islam.

Economy (Snapshot)

- GDP: $30.873 billion (Nominal, 2019 est.); $175.228 billion (PPP. 2019 est.). (UK: GDP: $2.64 trillion (nominal, 2020 est.); $2.98 trillion (PPP 2020)

- GDP by sector: Agriculture: 39.6%; Industry: 2.6%, Services: 57.8% (2017 est.).

- Population below poverty line: 46.5% in poverty (2009 CE); 41% on less than $3.20/day (2009 CE).

- Labour force: 12 064 673 (2019); 41.1% employment rate (2011).

- Labour force by occupation: Agriculture: 80%; Industry: 7%; Services: 13% · (1998 CE est.).

CHAPTER 9: THE SAUDI PENINSULA: THE GCC AND YEMEN

The GCC comprises, with Kuwait and offshore Bahrain, the countries of the Saudi Peninsula. The exception is Yemen in the southeast of the peninsula. The GCC is a regional political grouping of the main six countries in the Saudi Peninsula. They are all Sunni Muslim with the exception of Oman which has a more mixed religious base. Yemen is predominantly Shia Muslim, as is Bahrain. There are other religions, some animist.

The Saudi Peninsula protrudes into the Indian Ocean with the Gulf to the east and the Red Sea to the west.

Saudi Arabia

Saudi Arabia is bordered by Jordan and Iraq to the north, Kuwait to the northeast, Qatar, Bahrain, and the United Arab Emirates to the east, Oman to the southeast and Yemen to the south. It is separated from Egypt and Israel in the northwest by the Gulf of Aqaba. With a land area of approximately 2 150 000 sq.km, Saudi Arabia is geographically the largest sovereign state in Western Asia, the second largest in the Arab world (after Algeria in northwest Africa), the fifth largest in Asia, and the 12th-largest in the world. Its capital is Riyadh and as with many other Arab countries it has a large young population.

General Geography and Topography

Saudi Arabia's geography is dominated by the Arabian Desert, associated semi-desert, shrubland, steppes, several mountain ranges, volcanic lava fields and highlands. The 647 500 sq.k-m Rub' al Khali ('Empty Quarter') in the southeastern part of the country is the world's largest contiguous sand desert. Though there are lakes in the country, Saudi Arabia is the largest country in the world by area with no permanent rivers. Wadis, non-permanent rivers, however, are very numerous.

Fertile areas are to be found in the alluvial deposits in wadis, basins, and oases. The main topographical feature is the central plateau which rises abruptly from the Red Sea and gradually descends into the Nejd and toward the Persian Gulf. On the Red Sea coast, there is a narrow coastal plain, known as the Tihamah parallel to which runs an imposing escarpment. The southwest province of Arir is mountainous and contains the 3 133 m Mount Sawda, which is the highest point in the country.

Climate

Except for the southwestern regions such as Asir, Saudi Arabia has a desert climate with very high day-time temperatures during the summer and a sharp temperature drop at night. Average summer temperatures are around 45 °C but can be as high as 54 °C at its most extreme. In the winter the temperature rarely drops below 0 °C with the exception of mostly the northern regions of the country where annual snowfall, in particular in the mountainous regions of Tabuk province, is not uncommon. The lowest recorded temperature to date, -12.0 °C was measured in Turaif.

In the spring and autumn, the heat is temperate, temperatures average around 29 °C. Annual rainfall is very low. The southern regions differ in that they are influenced by the Indian Ocean monsoons, usually occurring between October and March. An average of 300 mm of rainfall occurs during this period, which is about 60 % of the annual precipitation. Saudi Arabia has approximately 1300 islands.

As with other regions the climate over the last few years has diverged from the mean. There has been more rain and heavy flooding in all areas.

Soils

Almost all soils are desert soils. There are exceptions in the alluvial deposits and in the southwest.

Minerals and Natural Resources

The overwhelming mineral and natural resource is oil and gas. This was discovered in the 1920s CE and 1930s CE as a commercial prospect, led to the development of Saudi Aramco, and has provided most of Saudi Arabia's development finance.

Since 2010 CE the production of low-grade iron ore, low-grade bauxite, cement, clays, ethane, methane, propane, direct-reduced iron, lead, and pozzolana has increased.

The country does not have enough water, without relying on desalination plants.

Food, Agriculture, Flora and Fauna

Saudi Arabia is not self-sufficient in food.

Agriculture has historically tended to be of a subsistence type, except, principally, in the southwest. Nomadic tribes raised goats and camels, collected dates and other tree products, to subsist in a difficult climate. These days huge artificial and irrigated farms have been created to deliver milk, beef and some green crops in large quantities. All of these, however, are very expensive and are being phased out.

Saudi Arabia is home to five terrestrial ecoregions: Arabian Peninsula coastal fog desert, Southwestern Arabian foothills savanna, Southwestern Arabian montane woodlands, Arabian Desert, and Red Sea Nubo-Sindian tropical desert and semidesert.

Wildlife remains diverse but limited in numbers and includes the Arabian leopard, wolf, striped hyena, mongoose, baboon, hare, sand cat, and jerboa. Animals such as gazelles-, oryx, leopards and cheetahs were relatively numerous until the 19th century CE, when extensive hunting reduced these animals almost to extinction. Birds include falcons (which are caught and trained for hunting), eagles, hawks, vultures, sandgrouse, and bulbuls. There are several species of snakes, many of which are venomous. Saudi Arabia is home to a rich marine life. The Red Sea in particular has a rich and diverse ecosystem. More than 1200 species of fish have been recorded in the Red Sea, and around 10 percent of these are found nowhere else. This also includes 42 species of deep-water fish.

Population

The population of Saudi Arabia is around 40 million, of whom some 20 million are under 30. The population is concentrated in urban areas.

Politics

The country is a hereditary and absolute monarchy. The ruling family is the House of Saud. As noted in earlier chapters the House of Saud can trace its ancestry, with a little licence, back many centuries. There are many factions within Saudi Arabia but the key to stability has been the Sudairi Seven. The Sudairi Seven is the commonly used name for a powerful alliance of seven full brothers within the Saudi royal family. They are among the forty-five sons of the country's founder, King Abdulaziz. The King had more sons with their mother, Hussa bint Ahmed Al Sudairi, than he did with any of his other wives. The seven sons, with their father, have provided leadership over the last century. This tradition has changed recently with the ascent of King Salman and Crown Prince Mohammad bin Salman. A parallel family group now reigns. This has caused some disruption in the royal ranks, to put it mildly. This disruption is likely to continue.

The politics of Saudi Arabia will be discussed further later. However, it is is important to understand that Saudi Arabia has never been colonised, is the Guardian of the Two Holy Mosques in Mecca and Medinah (Sunni Muslim), the Royal Family and the religious leaders work hand in hand, and that there are many alliances across the Muslim world both good and bad. The important recent alliance has been with the UAE, the major partner in the Yemen war, and another Sunni Muslim leadership state. The GCC was plunged into chaos in 2017 CE when Qatar was expelled for links, it is claimed, with Iran and for the financing of terrorist organisations. Qatar returned to the fold in 2020 CE and the GCC is now complete, if not fully functioning, once again. Relations with the UAE are more strained than usual.

Language

The language spoken in Saudi Arabia is Modern Standard Arabic; most management speaks English (American).

Religion

Religion is predominantly Sunni Muslim, with the Kingdom being the Custodian of the Two Holy Mosques in Mecca and Medinah. There is a sizeable Shia population in the Eastern Province which is often viewed as a threat.

Economy (Snapshot)

- GDP: $680 billion (nominal; 2020 CE est.); $1.6 trillion (PPP 2020 CE est.). (UK: GDP: $2.64 trillion (nominal, 2020 CE est.); $2.98 trillion (PPP 2020 CE).

- GDP by sector: Agriculture: 2.6%; Industry: 44.2%; Services: 53.2% (2017 CE est.).

- Main export partners: Japan (+) 12.2%; China (-) 11.7%; South Korea (+) 9% · India (+) 8.9%; United States (+) 8.3%.

- Main import partners: China (-) 15.4%; United States (+) 13.6%; United Arab Emirates (+) 6.5%; Germany (+) 5.8%; Japan (+) 4.1%.

- Fiscal year: Calendar year

Yemen

Yemen is a country situated at the southwest of the Saudi Peninsula. It has Saudi Arabia to the North, Oman to the East, the Indian Ocean to the south and the Red Sea to the west. It has an area of 527 970 sq.km. – about a quarter the size of Saudi Arabia.

General Geography and Topography

The country's mountainous interior is surrounded by narrow coastal plains to the west, south, and east and by upland desert to the north along the border with Saudi Arabia. The Tihamah is a nearly 419 km long, semidesert coastal plain that runs along the Red Sea and is part of the Arabian Peninsula coastal fog desert ecoregion. The highland regions are interspersed with wadis, or river valleys, that are dry in the winter months (Yemen has no permanent rivers.) Most notable is the Wadi Hadhramaut in eastern Yemen, the upper portions of which contain alluvial soil and floodwaters and the lower portion of which is barren and largely uninhabited. Both the eastern plateau region and the desert in the north are hot and dry with little vegetation.

Climate

The climate of Yemen can be described as subtropical dry, hot desert climate with low annual rainfall, very high temperatures in summer and a big difference between maximum and minimum temperatures, especially in the inland areas. Summer (June to September) is very low rainfall. Daily maximum temperatures can easily reach 40°C or more.

Soils

Yemen contains the most fertile land in the Arabian Peninsula. The arable land in the country is approximately 1.2 million hectares or 2.4% of the total land area. The highest value of agricultural land over 54 years was 3.12% of the total land in 1996 CE.

Minerals and Natural Resources

Yemen has vast metal resources including silver, gold, copper, zinc, cobalt, and nickel. Several companies have been licensed to prospect and explore several metal deposits in the country. Cantex Mine Development Corporation of Canada has been exploring the Al Hariqah gold deposit since 2010 CE. Thani Daubi Mining of the UAE found some gold deposits in Wadi Sharis, which was estimated to produce 7 grams of gold per tonne. It is estimated that there are 40 gold and silver deposits in Yemen, with Medden area having the largest deposit of about 600,000 tonnes which can yield 15 g and 11 g of gold and silver per tonne respectively. The Jabali silver and zinc mines owned and operated by the Jabal Salab Company is estimated to contain 12 million metric tons of oxide ores in the grade of 68 g/Mt of silver, 18.9% of zinc, and 1.2% lead. Apart from the metal resources, Yemen also has plenty of non-metal resources or industrial mineral deposits such as limestone, magnesite, scoria, sandstone, gypsum, marble, perlite, dolomite, feldspar, and Celestine.

Yemen has little oil, but a large natural gas field.

It has very little fresh water.

Food, Agriculture, Flora and Fauna

Agriculture is one of the country's main economic activities and contributes 20% of the GDP and employs almost half of the working population. Agriculture is mainly practiced in the coastal plains, highlands, wadis, and in the eastern plateaus. These areas are considered fertile and also have favourable climates. Due to the low levels of rainfall, agriculture relies on the use of groundwater. Irrigation has made it possible for vegetables and fruits to thrive as Yemeni's primary cash crop. Other major commodities produced include cereals and industrial crops. Increased population has led to increased pressure on agricultural land, especially along the coastal areas.

Yemen has one of the most diverse and important populations of fauna and flora on the planet, the island of Socotra being particularly important. It is a meeting point of Asian and African wildlife and has important sea resources.

Population

The population of Yemen was about 28 million according to 2015 CE estimates, with 46% of the population being under 15 years old and 2.7% above 65 years. In 1950 CE, it was 4.3 million. By 2050 CE, the population is estimated to increase to about 60 million.

It is unclear what effect the recent war with Saudi Arabia, which has caused a humanitarian disaster, will have on the population of the country long-term.

Politics

Yemen's civil war began in 2014 CE when Houthi insurgents, Shiite rebels with links to Iran and a history of rising up against the Sunni government, took control of Yemen's capital and largest city, Sana'a, demanding lower fuel prices and a new government. Following failed negotiations, the rebels seized the presidential palace in January 2015 CE, leading President Abd Rabbu Mansour Hadi and his government to resign. Beginning in March 2015 CE, a coalition of Gulf states led by Saudi Arabia launched a campaign of economic isolation and air strikes against the Houthi insurgents, with U.S. logistical and intelligence support.

Hadi rescinded his resignation and returned to Aden in September 2015 CE, and fighting has continued since. A UN effort to broker peace talks between allied Houthi rebels and the internationally recognized Yemeni government stalled in the summer of 2016 CE. As of December 2017 CE, Hadi has reportedly been residing in exile in Saudi Arabia.

In July 2016 CE, the Houthis and the government of former President Ali Abdullah Saleh, ousted in 2011 CE after nearly thirty years in power, announced the formation of a 'political council' to govern Sana'a and much of northern Yemen. However, in December 2017 CE, Saleh broke with the Houthis and called for his followers to take up arms against them. Saleh was killed and his forces defeated within two days.

The intervention of regional powers in Yemen's conflict, including Iran and Gulf states led by Saudi Arabia, threatens to draw the country into the broader Sunni-Shia divide. Numerous Iranian weapons shipments to Houthi rebels have been intercepted in the Gulf of Aden by a Saudi naval blockade in place since April 2015 CE. In response, Iran has dispatched its own naval convoy, which further risks military escalation between the two countries.

By 2020 CE there was a certain weariness on all sides; and the UAE withdrew from the coalition. On 9 February 2020 CE, after five years of involvement in Yemen's civil war as part of the Saudi-led coalition, the UAE's leadership celebrated the completion of its phased military withdrawal from the country in a ceremony at Zayed Military City. With the December 2018 CE Stockholm Agreement constraining forces fighting for control of the port city of Hodeida and raising tensions in the Gulf, the prospects for a military end to the conflict dimmed substantially, calling into question the usefulness of the UAE's continued presence. Although the UAE's withdrawal has provided an exit strategy from the stalemate in Yemen, it neither suspends Abu Dhabi's role in the coalition nor curtails Emirati influence on the ground. The bedrock of the UAE's 'Peace First' strategy is a switch from direct to indirect engagement in the country through increased reliance on local proxies and partners, as the deputy chief of staff of the UAE's armed forces, Lieutenant General Eisa Saif al-Mazrouei, recently reiterated.

Before its phased withdrawal strategy, initially introduced as a military drawdown in July 2019 CE, the UAE publicly and directly fought two primary enemies: first, the Houthis as part of the Arab coalition, and second, violent extremist groups, most notably al-Qaeda in the Arabian Peninsula (AQAP) and ISIS, with the U.S. On the first front, there is no doubt that the UAE's engagement alongside Yemeni and coalition troops curbed the expansion of the Houthis in the southern and eastern governorates and, more importantly, through its operational command on a number of frontlines, helped to liberate Aden via Operation Golden Arrow in July 2015 CE and Mocha in January 2017 CE via Operation Golden Spear. These robust efforts have not only reduced the Houthis' territorial control and curtailed their presence on the Red Sea and the Gulf of Aden, but they have also mitigated threats to maritime security.

The UAE remains in occupation of Socotra.

Language

The language of Yemen is Modern Standard Arabic; but a variety of dialects are spoken.

Religion

Sunni Muslims dominate with over 50% of the population, concentrated in the south. Shia Muslims at around 44% dominate in the north. Roughly these splits equate with the old North Yemen and South Yemen and are an obvious real and proxy catalyst for the current conflict.

Economy (Snapshot)

· GDP: $27.591 billion (nominal, 2018 CE est.); $69.439 billion (PPP 2018 CE est.). (UK: GDP: $2.64 trillion (nominal, 2020 CE est.); $2.98 trillion (PPP 2020 CE).

· GDP per capita: $895 (nominal, 2018 CE est.); $2 253 (PPP 2018 CE est.).

· GDP by sector: Agriculture: 20.3%; Industry: 11.8%; Services; 67.9% (2017 CE est.).

· Population below poverty line: 48.6% (2014); 18.8% on less than $1.90/day (2014 CE).

· Labour force: 6 814 000 (2019 CE); 31.4% employment rate (2014 CE).

Oman

Oman is a country on the southeastern coast of the Arabian Peninsula in Western Asia and the oldest independent state in the Arab world (except Egypt). Located in a strategically important position at the mouth of the Persian Gulf, the country shares land borders with the United Arab Emirates to the northwest, Saudi Arabia to the west, and Yemen to the southwest. Marine borders are with Iran and Pakistan. The coast is formed by the Arabian Sea to the southeast and the Gulf of Oman to the northeast. The Madha and Musandam exclaves are surrounded by the UAE on their land borders, with the Strait of Hormuz (which it shares with Iran) and the Gulf of Oman forming Musandam's coastal boundaries.

General Geography and Topography

Oman comprises a narrow coastal plain backed by hill ranges and an interior desert plateau. The highest point is Jebel Sham 3 018 m.

Climate

With the exception of the Dhofar region, which has a strong monsoon climate and receives warm winds from the Indian Ocean, the climate of Oman is extremely hot and dry most of the year.

Soils

Most soils are desert soils, with the exception of Dhofar which has extremely fertile soils both natural and man-made (from centuries of irrigation and development, though now in disrepair).

Minerals and Natural Resources

The major product is oil, which was discovered in Oman in 1964 CE and first exported in 1967 CE. Crude oil is produced and refined; other industrial products include natural gas, copper, steel, chemicals, and optic fibre. Petroleum, reexported goods, fish, metals, and textiles are important exports.

Food, Agriculture, Flora and Fauna

In the extreme north, dates, limes, nuts, bananas, alfalfa, and vegetables are cultivated, and in the southwest there is an abundance of camels, cattle and other livestock. Fishing is an important industry.

Most of the country has a desert fauna and flora, with the oryx having been successfully reintroduced. In the southwest is a much lusher vegetation and a wide variety of tropical, sub-tropical, temperate and desert flora and fauna.

Population

Oman has a population of around 4.7 million residents (2019 CE), of which about 56 % are Omani citizens, the rest are immigrants (guest workers). Much of Oman is desert, and the twin cities of Muscat and Matrah are the most important population centres. Islam is the dominant religion.

The inhabitants are mostly Arabs; there are also minorities of Baluchis, South Asians, East Africans, and migrant workers of varied ethnicities.

Politics

Under the last Sultan, Qaboos, Oman was an absolute monarchy, albeit a benign one. The new Sultan has only been in power since January 2020 CE but has shown some signs of distributing his absolute power. Oman has led a balanced political existence between the Sunni dominated peninsula and the Shia powerhouse of Iran, the latter less than 20 km from the coast of Oman's Musandam Peninsula.

Language

The common language of Oman is Arabic, with English as a second official language.

Religion

A majority of Omanis are Muslim most of whom, 75%, follow the Ibadi School of Islam (and who are neither strictly Sunni nor Shia), followed by the Twelver school of Shia Islam, the Shafi`i school of Sunni Islam, and the Nizari Isma'ili school of Shia Islam. Thus, Oman is not a majority Sunni Islam state.

Economy (Snapshot)

Although an oil producing state Oman has acquired a large debt, much of it outstanding to China.

- GDP: $79.277 billion (nominal, 2018 CE); $200.314 billion (PPP 2018 CE); (UK: GDP: $2.64 trillion (nominal, 2020 CE est.); $2.98 trillion (PPP 2020 CE).

- GDP rank: 67th (nominal, 2019 CE); 64th (PPP 2019 CE).

- GDP growth:1.8% (2018 CE); 0.5% (2019 CE est.); –3.5% (2020 CE); 2.7% (2021 CE).

- GDP per capita: $18 970 (nominal, 2018 CE); $47 933 (PPP 2018).

- GDP per capita: rank 41st (nominal, 2018 CE) 23rd (PPP 2018 CE).

- GDP by sector: agriculture 1.7% industry 45.2% services 53% (2017 CE est.).

UAE

The United Arab Emirates, or UAE, is a country in Western Asia located at the eastern end of the Arabian Peninsula. It borders Oman to the south and Saudi Arabia to the west and north; and has maritime borders in the Persian Gulf with Qatar and Iran. It is a federal elective constitutional monarchy formed from a federation of seven emirates: Abu Dhabi (which serves as the capital), Ajman, Dubai, Fujairah, Ras Al Khaimah, Sharjah and Umm Al Quwain. All have slightly different laws and approaches to both religion and westerners/visitors. Their boundaries have numerous enclaves within each other. Each emirate is governed by a ruler, who together form the Federal Supreme Council, and one of whom serves as President of the United Arab Emirates. In practice the UAE is ruled by the leader of Abu Dhabi, and his deputy the leader of Dubai. To all intents and purposes, it is an authoritarian regime.

General Geography and Topography

The United Arab Emirates (UAE) covers an area of around 83 600 sq. kms in the Arabian Peninsula. Most of the United Arab Emirates is a desert wasteland, with large, rolling sand dunes, as the outer reaches of the Rub' Al Khali Desert stretch into the country. The coastal areas fronting the Persian Gulf are flat, while the Hajar Mountains dominate the landscape in the northeast. Jabal Yibir, the country's highest point, is located there, which rises to 1,727 m. The United Arab Emirates has no significant rivers or lakes of note. Numerous small islands and inlets are situated offshore in the Persian Gulf.

Climate

The climate of the UAE is subtropical-arid with hot summers and warm winters. The climate is categorized as desert climate. The hottest months are July and August when average maximum temperatures reach above 45 °C on the coastal plain. In the Al Hajar Mountains, temperatures are considerably lower, a result of increased elevation. Average minimum temperatures in January and February are between 10 and 14 °C. During the late summer months, a humid southeastern wind known as *Sharqi* (i.e. 'Easterner') makes the coastal region especially unpleasant. The average annual rainfall in the coastal area is less than 120 mm but in some mountainous areas annual rainfall often reaches 350 mm Rain in the coastal region falls in short, torrential bursts during the summer months, sometimes resulting in floods in ordinarily dry wadi beds. The region is prone to occasional, violent dust storms, which can severely reduce visibility. On 28 December 2004, there was snow recorded in the UAE for the first time, in the Jebel Jais mountain cluster in Ras al-Khaimah. A few years later, there were more sightings of snow and hail. The Jebel Jais mountain cluster has experienced snow only twice since records began. As elsewhere in the region rainfall is increasing, as is flooding. In 2016 there was a severe hurricane in Abu Dhabi accompanied by flash flooding.

Soils

UAE soils are almost exclusively desert soils.

Minerals and Natural Resources

Compared to the global average, the UAE has a considerable amount of energy reserves. It is the 7th largest crude oil producer in the world and the 4th largest producer of petroleum liquid in the OPEC. According to the Government of the United Arabs Emirates, there are approximately 99 billion barrels of oil reserves in the country, almost as big as Kuwait claims to have. Of the Emirates, Abu Dhabi has the highest reserve at 92 billion barrels or 90% of the total reserves while Dubai has only 4 billion barrels and Sharjah has 1.5 billion barrels. The country produces 2.9 million barrels of crude oil per day but has an intention of increasing the production to 5 million barrels per day by 2020 CE, which it aims to maintain until 2027 CE. Since proven reserves are estimated to remain relatively constant, increased production will mainly rely on enhanced oil recovery practices. The Emirates' reserve-to-production is estimated to be about 18 years.

The petroleum related policies in the Abu Dhabi are established by the Supreme Petroleum Council. SPC is one of the key players in the UAE's oil industry and the wider economy. Other players include the Abu Dhabi National Oil Company. The country has an advanced domestic pipeline network linking producing oil fields with the processing plants and export terminals. The 400 km Abu Dhabi Crude Oil Pipeline links the rich oil fields in Habshan to Fujairah.

Natural Gas

The UAE is an important country with regard to natural gas due to the large proven reserves and consumption. It has a substantial 6 trillion cubic meters of proven natural gas, with Abu Dhabi again holding the largest reserve (94%) with Sharjah holding 4% while Dubai and Ras al-Khaimah holding 1.5% and 0.5% respectively. This level of natural gas reserve gave the country the 4th largest in the Middle East and the 7th largest in the world. The production of natural gas has been growing over the recent years and the country currently produce 4.6 billion cubic feet per day, making it the 17th largest producer in the world. The UAE has the potential to produce even more gas, but the production is generally low because the majority of its natural gas contains high sulphur. The high sulphur makes the development and processing of natural gas technically difficult and economically challenging.

The Emirates is also a significant consumer of natural gas. In 2014 CE, the country consumed about 69 billion cubic meters of natural gas, making them the world's 9th largest natural gas consumer. It is the country's primary source of energy, accounting for 60% of the UAE's primary energy consumption. Natural gas is also used in the generation of electricity and desalination of water. Even with the massive reserves, the UAE still import natural gas to meet the demand. It is a major importer of pipeline natural gas.

Solar Energy

The UAE is one of the countries with the highest sun exposure rates in the world, making it a potential place for renewable energy. The government is taking advantage of sun exposure and the potential for renewable energy to establish a clean energy strategy. By 2050 CE, the country hopes to have a balance between energy production and consumption, with solar energy playing a key role in achieving this. The energy equation targeted by then is as follows; 44% renewable energy, 38% gas, 13% coal, and 6% nuclear.

Food, Agriculture, Flora and Fauna

The UAE is not self-sufficient in food.

As a desert country there is little livestock production apart from camels; and little formal agriculture. Much subsistence agriculture still abounds.

Flora and fauna are typical of the desert areas of the peninsula. Much flora and fauna are under threat from development and hunting.

Given that the country experiences mainly a desert climate, the arable land is estimated to be approximately 1% of the total land area. The total area under permanent crop is 2.4% of the total land area, most of which is artificially irrigated. The UAE has been working on increasing the size of land under agriculture, with research on fertilization and soil fertility technologies. Approximately 16% of the population live in rural areas and depend mainly on agriculture. The fertile agricultural land is common around the oases and seasonal riverbanks. Despite the aridity, the Emirates has developed thriving agriculture leading to self-sufficiency in certain vegetable crops. The UAE has approximately 40 million date palm trees, the highest concentration of palm trees in the world. Meat and dairy industries are also growing in the country; although these are expensive to produce.

Population

In 2013 CE, the UAE's population was 9.2 million, of which only 1.4 million were Emirati citizens and 7.8 million were expatriates. The estimated population of the UAE in 2020 CE was 9.89 million.

Politics

In early 2007 CE, the United Arab Emirates launched the 'UAE Government Strategy' for the years ahead, which covered twenty-one topics in six different sectors including social development, economic development, public sector development, justice and safety, infrastructure and rural areas development. The initiative is meant to re-evaluate and advance these sectors towards top global standards by facilitating better continuous cooperation between federal and local governments with increased efficiency, training, Emiratisation, ministry empowerment, upgrading of services, improving civil service and legislation review.

Subsequently, Abu Dhabi announced implementation of its own policy to modernize public administration practices and government performance in 2007–2008 CE. Plans for re - evaluation were laid out in areas including economy, energy, tourism, health, education, labour, civil services, culture and heritage, good control, urban planning, transport, environment, health and safety, municipal affairs, police and emergency services, electronic government, women and legislative reform. Abu Dhabi hopes advancements towards global standards in these areas will improve the quality of services for its residents as well as attract future investment towards further modernizing the Emirate.

The country did not see the type of trouble other Arab countries saw during the Arab spring. There were minor protests. Some people were arrested, and some had their nationality revoked.

Currently, 2021, relations with Saudi Arabia are more strained than is usual.

Language

The language of the UAE is Modern Standard Arabic, with English widely spoken.

Religion

The religion in the UAE is Sunni Islam.

Economy (Snapshot)

The UAE economy is the second largest in the GCC, after Saudi Arabia. Although UAE has the most diversified economy in the GCC, the UAE's economy remains extremely reliant on oil. With the exception of Dubai, most of the UAE is dependent on oil revenues. Petroleum and natural gas continue to play a central role in the economy, especially in Abu Dhabi. More than 85% of the UAE's economy was based on the oil exports in 2009 CE. While Abu Dhabi and other UAE emirates have remained relatively conservative in their approach to diversification, Dubai, which has far smaller oil reserves, was much more risk tolerant.

- GDP: $421.142 billion (nominal, 2020 CE); $647.650 billion (PPP 2020 CE est.). (UK: GDP: $2.64 trillion (nominal, 2020 CE est.); $2.98 trillion (PPP 2020 CE)

- GDP per capita: $43 103 (nominal, 2019 CE) · $58 466 (PPP 2020 CE est.).

- GDP by sector: Agriculture: 0.9%; Industry: 49.8% ; Services : 49.2% (2017 est.).

- Labour force: 6 922 233 (2020 CE) · 78.3% employment rate (2019 CE); expatriates account for about 85% of the workforce

- Labour force by occupation: Agriculture: 7%; Industry: 15%; Services: 78%; (2000 est.).

Qatar

Qatar is a country located in Western Asia, occupying the small Qatar Peninsula on the northeastern coast of the Arabian Peninsula. Its sole land border is with neighbouring Gulf Cooperation Council (GCC) monarchy Saudi Arabia to the south, with the rest of its territory surrounded by the Persian Gulf. The Gulf of Bahrain, an inlet of the Persian Gulf, separates Qatar from nearby Bahrain. The capital is Doha, and most people live within the capital area.

General Geography and Topography

Qatar is a peninsula in the east of the Arabian Peninsula, bordering the Persian Gulf and Saudi Arabia, in a strategic location near major petroleum deposits. The state of Qatar occupies 11 437 sq.km on a peninsula that extends approximately to 160 km north into the Persian Gulf from the Arabian Peninsula.

Varying in width between 55 and 90 km the land is mainly flat (the highest point is 103 m and rocky. Notable features include coastal salt pans, elevated limestone formations along the west coast under which lies an oil field, and massive sand dunes surrounding Khawr al Udayd, an inlet of the Persian Gulf in the southeast.

Climate

The long summer (May through September) is characterized by intense heat and alternating dryness and humidity, with temperatures reaching 50 °C. Temperatures are moderate from November to April, ranging from as high as 39 °C in April to as low as 7 °C in January. Rainfall is negligible, averaging 100 mm per year, confined to the winter months, and falling in brief, sometimes heavy, storms that often flood the small ravines and the usually dry wadis.

Sudden, violent dust storms occasionally descend on the peninsula, blotting out the sun, causing wind damage, and temporarily disrupting transport and other services.

Soils

Most of Qatar's soils are desert soils.

Qatar's soils vary in soil texture, ranging from sandy loam to heavy calcareous clay. The majority of cultivation that occurs is on clay loam soil. However, there are numerous problems with this soil, including high salinity levels, low amounts of nutrients, and a bad water-infiltration rate.

Minerals and Natural Resources

Qatar sits on the third largest natural gas field in the world (which it shares with Iran) and substantial oil reserves.

Apart from oil and gas, fishing and pearl hunting are also important components of the economy. Qatar is also a major producer of helium.

The scarcity of rainfall and the limited underground water, most of which has such a high mineral content that it is unsuitable for drinking or irrigation, restricted the population and the extent of agricultural and industrial development the country could support until desalination projects began. Although water continues to be provided from underground sources, most is obtained by desalination of seawater.

Food, Agriculture, Flora and Fauna

Qatar is not self-sufficient in food. Agriculture is limited because of the sandy deserts.

Flora is curtailed to depressions, wadis and the east coast.

There is a wide variety of fauna still evident including twenty-two mammals. The sea coasts are rich in wildlife; the sea offshore and is a centre for whale sharks and dugongs.

Population

Natives of the Arabian Peninsula, many Qataris are descended from several migratory Arab tribes that came to Qatar in the 18th century CE from mainly the neighbouring areas of Nejd and Al-Hasa. Some are descended from Omani tribes. Qatar has about 2.5 million inhabitants as of early 2018, the vast majority of whom (about 92%) live in Doha, the capital. Foreign workers amount to around 88% of the population,

Politics

Qatar has been ruled by the House of Thani since Mohammed bin Thani signed a treaty with the British in 1868 CE that recognised its separate status. Following Ottoman rule, Qatar became a British protectorate in the early 20th century CE until gaining independence in 1971 CE. In 2003 CE, the constitution was overwhelmingly approved in a referendum, with almost 98% in favour. In the 21st century CE, Qatar emerged as a significant power in the Arab world both through its globally expanding media group, Al Jazeera Media Network, its sovereign wealth fund, and reportedly supporting several rebel groups financially during the Arab Spring. For its size, Qatar wields disproportionate influence in the world, and has been identified as a middle power.

Language

Qatar uses Modern Standard Arabic, English is widely spoken and used for business.

Religion

The religion of Qatar is Sunni Muslim.

Economy (Snapshot)

- GDP: $147.791 billion (nominal 2020 CE est.); $257.464 billion (PPP 2020 est.). (UK: GDP: $2.64 trillion (nominal, 2020 est.); $2.98 trillion (PPP 2020)

- Main export partners: Japan (+) 17.3%; South Korea (+) 16%; India (+) 12.6%; China (+) 11.2%; Singapore (+) 8.2%. (2017).

- Main import partners: United States (+) 13.7%; Germany (+) 9.8%; China (+) 8.6%; Japan (+) 7.2%; United Kingdom (+) 5.5%; Italy (+) 4.8%.

- Indigenous population below poverty line: 0%.

Bahrain

Bahrain, or the Kingdom of Bahrain, is a country in the Persian Gulf. The island nation comprises a small archipelago made up of 51 natural islands and an additional 33 artificial islands, centred around Bahrain Island which makes up around 83% of the country's landmass. The country is situated between the Qatari peninsula and the northeastern coast of Saudi Arabia to which it is connected by the 25 km King Fahd Causeway.

At 780 sq.km in size, it is the third-smallest nation in Asia after the Maldives and Singapore. The capital and largest city is Manama.

General Geography and Topography

Around most of Bahrain is a relatively shallow inlet of the Persian Gulf known as the Gulf of Bahrain. The seabed adjacent to Bahrain is rocky and, mainly off the northern part of the island, covered by extensive coral reefs. Most of the island is low-lying and barren desert. Outcroppings of limestone form low rolling hills, stubby cliffs, and shallow ravines. The limestone is covered by various densities of saline sand, capable of supporting only the hardiest desert vegetation, chiefly thorn trees and scrub. There is a fertile strip five kilometres wide along the northern coast on which date, almond, fig, and pomegranate trees grow. The interior contains an escarpment that rises to 134 m, the highest point on the island, to form Jabal al Dukhan (Mountain of Smoke), named for the mists that often wreathe the summit. Most of the country's oil wells are situated in the vicinity of Jabal al Dukhan.

Climate

The climate of Bahrain is an arid type; mean annual rainfall is small (70.8mm) and irregular. Broadly speaking, the year may be divided into two main climatic periods from June to September and from December to March, separated by two transitional periods April/May and October/November. The mean number of days per annum with measurable rain of 1mm or more are 9.9 with the highest being 2 days in the month of January. Thunderstorms occur on average on 7.8 days per annum with March having the highest average of 1.9 days. The average number of days per annum that visibility is reduced to 1 000 m or less by fog is 6.6 and by thick dust haze is 4.5. January averages 1.7 days of fog and is the highest monthly frequency. July has the highest frequency of thick dust haze occurrence (1.1

days on average).

Recently, particularly in the early part of the year, there has been much heavy rain and flooding. This is changing the climate profile as described above.

Soils

Soils were once much more fertile than they are today. The island was famous for having over a million date palms, many of which have gone. The soils have been affected by development, and a lowering of the freshwater table (which has become more saline). The soils are more arid, more desert in nature; and tougher, harder.

Minerals and Natural Resources

Fossil fuels, particularly oil and natural gas, are the most critical natural resources in Bahrain. Apart from fossil fuels, Bahrain also relies on other natural resources such as arable land and minerals such as aluminium.

In recent years there have been further discoveries of both oil and gas linked to fields in Saudi Arabia and Qatar. (Though these have clearly been assessed many years ago).

Food, Agriculture, Flora and Fauna

Before oil was discovered in the country, the most important crop was dates. The country produced sufficient dates to satisfy the local demand, and the surplus was sold to other nations. According to the country's agricultural experts, more than 20 types of dates thrive in Bahrain's climate. Apart from the fruit of the date trees, the other parts of the tree such as the flowers, the buds, and the leaves were also used. Date farming experienced a significant decline in the mid-20th centuries CE due to several reasons. The most notable factor was the change in the Bahraini dietary patterns. Another factor that led to the decline in date production in the country was the reduction of water available to irrigate the dates.

Livestock is one of Bahrain's most important natural resources. Bahraini livestock farmers keep a variety of animals such as cattle, camels, sheep, and goats. Because Bahrain is a Muslim country, livestock farmers do not keep pigs. Despite the presence of the livestock industry in the country, Bahrain must rely on imports from other countries to satisfy the local demand.

Because Bahrain is an island nation it has a wealth of fishing resources. Fish constitutes a vital part of the diet of most Bahraini people. According to several experts, Bahrain's territorial waters are home to more than 200 kinds of fish. Before the Bahraini oil boom, fishing was an essential economic activity for most of the country's young men. Apart from fishing Bahraini young men were also involved in pearling. In the past, pearls from Bahrain were famous all around the world due to their high quality. Bahrain's pearl industry declined due to two main reasons; the oil industry attracted most of the young Bahraini men and stiff competition from the Japanese pearl industry.

Population

According to the 2010 CE census, Bahrain's 2020 CE population is estimated at 1 701 575 people mid-year according to UN data. Half of people counted are non-nationals willing to report their status.

Politics

The politics of Bahrain has, since 2002 CE, taken place in a framework of a constitutional monarchy where the government is appointed by the King of Bahrain, King Hamad bin Isa Al Khalifa. The head of the government since 1971 CE has been Prime Minister Prince Khalifa bin Salman Al Khalifa and the Crown Prince is Prince Salman bin Hamad Al Khalifa, who also serves as Deputy Commander of the Bahrain Defence Force. The parliament is a bi-cameral legislature, with the Council of Representatives elected by universal suffrage, and the Consultative Council (also called the Shura Council) appointed directly by the king.

Language

The language in Bahrain is Modern Standard Arabic, with English the key language for business.

Religion

The state religion of Bahrain is Sunni Muslim, however there is a majority of Shia Muslim in the indigenous population.

Economy (Snapshot)

- GDP: $34.624 billion (nominal, 2020 CE est.) · $74.245 billion (PPP 2020 CE est.). (UK: GDP: $2.64 trillion (nominal, 2020 CE est.); $2.98 trillion (PPP 2020 CE).

- GDP by sector: Agriculture: 0.3%; Industry: 39.3%; Services: 60.4% · (2017 CE est.).

- Labour force: 977 302 (201CE 9) 70.9% employment rate (201CE5); 44% of the population in the 15-64 age group is non-national.

- Main export partners: United Arab Emirates 19.6%; Saudi Arabia 11.7%; United States 10.8%; Oman 8.1%; China 6.5%; Qatar 5.7%

- Main import partners: China 8.8%; United Arab Emirates 7.2%; United States 7.1%; Australia 5.8%; Japan 4.8% (2017 est.).

Kuwait

Kuwait, or the State of Kuwait, is a country in Western Asia. It is situated at the northern edge of the eastern Arabian Peninsula at the tip of the Persian Gulf, bordering Iraq to the north and Saudi Arabia to the south. As of 2016 CE, Kuwait has a population of 4.5 million people: 1.3 million are Kuwaitis and 3.2 million are expatriates. Expatriates account for approximately 70% of the population. As of 2018 CE, more than 70 % of the country's population lived in the urban agglomeration of the capital Kuwait City.

General Geography and Topography

Kuwait is a small, generally flat (highest point is just over 300m desert with a small marine economic zone.

Climate

Kuwait has a subtropical desert climate, with mild winters and very hot summers. Summers can reach over 50 °C. Rainfall, slightly higher than 100 mm per year, occurs mainly from November to April, in the form of rare showers, which can sometimes be so intense and concentrated as to cause flooding. This has become a more common occurrence in recent years.

Soils

Kuwait soils are desert soils.

Minerals and Natural Resources

The most critical natural resource in Kuwait is the oil. Geological research indicates that the oil reserves in Kuwait comprise slightly below 10% of the world's total reserves. Part of Kuwait's oil reserves is situated in the Saudi-Kuwait neutral zone. Kuwait is home to the world's second largest oil reserve, the Burgan field. The oil industry is Kuwait's most important industry.

Food, Agriculture, Flora and Fauna

Arable land is one of the most critical natural resources in Kuwait. A study carried out in 2014 indicated that approximately 1500 sq.kms of land in Kuwait were used for agricultural purposes. However, despite its importance, the agricultural sector

175

in Kuwait has not had significant improvement because the nation is situated in a relatively dry area. Due to the lack of development in the sector, it does not provide a large number of jobs. Research from the World Bank indicates that only 4% of the Kuwaiti workforce was employed in the agricultural sector. Most of the people who work in the agricultural sector are foreigners. Foreign investors own a large number of farms in Kuwait. The contribution of Kuwait's agricultural sector to the gross domestic product is also minimal as in 2017 CE it contributed less than 0.5% of the total GDP. Most of the agricultural produce from Kuwait include fruits and vegetables for local consumption. To increase the nation's agricultural output, the Kuwaiti government has experimented with some modern farming methods such as the use of hydroponics and growing food in a carefully controlled situation. Apart from the dry climate, another factor that limits the agricultural potential of Kuwait is the fact that much of its agricultural land was destroyed during the war with Ir

Another primary natural resource in Kuwait is the livestock. Some of the most commonly kept animals in Kuwait include cattle, sheep, and goats. Livestock keeping contributes significantly to the country's agricultural output as its contribution was roughly 67%. Due to the low amount of water in the country, the government supplies the livestock farmers with water.

Due to its position, Kuwait has access to large fishing grounds with a wide array of fish. Despite the availability of a variety of fish species, fishing only contributes a small portion to Kuwait's gross domestic product. Most of the fish caught in Kuwait's territorial waters are consumed locally by the Kuwaiti people. Large-scale fishing is primarily carried out by the United Fisheries of Kuwait. Apart from fishing in Kuwait's territorial waters, the organization also fishes in international waters of the Indian Ocean, the Atlantic Ocean, as well as the Red Sea. The organization is well known for the quality of its shrimp. One of the factors that limit Kuwait's ability to exploit its fish resources in its territorial waters is the rampant over-fishing that occurred in the Gulf during the 1970s CE. Apart from the overfishing, other factors that limit Kuwait's fishing industry is the impact of war and the environmental damage caused by frequent oil spills in the region.

Population

Expatriates account for around 70% of Kuwait's (per-haps 5 million) total population, with Kuwaitis constituting 28%-32% (Nearly 2 million by 2020) of the total population. The government and some Kuwaiti citizens consider the pro-portion of expatriates (which has been relatively stable since the mid-1970s CE) to be a problem, and since 2016 CE the number of deportations has increased.

Politics

Kuwait is a constitutional emirate with a semi-democratic pol-itical system. The hybrid political system is divided between an elected parliament and appointed government. Kuwait is among the Middle East's freest countries in civil liberties and political rights. The Constitution of Kuwait was promulgated in 1962 CE. Freedom House rates the country as 'partly free' in the Freedom in the World survey. Kuwait is the only one among the Arab states of the Persian Gulf which is ranked "partly free". In 2020 CE elections, following some repression since the last elections in 2016 CE, the number of opposition leaning elected members increased. The effect of this has yet to be seen.

Language

The language of Kuwait is Modern Standard Arabic.

Religion

Kuwait's religion is Sunni Muslim with perhaps 5 -15% Shia.

Economy (Snapshot)

Kuwait has reportedly saved 10% of its oil revenues against

future oil shocks; but is still finding itself in difficulty as a result of low oil prices and COVID.

- GDP: $108.656 billion (nominal, 2020 CE est.) · $203.786 billion (PPP 2020 CE est.) (UK: GDP: $2.64 trillion (nominal, 2020 CE est.); $2.98 trillion (PPP 2020 CE).

- GDP per capita: $22 252 (nominal, 2020 CE est.) · $41 735 (PPP 2020 CE est.).

- Main export partners: South Korea (+) 18.3%; China (-) 17.4%; Japan (+) 11.5%; India (+) 11.2%; Singapore (+) 6.3%; United States (+) 5.7% (2017).

- Main import partners: China (-) 13.5%; United States (+) 13.3%; UAE (+) 9.5%; Saudi Arabia (+) 5.8%; Germany (+) 5.4%; Japan (+) 5.0%.

- Fiscal year: 1 April – 31 March

CHAPTER 10: IRAN

Iran, also called Persia, and officially the Islamic Republic of Iran is a country situated in Western Asia. It is bordered to the northwest by Armenia and Azerbaijan, to the north by the Caspian Sea, to the northeast by Turkmenistan, to the east by Afghanistan, to the southeast by Pakistan, to the south by the Persian Gulf and the Gulf of Oman, and to the west by Turkey and Iraq. Iran covers an area of 1 648 195 sq. kms with a population of 83 million. It is the second largest country in the Middle East, and its capital and largest city is Tehran.

General Geography and Topography

Iran covers such a large area of land that the country contains a vast variety of landscapes and terrains. Much of Iran is made up of the Iranian Plateau, which except for the Caspian Sea and Persian Gulf coastlines are where the only large plains are found. Iran is also one of the most mountainous countries in the world. These large mountain ranges cut through the landscape and divide the numerous basins and plateaus. The western side of the country possesses the largest mountain ranges such as the Caucasus, Alborz, and Zagros Mountains. The Alborz contains Iran's highest point on Mount Damavand. The northern part of the country is marked by dense rainforests and jungles, whereas eastern Iran is mostly desert basins which also contain some salt lakes formed due to the convection rain from mountain ranges.

Climate

Iran has what is considered a variable climate that ranges from semi-arid to subtropical. In the northwest, winters are cold with heavy snowfall and subfreezing temperatures during December and January. Spring and autumn are relatively mild, while summers are dry and hot. In the south, however, winters are mild, and the summers are very hot, with average daily temperatures in July exceeding 38°C. On the Khuzestan plain, the extreme summer heat is accompanied by high humidity.

In general, Iran has an arid climate in which most of the relatively scant annual precipitation falls from October through April. In most of the country, yearly precipitation averages only 25 cm or less. The major exceptions to this semiarid and arid climate are the higher mountain valleys of the Zagros and the Caspian coastal plain, where precipitation averages at least 50 cm annually. In the western part of the Caspian, Iran sees the greatest rainfall in the country where it exceeds 100 cm annually and is distributed relatively evenly throughout the year rather than being confined to a rainy season. This climate contrasts greatly with some basins of the Central Plateau that receive 10 cm or less of precipitation annually. It has been said that water scarcity poses the most severe human security challenge in Iran today.

Soils

Soil patterns vary widely. The abundant subtropical vegetation of the Caspian coastal region is supported by rich brown forest soils. Mountain soils are shallow layers over bedrock, with a high proportion of unweathered fragments. Natural erosion moves the finer-textured soils into the valleys. The alluvial deposits are mostly chalky, and many are used for pottery. The semiarid plateaus lying above 900 metres are covered by brown or chestnut-coloured soil that supports grassy vegetation. The soil is slightly alkaline and contains 3 - 4% organic material. The saline and alkaline soils in the arid regions are light in colour and infertile. The sand dunes are composed of loose quartz and fragments of other minerals and, except where anchored by vegetation, are in almost constant motion, driven by high winds.

Climate

Iran's climate ranges from subtropical to subpolar. In winter a high-pressure belt, centred in Siberia, slashes west and south to the interior of the Iranian plateau, and low-pressure systems develop over the warm waters of the Caspian Sea, the Persian Gulf, and the Mediterranean Sea. In summer one of the world's lowest-pressure centres prevails in the south. Low-pressure systems in Pakistan generate two regular wind patterns: the *Shamal*, which blows from February to October north-westerly through the Tigris-Euphrates valley, and the '120-day' summer wind, which can reach velocities of 110 km per hour in the Sistani region near Pakistan. Warm Arabian winds bring heavy moisture from the Persian Gulf.

Elevation, latitude, maritime influences, seasonal winds, and proximity to mountain ranges or deserts play a significant role in diurnal and seasonal temperature. Average daytime summer temperature fluctuation in Abadan in Khuzestan province tops 43 °C, and the average daytime winter high in Tabriz in the East Azarbayjan province barely reaches freezing. Precipitation also varies widely, from less than 50 mm in the southeast to about 1 980 mm in the Caspian region. The annual average is about 400 mm. Winter is normally the rainy season for the country; more than half of the annual precipitation occurs in that three-month period. The northern coastal region presents a sharp contrast. The high Elburz Mountains, which seal off the narrow Caspian plain from the rest of the country, wring moisture from the clouds, trap humidity from the air, and create a fertile semitropical region of luxuriant forests, swamps, and rice paddies. Temperatures there may soar to 38 °C and the humidity to nearly 100%, while frosts are extremely rare. Except in this region, summer is a dry season.

The northern and western parts of Iran have four distinct seasons. Toward the south and east, spring and autumn become increasingly short and ultimately merge in an area of mild winters and hot summers.

Minerals and Natural Resources

As of 2010 CE, Iran's crude oil and natural gas liquids production ranked fourth in the world. It is said to have 15.8% of the world's proven natural gas reserves and 9.9% of the world's proven oil reserves.

Production statistics of mineral commodities in 2010 are:

- Gypsum and pumice - 9% of the world's total production.
- Barite - 4%.
- Feldspar - 3%.
- Molybdenum - 2%.
- Nitrogen - 2%.
- Sulphur - 2%.
- Cement, iron ore, and silica sand - more than 1%.

Through the Iranian Mines and Mining Industries Development and Renovation Organization (IMIDRO), the government controls most of the big mining and mining-related companies such as those producing natural gas, petroleum, coal, aluminium, copper, iron and steel, salt, ammonia, and sulphur.

Metals

In the beginning of 2010 CE, the 147 000 t/yr-capacity Hormozgan aluminium complex (Hormozal) began operations. Similarly, two other aluminium projects, namely, a 276 000-t/yr-capacity smelter construction project of South Aluminium Co. and an 110 000-t/yr-capacity expansion project of Iran Aluminium Co. progressed that year.

The Zarshoran gold project went ahead as planned in 2010 CE. The new mining facility is designed with a production capacity of 3 000 kg/yr of gold, 1 000 kg/yr of silver, and 800 kg/yr of mercury.

The Gharb Asia Steel Company with a capacity of producing 550 000 t/yr of cold-rolled steel plates began operation in 2011 CE.

Industrial Minerals and Gemstones

In 2010 CE, Iran had many petrochemical projects lined up including two large fertilizer projects. One of them was the construction of a 770,000-t/yr-capacity ammonia plant by a joint venture between the National Petrochemical Co. of Iran and Nagarjuna Fertilisers and Chemicals Limited Co. of India. Construction is scheduled to be completed in 2014 CE.

Reports claim that Iran's current annual cement production capacity is estimated at 72 million tonnes.

Fossil Fuels

As of 2010 CE, Iran had about 40 oil fields in operation. There were many other oil fields that were under development.

Some of the hydrocarbon refineries under construction were:

- Anahita refinery at Kermanshah.
- Caspian refinery in Golestan Province.
- Horumuz refinery.
- Khuzestan extra-heavy crude oil refinery at Abadan.
- Pars refinery at Shiraz.
- Persian Gulf Star refinery at Bandar Abbas.
- Shahriyar refinery at Tabriz.

These refineries are likely to increase the domestic supply of gasoline from 2013 CE onwards.

Food, Agriculture, Flora and Fauna

Roughly 33% of Iran's total surface area is suited for farmland, but because of poor soil and lack of adequate water distribution in many areas, most of it is not under cultivation. Only 12% of the total land area is under cultivation (arable land, orchards and vineyards) but less than one-third of the cultivated area is irrigated; the rest is devoted to dryland farming. Some 92% of agricultural products depend on water. The western and northwestern portions of the country have the most fertile soils. Iran's food security index stands at around 96%.

3% of the total land area is used for grazing and small fodder production. Most of the grazing is done on mostly semi-dry rangeland in mountain areas and on areas surrounding the large deserts ('Dasht's') of Central Iran.

The non-agricultural surface represents 53% of the total area of Iran, as follows:

- About 39% of the country is covered by deserts, salt flats ('kavirs') and bare-rock mountains, not suited for agricultural purposes.

- An additional 7% of Iran's total surface is covered by woodlands.

- And 7% is covered by cities, towns, villages, industrial areas and roads.

At the end of the 20th century CE, agricultural activities accounted for about 20% of Iran's gross domestic product (GDP) and employed a comparable proportion of the workforce. Most farms are small, less than 10 hectares, and are not economically viable, which has contributed to the wide-scale migration to cities. In addition to water scarcity and areas of poor soil, seed is of low quality and farming techniques are antiquated.

All these factors have contributed to low crop yields and poverty in rural areas. Further, after the 1979 CE revolution many agricultural workers claimed ownership rights and forcibly occupied large, privately owned farms where they had been employed. The legal disputes that arose from this situation remained unresolved through the 1980s CE, and many owners put off making large capital investments that would have improved farm productivity, further deteriorating production. Progressive government efforts and incentives during the 1990s CE, however, improved agricultural productivity marginally, helping Iran toward its goal of re-establishing national self-sufficiency in food production.

Topography, elevation, water supply, and soil determine the character of the vegetation. Approximately 10% of Iran is forested, most extensively in the Caspian region. In the area are found broad-leaved deciduous trees—oak, beech, linden, elm, walnut, ash, and hornbeam—and a few broad-leaved evergreens. Thorny shrubs and ferns also abound. The Zagros Mountains are covered by scrub oak forests, together with elm, maple, hackberry, walnut, pear, and pistachio trees. Willow, poplar, and plane trees grow in the ravines, as do many species of creepers. Thin stands of juniper, almond, barberry, cotoneaster, and wild fruit trees grow on the intermediate dry plateau. Thorny shrubs form the ground cover of the steppes, while species of *Artemisia* (wormwood) grow at medium elevations of the desert plains and the rolling country. Acacia, dwarf palm, *kunar* trees (of the genus *Ziziphus*), and scattered shrubs are found below 900 metres. Desert sand dunes, which hold water, support thickets of brush. Forests follow the courses of surface or subterranean waters. Oases support vines and tamarisk, poplar, date palm, myrtle, oleander, acacia, willow, elm, plum, and mulberry trees. In swamp areas reeds and grass provide good pasture.

Wildlife includes leopards, bears, hyenas, wild boars, ibex, gazelles, and mouflons, which live in the wooded mountains. Jackals and rabbits are common in the country's interior. Wild asses live in the *kavīrs* (salt flats). cheetahs and pheasants are found in the Caspian region, and partridges live in most parts of the country. Aquatic birds such as seagulls, ducks, and geese live on the shores of the Caspian Sea and the Persian Gulf, while buzzards nest in the desert. Deer, hedgehogs, foxes, and 22 species of rodents live in semidesert, high-elevation regions. Palm squirrels and Asiatic black bears are found in Baluchistan. Tigers once inhabited the forests of the Caspian region but are now extinct; and many of the other animals are threatened with extinction.

Studies made in Khuzestan province and the Baluchistan region and along the slopes of the Elburz and Zagros mountains have revealed the presence of a remarkably wide variety of amphibians and reptiles. Examples are toads, frogs, tortoises, lizards, salamanders, racers, rat snakes (*Ptyas*), cat snakes (*Tarbophis fallax*), and vipers.

Population

Iran's population increased dramatically during the latter half of the 20th century CE, reaching about 85 million by 2020 CE. In recent years, however, Iran's birth rate has dropped significantly to around 2 to 2.1 per woman – which is just about replacement rate. Studies project that Iran's rate of population growth will continue to slow until it stabilizes above 100 million by 2050 CE. More than half of Iran's population is under 30 years old (2020 CE).

In 2009 CE, the number of households stood at 15.3 million (4.8 persons per household). Families earn some 11.8 million-rials (about $960) per month on average (2012 CE).

According to the OECD/World Bank statistics population growth in Iran from 1990 CE to 2008 CE was 17.6 million and 32%. The literacy rate was 80% in 2002 CE, and 85% in 2016 CE.

Politics

Iran is the Guardianship of the Islamic Jurist and Islamic Republic in which the president, parliament (Majles) and judicial system share powers reserved to the national government, according to its constitution. The politics of Iran take place in a framework that officially combines elements of theocracy and presidential democracy. The December 1979 CE constitution, and its 1989 CE amendment, define the political, economic, and social order of the Islamic Republic of Iran, declaring that Shia Islam is Iran's official religion where around 90–95% of Iranians associate themselves with the Shia branch of Islam.

Iran has a democratically elected president, a parliament (or Majlis), an Assembly of Experts which elects the Supreme Leader, and local councils. According to the constitution, all candidates running for these positions must be vetted by the Guardian Council before being elected.

In addition, there are representatives elected from appointed organizations (usually under the Supreme Leader's control) to 'protect the state's Islamic character'. Prior to 1979 CE, Iran had its political system as a parliamentary democratic constitutional monarchy with parliamentary system. The Shah served as its head of state while the Prime Minister held the post of the head of government from the 1906 Persian Constitution. While the political system is secular in nature, it has been described as authoritarian in the later years of the Imperial State.

The Armed Forces of the Islamic Republic of Iran comprise the Army (*Artesh*), the Revolutionary Guard Corps (*Sepāh*) and the Law Enforcement Force (Police) of the Islamic Republic of Iran.

The Iranian Armed Forces are numerically the largest and arguably the most powerful in the Middle East. These forces total about 610 000 active personnel (not including the Law Enforcement Force) plus 1 050 000 reserve and trained personnel that could be mobilized when needed. That makes a total of 2 010 000 military personnel that Iran could mobilize. All branches of the armed forces fall under the command of General Staff of Armed Forces. The Ministry of Defence and Armed Forces Logistics is responsible for planning logistics and funding of the armed forces and is not involved with in-the-field military operational command.

Iran's military was described in 2015 CE as the Middle East's *"most powerful military force"* by retired U.S General and former CENTCOM commander John Abizaid.

In March 2021 CE state TV in Iran showed footage of a 'missile city' armed with ballistic and cruise weapons described as 'a new Revolutionary Guard base' along the Gulf coast.

The Islamic Revolutionary Guard Corps (IRGC), also called Pasdaran, branch of the Iranian armed forces, is independent of Iran's regular army. Iran's current leader Ruhollah Khomeini established the Islamic Revolutionary Guard Corps (IRGC) in April 1979 CE by decree and tasked it with safeguarding the Islamic republic that was formed after the Iranian Revolution (1978–79 CE). The participation of the IRGC in the Iran-Iraq War (1980–88 CE) led to the expansion of both its role and its might, making it Iran's dominant military force, with its own army, navy, and air force and, later, its own intelligence wing.

Establishment And Development

Following a year of unrest, Mohammad Reza Shah Pahlavi fled Iran in January 1979 CE. A referendum in March approved the establishment of an Islamic republic under the leadership of Khomeini, who had laid out the intellectual basis of an Islamic republic in the decades prior to the revolution. Although Iran's armed forces had declared their neutrality to the revolution in February, many of the revolutionaries were fearful of a repeat of the 1953 CE countercoup, in which the military aided in the removal of Mohammad Mosaddegh and the restoration of the Shah. Khomeini established the IRGC to unify and organize paramilitary forces that were committed to the revolution; the unified force would thus serve as a counterweight to the regular army, which had originally been loyal to the shah. The permanence of the IRGC was formalized in the new constitution adopted later that year.

The IRGC resisted attempts to subjugate it to political control and bring it within the fold of the regular armed forces. Tension was particularly pronounced between the IRGC and Iran's first president, Abolhasan Bani-Sadr (1980–81 CE), whose friction with various government figures led to his impeachment and removal from office in 1981 CE. The two subsequent presidents, however, Mohammad Ali Raja'i (August 1981 CE) and Ali Khamenei (1981–89 CE), were favourable to the IRGC, and Khamenei aided the organization with expansive resources. Although the IRGC was initially deployed in the Iran-Iraq War to bolster the efforts of the regular army, it grew in force, structure, and complexity with the support of the political establishment. A contingent for foreign operations, known as the Quds Force, became active in the Lebanese Civil War in 1982 CE, and Khomeini authorized the creation of a navy and an air force in 1985 CE.

Language

The largest linguistic group comprises speakers of Iranian languages, like modern Persian, Kurdish, Gilaki, Mazandarani, Luri, Talysh, and Balochi. Speakers of Turkic languages, most notably Azerbaijanis, which is by far the second-most spoken language in the country, but also the Turkmen, and the Qashqai peoples, comprise a substantial minority. The remainder are primarily speakers of Semitic languages such as Arabic and Assyrian. There are small groups using other Indo-European languages such as Armenian, Russian,

Georgian (a member of the Kartvelian language family), spoken in a large pocket only by those Iranian Georgians that live in Fereydan, Fereydunshahr. Most of those Georgians who live in the north Iranian provinces of Gilan, Mazandaran, Isfahan, Tehran Province and the rest of Iran no longer speak the language but keep a Georgian conscience. The Circassians in Iran, a very large minority in the past and speakers of the Circassian language, have been strongly assimilated and absorbed within the population in the past few centuries. However, significant pockets do exist spread over the country, and they are the second-largest Caucasus-derived group in the nation after the Georgians.

Jews have had a continuous presence in Iran since the time of Cyrus the Great of the Achaemenid Empire. In 1948, there were approximately 140,000–150,000 Jews living in Iran. According to the Tehran Jewish Committee, the Jewish population of Iran was (more recently) estimated at about 25,000 to 35,000, of which approximately 15,000 are in Tehran with the rest residing in Hamadan, Shiraz, Isfahan, Kermanshah, Yazd, Kerman, Rafsanjan, Borujerd, Sanandaj, Tabriz and Urmia. However, the official 2011 state census recorded only 8,756 Jews in Iran.

Religion

Iran is an Islamic state where close to 98% of the population identifies as being Muslim. The nation's constitution is largely based on Islamic law. The dominant religious group in Iran is the Shia Muslims. Sunni Muslims are the second largest religious group. The other religious minorities recognized by the State are Zoroastrian, Jewish, and Christian Iranians. The constitution allows for religious freedom as long as it is within the provisions of the law.

Shia Islam

Shia Muslims make up the largest religious group in Iran, comprising an estimated 93% share of the population. Shia

Islam was established as the state religion during the Safavid dynasty of 1501. In that period, Sunni Muslims were forced to convert to Shia Muslims in a nationwide campaign. Shia Islam has three main divisions which are Zaidis, Ismailis and Ithna Asharis (Twelvers or Imamis). The Twelvers are the largest group of Shia Muslims. They believe that the 12th Imam, Muhammad al-Mahdi, did not die and that he will return to proclaim justice on earth. Although Shia Muslims are the largest religious group in Iran, they are a minority group in the Muslim faith. The world's Muslim population is made up of approximately 80% Sunni Muslims and close to 20% Shia Muslims.

Sunni And Other Muslims

All other types of Islam combine to make up 6% of the total population in the country. Sunni Muslims are the second largest religious group in Iran. They are concentrated in the mountainous region of Larestan in Iran. The Sunnis are said to be indigenous Iranians who escaped conversion to Shia Muslims during the time of Safavid dynasty. Sunni Muslims put much emphasis on the Sunnah, in contrast to Shia Muslims. Sunnis heavily rely on the Prophet Muhammad's (pbuh) actions and teachings. They view Shia Muslims as heretics. Sunnis dogmatic beliefs are a reason for the emergence of extremist sects in Islam.

Non-Muslims

All other non-Muslim religions combined constitute 1% of the country's population. The religious minority groups in Iran include Christians, Baha'is, Jews, Zoroastrians, and Mandaeans. The largest non-Muslim religious group in Iran are its Christians. Christians in Iran date back to the early years of Christianity in the 1st Century CE. Iran has numerous churches. Christianity is the fastest growing religion in Iran currently.

Zoroastrianism was the predominant religion in Iran before the Islamic conquest in 640 CE. After the conquest, Islam became the predominant religion. Currently a few Iranians still practice Zoroastrianism. The religion is recognized by the state. Zoroastrian believers enjoy representation in the Iranian government. Judaism is among the oldest religions in Iran. It dates back to the old biblical times. Jews in Iran are recognized by the state as a minority religious group. Baha'i is another significant religious minority in Iran. Baha'is are said to have emerged from the Shia Islamic group. The group is not recognized by Iranian Government. They do not have any representation in government. Baha'i followers have suffered discrimination in access to higher education and employment in Iran. They are an oppressed religious minority group.

Economy

The economy of Iran is a mixed and transition economy with a large public sector. It is the world's eighteenth largest by purchasing power parity (PPP). Some 60% of Iran's economy is centrally planned. It is dominated by oil and gas production, although over 40 industries are directly involved in the Tehran Stock Exchange, one of the best performing exchanges in the world over the past decade. With 10% of the world's proven oil reserves and 15% of its gas reserves, Iran is considered an 'energy superpower'. A unique feature of Iran's economy is the presence of large religious foundations called Bonyad, whose combined budgets represent more than 30 percent of central government spending.

Price controls and subsidies, particularly on food and energy, are heavily prominent in the economy. Contraband, administrative controls, widespread corruption, and other restrictive factors undermine private sector-led growth. The government's 20-year vision (as of 2020 CE) involves market-based reforms with a five year development plan (FY 2016 CE to FY 2021 CE) focusing on 'a resilient economy' and "progress in science and technology".

Most of the country's exports are oil and gas, accounting for a majority of government revenue in 2010 CE and since.

GDP contracted in 2018 CE and 2019 CE and modest rebound is expected in 2020 CE.[Challenges include COVID-19 outbreak starting in February 2020 CE and U.S sanctions reimposed in mid-2018 CE, causing increased unemployment, inflation, a chronically weak and undercapitalised banking system, and an anaemic private sector. Iran's currency (Iranian rial) has fallen, and Iran has a relatively low rating in "Economic Freedom", and "ease of doing business".

Iran's educated population, high human development, constrained economy and insufficient foreign and domestic investment prompted an increasing number of Iranians to seek overseas employment, resulting in a significant 'brain drain'. However, in 2015, Iran and the P5+1 reached a deal on the nuclear program which removed most international sanctions. Consequently, the tourism industry was significantly improved, and inflation decreased. This all changed during the Trump administration.

Economy (Snapshot)

- GDP: $610.6 billion (nominal, 2020 CE est.) $1.007 trillion (PPP, 2020 CE est.). (UK: GDP: $2.64 trillion (nominal, 2020 CE est.); $2.98 trillion (PPP, 2020 CE).

- GDP Rank: 22nd (nominal, 2019 CE) 26th (PPP 2020 CE).

- GDP Growth: −5.4% (2018 CE); −7.6% (2019 CE); −6.0% (2020 CE e); 3.1% (2021 CE e).

- GDP per capita: $5,506 (nominal, 2019 CE est.); $17 662 (PPP, 2019 est.).

- GDP per capita (rank): 98th (nominal, 2019 CE); 100th (PPP, 2019 CE).

- GDP by sector: Agriculture: 6.9% (2016 CE est.); Industry: 35.3% (2016 CE est.); Services: 55% (2017 CE est.).

- GDP by component: Household consumption: 49.7%; Government consumption: 14%; Investment in fixed capital: 20.6%; Investment in inventories: 14.5%; Exports of goods and services: 26%; Imports of goods and services: −24.9% (2017 CE est.)

- Inflation: 35% Approx. (2020 CE est.).

- Population below poverty line: 55% (2019 CE Majlis Research Centre).

CHAPTER 11: IRAQ

Iraq, the Republic of Iraq, is a country in Western Asia, bordered by Turkey to the north, Iran to the east, Kuwait to the southeast, Saudi Arabia to the south, Jordan to the southwest and Syria to the west. The capital and largest city is Baghdad.

Iraq is home to diverse ethnic groups including Arabs, Kurds, Turkmens, Assyrians, Yazidis, Shabakis, Armeians, Mandeans, Circassians, Sabians, and Kawliya. Around 99% of the country's population of around 40 million are Muslims, with small minorities of Christians, Yarsans, Yazidis, and Mandeans also present. The official languages are Arabic and Kurdish.

General Geography and Topography

The geography of Iraq is diverse and falls into five main regions: the desert (west of the Euphrates), Upper Mesopotamia (between the upper Tigris and Euphrates rivers), the northern highlands of Iraq, Lower Mesopotamia, and the alluvial plain extending from around Tikrit to the Persian Gulf.

The mountains in the northeast are an extension of the alpine system that runs eastward from the Balkans through southern Turkey, northern Iraq, Iran, and Afghanistan, eventually reaching the Himalayas in Pakistan. The desert lies in the southwest and central provinces along the borders with Saudi Arabia and Jordan and geographically belongs in the Arabian Peninsula.

Climate

Iraq has two climatic provinces: the hot, arid lowlands, including the alluvial plains and the deserts; and the damper north-east, where the higher elevation produces cooler temperatures. In the northeast cultivation fed by precipitation is possible, but elsewhere irrigation is essential.

In the lowlands there are two seasons, summer and winter, with short transitional periods between them. Summer, which lasts from May to October, is characterized by clear skies, extremely high temperatures, and low relative humidity; no precipitation occurs from June through September. In Baghdad, July and August mean daily temperatures are about 35 °C, and summer temperatures of 51 °C have been recorded. The diurnal temperatures range in summer is considerable.

In winter the paths of westerly atmospheric depressions crossing the Middle East shift southward, bringing rain to southern Iraq. Annual totals vary considerably from year to year but mean annual precipitation in the lowlands ranges from about 100 to 180 mm; nearly all of this occurs between November and April.

Winter in the lowlands lasts from December to February. Temperatures are generally mild, although extremes of hot and cold, including frosts, can occur. Winter temperatures in Baghdad range from about 2 to 15 °C.

In the northeast the summer is shorter than in the lowlands, lasting from June to September, and the winter considerably longer. The summer is generally dry and hot, but average temperatures are some 3–6 °C cooler than those of lowland Iraq. Winters can be cold because of the region's high relief and the influence of northeasterly winds that bring continental air from Central Asia. In Mosul (Al-Mawṣil), January temperatures range between 4 and 17 °C; readings as low as –11 °C have been recorded.

In the foothills of the northeast, annual precipitation of 300 to 560 mm, enough to sustain good seasonal pasture, is typical. Precipitation may exceed 1 000 mm in the mountains, much of which falls as snow. As in the lowlands, little rain falls during the summer.

A steady northerly and north westerly summer wind, the 'Shamal', affects all of Iraq. It brings extremely dry air, so hardly any clouds form, and the land surface is thus heated intensively by the sun. Another wind, the 'Sharqi' (Arabic: 'easterly'), blows from the south and southeast during early summer and early winter; it is often accompanied by dust storms. Dust storms occur throughout Iraq during most of the year and may rise to great height in the atmosphere. They are particularly frequent in summer, with five or six striking central Iraq in July, the peak of the season.

Soils

The work of soil survey and classification in Iraq was started before 1950. At this point in time, the number and type of soil units in Iraq are incomplete due to the lack of semi-detailed or detailed surveys covering all of Iraq. Non-systematic work of soil survey has been the dominant type of work to date. Only 35% of Iraq is considered covered by a semi-detailed survey work with 1:50 000 to 1:25 000 soil maps. There is no general soil map covering the whole country up to now, using soil Taxonomy or other system. The exploration work of Buringh in 1960 using 1938 system, is the common work done on Iraqi soils. He recognized 18 great groups. So the need for detail soil survey to developing soil map at large scale is very necessary. In order to develop general soil map for Iraq following USDA soil taxonomy, 300 pedons representing all expected Iraqi soils were collected from the previous works. The collected data were reclassified using the key of soil classification, 2012. Digitized soil map at 1:500000scale was developed. The results indicated the presence of five soil orders each one shows some variations with the common properties reflecting the effect of the dominant soil formation factors. The soil orders are arranged according to their dominance as following: Aridisols

(62.2%), Entisols (16.2%), Inceptisols (12.6), Mollisols (3.8%) and Vertisols (1.2%), respectively. Twelve suborders belong to the dominant orders were recognized, with twenty-five great groups.

Minerals and Natural Resources

Petroleum is Iraq's most valuable mineral—the country has some of the world's largest known reserves and, before the Iran-Iraq War, was the second largest oil-exporting state. Oil production contributes the largest single portion to GDP and constitutes almost all of Iraq's foreign exchange. Iraq is a founding member of the Organization of Petroleum Exporting Countries (OPEC), but disagreements over production quotas and world oil prices have often led Iraq into conflict with other members.

Oil was first discovered in Iraq in 1927 CE near Kirkuk by the foreign-owned Turkish Petroleum Company, which was renamed the Iraq Petroleum Company (IPC) in 1929. Finds at Mosul and Basra followed, and several new fields were discovered and put into production in the 1940s CE and 1950s CE. New fields have continued to be discovered and developed.

The IPC was nationalized in 1972 CE, as were all foreign-owned oil companies by 1975 CE, and all facets of Iraq's oil industry were thereafter controlled by the government through the Iraq National Oil Company and its subsidiaries. During the war with Iran, production and distribution facilities were badly damaged, and after Iraq's invasion of Kuwait, which was itself partly prompted by disagreements over production quotas and disputes over oil field rights, the UN embargo on Iraq halted all exports. Under the embargo Iraq exported little or no oil until the oil-for-food program was implemented. By the early 21st century CE, oil production and exports had risen to roughly 75% of the levels achieved prior to the Persian Gulf War. Oil production rebounded slowly following the initial phase of the Iraq War.

Oil Pipelines

Because Iraq has such a short coastline, it has depended heavily on transnational pipelines to export its oil. This need has been compounded by the fact that Iraq's narrow coastline is adjacent to that of Iran, a country with which Iraq frequently has had strained relations. Originally (1937–48 CE) oil from the northern fields (mainly Kirkuk) was pumped to the Mediterranean Sea through Haifa, Palestine (now in Israel), a practice that the Iraqis abandoned with the establishment of the Jewish state. Soon thereafter pipelines to the Mediterranean were built to Baniyas, Syria, and through Syria to Tripoli, Lebanon. In 1977 CE a large pipeline was completed to the Turkish Mediterranean coast at Ceyhan. When the first Turkish line was completed, Iraq ceased using the Syrian pipelines and relied on the outlet through Turkey and on new terminals on the Persian Gulf (although export through Syria briefly resumed in the early 1980s CE). By 1979 CE Iraq had three gulf terminals —Mina,' al-Bakr, Khawr al-Amaya, and Khawr al-Zubayr; all of which were damaged during one or the other of Iraq's recent wars. In 1985 Iraq constructed a new pipeline that fed into the Petroline (in Saudi Arabia), which terminated at the Red Sea port of Yanbu. In 1988 that line was replaced with a new one, but it never reached full capacity and was shut down, along with all other Iraqi oil outlets, following Iraq's invasion of Kuwait.

In December 1996, the Turkish pipeline was reopened under the oil-for-food program. Later the gulf terminal of Mina al-Bakr also was revived, and in 1998 CE repairs were begun on the Syrian pipeline. Following the start of the Iraq War in 2003, Iraq's pipelines were subjected to numerous acts of sabotage by guerrilla forces.

Other minerals and energy

Exploitation of other minerals has lagged far behind that of oil and natural gas. It seems likely that Iraq has a good range of these untapped resources. Huge rock sulphur reserves—estimated to be among the largest in the world—are exploited at Mishraq, near Mosul, and in the early 1980s CE phosphate production began at Akashat, near the Syrian border; the phosphates are used in a large fertilizer plant at Al-Qaim. Lesser quantities of salt and steel are produced, and construction materials, including stone and gypsum (from which cement is produced), are plentiful.

Iraq's electrical production fails to meet its needs. Energy rationing is pervasive, and mandatory power outages are practiced throughout the country. This is largely because of damage by the Persian Gulf War, which destroyed the bulk of the country's power grid, including more than four-fifths of its power stations and a large part of its distribution facilities. Despite a shortage of spare parts, Iraq was able—largely through cannibalizing equipment—to reconstruct roughly 75% of its national grid by 1992 CE. By the end of the decade, however, this level of energy production had decreased, in part as a result of a reduced level of hydroelectric generation caused by drought but also because there continued to be a lack of replacements for aging components. Damage from the Iraq War has been less severe, but energy production remains below installed capacity.

The bulk of electricity generation is by thermal plants. Even in the best of times—despite the many dams on Iraq's rivers—the hydroelectricity produced is below installed capacity. The largest hydroelectric plants are at the Mosul Dam on the Tigris, the Dokan Dam on the Little Zab River, the Darbandikhan Dam on the Diyata in eastern Kurdistan, and the Samarra Dam on Lake Al-Tharthar. A Chinese company completed a new plant near Kirkuk in 2000 CE.

Manufacturing

The manufacturing sector developed rapidly after the mid-1970s CE, when government policy shifted toward heavy industrialization and import substitution. Iraq's program received assistance from many countries, particularly from the former Soviet Union. The state generally has controlled all heavy manufacturing, the oil sector, power production, and the infrastructure, although private investment in manufacturing was at times encouraged. Until 1980 CE most heavy manufacturing was greatly subsidized and made little economic sense, but it brought prestige for the Ba'ath regime and later, during the Iran-Iraq War, served as a basis for the country's massive military build-up. Petrochemical and iron and steel plants were built at Khawr al-Zubayr, and petrochemical production and oil refining were greatly expanded both at Basra and at Al-Musayyib, 65 km south of Baghdad, which was designated as the site of an enormous integrated industrial complex. In addition, a wide range of industrial activities were started up, some of which were boosted by the Iran-Iraq War, notably aluminium smelting and the production of tractors, electrical goods, telephone cables, and tires. Petrochemical products for export also were expanded and diversified to include liquefied natural gas, bitumen, detergents, and a range of fertilizers.

The combined results of the Iran-Iraq War, both the Persian Gulf War and the Iraq War, and, most of all, the UN embargo eroded Iraq's manufacturing capacity. Within its first two years, the embargo had cut manufacturing—which was already well below its highs of the early 1980s CE—by more than half. After 199 CE7, however, there was an increase in manufacturing output, in both the public and the private sectors, as replacement parts and government credit became available. By the end of the decade, large numbers of products long unavailable to consumers were once again on the market, and almost all the factories that were operating before the imposition of the embargo had resumed production, albeit at somewhat lower levels

Finance

All banks and insurance companies were nationalized in 1964 CE. The Central Bank of Iraq (founded in 1947 CE and one of the first central banks in the Arab world) has the sole right to issue the dinar, the national currency. The Rafidain Bank (1941 CE) is the oldest commercial bank, but in 1988 CE the state founded a second commercial bank, the Rashid (Rasheed) Bank. There are also three state-owned specialized banks: the Agricultural Co-operative Bank (1936 CE), the Industrial Bank (1940 CE), and the Real Estate Bank (1949 CE). Beginning in 1991 CE the government authorized private banks to operate, although only under the strict supervision of the central bank. The Baghdad Stock Exchange opened in 1992 CE.

By 2004 CE, after three major wars and years of international isolation, the national accounts were in disarray, and the country was saddled with an enormous national debt. At the end of the Persian Gulf War, the value of the formerly sound dinar plummeted in the face of rampant inflation. The UN embargo made it difficult for Iraqi banks to operate outside the country, and, under UN auspices, numerous Iraqi assets and accounts, including those in Iraq's financial institutions, were frozen and later seized by host governments in order to pay the country's numerous outstanding debts. Under the stipulations of the oil-for-food program, all revenues derived from the export of Iraqi oil were placed in escrow and supervised by the international community. After the initial phase of the Iraq War, portions of Iraq's external debt were cancelled by creditor nations beginning in 2004 CE. By mid-2007 CE, inflation had returned to safe levels.

Food, Agriculture, Flora and Fauna

About one-eighth of Iraq's total area is arable, and another one-tenth is permanent pasture. A large proportion of the arable land is in the north and northeast, where rain-fed irrigation dominates and is sufficient to cultivate winter crops, mainly wheat and barley. The remainder is in the valleys of the Tigris and Euphrates rivers, where irrigation, approximately 50% of Iraq's arable land is irrigated, is necessary throughout the year. The cultivated area declined by about half during the 1970s, mainly because of increased soil salinity, but grew in the 1980s as a number of large reclamation projects, particularly in the central and northwestern areas, were completed. In addition, droughts in Turkey frequently reduced the amount of Euphrates water available for irrigation in the south. Although the Tigris is affected less by drought, because it has a wider drainage area, including tributaries in Iran, it has been necessary to construct several large dams throughout the river system to store water for irrigation. Careful management of the soils has been necessary to combat salinity. Increases in water usage in the upstream states, Turkey and Syria, and the poor condition of Iraq's water infrastructure have contributed to recurring severe water shortages, forcing farmers to abandon farmland.

Agriculture, which has traditionally accounted for 25 – 33% of Iraq's GDP, now accounts for about 10%. The country's agricultural sector faces many problems in addition to soil salinity and drought, including floods and siltation, which impede the efficient working of the irrigation system. A lack of access to fertilizer and agricultural spare parts after 1990 CE and a lengthy drought in the early 21st century CE led to a decrease in agricultural production.

Before the revolution of 1958 CE, most of the agricultural land was concentrated in the hands of a few powerful landowners. The revolutionary government began a program of land reform, breaking up the large estates and distributing the land to peasant families and limiting the size of private holdings. The Ba'athist government that took over in 1968 CE originally encouraged public ownership and established agricultural cooperatives and collective farms, but those proved to be inefficient. After 1983 CE the government rented state-owned land to private concerns, with no limit on the size of holdings, and from 1987 CE it sold or leased all state farms. Membership in a cooperative and the use of government marketing organizations ceased to be obligatory.

The chief crops are barley, wheat, rice, vegetables, corn (maize), millet, sugarcane, sugar beets, oil seeds, fruit, fodder, tobacco, and cotton. Yields vary considerably from year to year, especially in areas of rain-fed cultivation. Date production—Iraq was once the world's largest date producer—was seriously damaged during the Iran-Iraq War and approached pre-war levels only in the early 21st century CE. Animal husbandry is widely practiced, particularly among the Kurds of the northeast, and livestock products, notably milk, meat, hides, and wool, are important.

Timber resources are scarce and rather inaccessible, being situated almost entirely in the highlands and mountains of the northeast in Iraqi Kurdistan. The resources that are readily available are used almost exclusively for firewood and the production of charcoal. Limited amounts of timber are used for local industry, but most wood for industrial production (for furniture, construction, and other purposes) must be imported. Afforestation projects to supply new forest area and reduce erosion have met with limited success.

Iraq harvests both freshwater and marine fish for local consumption and also supports a modest aquaculture industry. The main freshwater fish are various species of the genus *Barbus* and carp, which are pulled from Iraqi national waters and from the Persian Gulf by Iraq's small domestic fleet. Inland bodies provide by far the largest source of fish. Various types of shad, mullet, and catfish are fished in the lakes, rivers, and streams, and fish farms mostly provide varieties of carp. There is no industrial fish-processing sector, and most fish is consumed fresh by the domestic market. Fishing contributes only a tiny fraction to GDP.

Plant and animal life

Vegetation in Iraq reflects the dominant influence of drought.

Some Mediterranean and alpine plant species thrive in the mountains of Kurdistan, but the open oak forests that formerly were found there have largely disappeared. Hawthorns, junipers, terebinths, and wild pears grow on the lower mountain slopes. A steppe region of open, treeless vegetation is located in the area extending north and northeast from the Ḥamrin Mountains up to the foothills and lower slopes of the mountains of Iraqi Kurdistan. A great variety of herbs and shrubs grow in that region. Most belong to the sage and daisy families: mugwort (*Artemisis vulgaris*), goosefoot, milkweed, thyme, and various rhizomic plants are examples. There also are many different grasses. Toward the riverine lowlands many other plants appear, including storksbill and plantain. Willows, tamarisks, poplars, liquorice plants, and bulrushes grow along the banks of the lower Tigris and Euphrates rivers. The juice of the licorice plant is extracted for commercial purposes. Dozens of varieties of date palm flourish throughout southern Iraq, where the date palm dominates the landscape. The lakesides and marshlands support many varieties of reeds, sedges, pimpernels, vetches, and geraniums. By contrast, vegetation in the desert regions is sparse, with tamarisk, milfoil, and various plants of the genera *Ziziphus* and *Salsola* being characteristic.

Birds are easily the most conspicuous form of wildlife. There are many resident species, though the effect of large-scale drainage of the southern wetlands on migrants and seasonal visitors—which were once numerous—has not been fully determined. The lion, oryx, ostrich, and wild ass have become extinct in Iraq. Wolves, foxes, jackals, hyenas, wild pigs, and wildcats are found, as well as many small animals such as martens, badgers, otters, porcupines, and muskrats. The Arabian sand gazelle survives in certain remote desert locations. Rivers, streams, and lakes are well stocked with a variety of fish, notably carp, various species of *Barbus*, catfish, and loach. In common with other regions of the Middle East, Iraq is a breeding ground for the unwelcome desert locust.

Population

During 2021 CE Iraq population is projected to increase by 1 356 521 people and reach 42 438 321 in the beginning of 2022 CE. The natural increase is expected to be positive, as the number of births will exceed the number of deaths by 1 222 594. If external migration will remain on the previous year level, the population will be increased by 133 927 due to migration. It means that the number of people who move into Iraq (to which they are not native) to settle there as permanent residents (immigrants) will prevail over the number of people who leave the country to settle permanently in another country (emigrants).

Politics

The politics of Iraq take place in a framework of a federal parliamentary representative democratic republic. It is a multi-party system whereby the executive power is exercised by the Prime Minister of the Council of Ministers as the head of government, as well as the President of Iraq, and legislative power is vested in the Council of Representatives and the Federation Council.

The current Prime Minister of Iraq is Mustafa Al-Kadhimi, who holds most of the executive authority and appointed the Council of Ministers, which acts as a cabinet and/or government.

The Economist Intelligence Unit rated Iraq an 'authoritarian regime' in 2019 CE.

A new political system was introduced in Iraq after Saddam Hussein's regime was brought down in 2003 CE. Based upon a new Constitution, approved on 15 October 2005 CE by referendum, Iraq is an Islamic, democratic federal republic, consisting of 18 governorates (*muhafazat*). The Kurdistan Autonomous Region forms part of the Federal Republic Iraq and is made up of the three northern provinces of Duhok, Erbil (Hewler) and al-Sulamaniya (Silemani). The region is governed by a regional administration, the Kurdistan Regional Government, and has its own armed forces. Article 114 of the Constitution leaves room for the formation of additional autonomous regions. The federal government is organized around a separation of powers – between the Executive, Legislative and Judiciary.

The Executive

The Executive is headed by the President, who is also head of state. The President is elected by a two-third majority of the Council of Representatives, Iraq's Parliament. The President is elected to serve a four-year term in office, after which he may be re-elected once. The President approves laws which have been passed by Parliament, and is the ceremonial head of the Armed Forces. He also fulfils ceremonial duties for Iraq. The President is aided by two Vice-Presidents. Together they form the Presidency Council, which makes decisions by unanimous vote.

There is also a Council of Ministers, consisting of the Prime Minister and other ministers. After the outcome of the parliamentary general election has been established, the Presidency Council summons the leader of the largest party or political block in Parliament to form a new government. It can assume its responsibilities once a majority in Parliament has adopted a vote of confidence. The Prime Minister chairs the Council of Ministers and thus leads the daily politics of decision-making. The Prime Minister can dismiss a minister, with the support of a majority in Parliament. The Prime Minister is also Commander-in-Chief of the Armed Forces.

The Legislative

The Legislative is formed by the 325 Members of Parliament (Council of Representatives), which is chaired by the Speaker.

317 of the 325 Members of Parliament are chosen in the general elections, which are held once every four years, and in which all Iraqi citizens who are eighteen years of age or older are allowed to participate. The remaining eight seats are reserved for chosen representatives of small minority groups. The Parliament choses the President, and offers a vote of confidence to the Prime Minister and the Council of Ministers (or else issues a motion of no confidence, dismissing the government). It also confirms important appointments, is responsible for the budget, submits and assesses laws, and ratifies treaties.

A Federation Council is also in place, alongside Parliament. On paper it is made up of representatives from the regions and governorates that are not separately organized, but it is not in force, as yet. The council is controlled by the Council of Representatives.

The Political Parties

Iraqi National Accord: also known as the National Reconciliation Movement, this party was founded in 1990 CE and led by former prime minister Ayad Allawi. It is considered a liberal party that seeks political action far from sectarian quotas. It was among the opposition groups that formed the Iraqi National List (INL), which won the majority of parliamentary seats in the 2010 CE elections. In the 2014 CE elections, and after the dissolution of the INL, the Iraqi National Accord entered into a new coalition called the National Coalition (Wataniya), taking 21 seats.

Islamic Dawa Party: led by Nouri al-Maliki, who was prime minister from May 2006 CE to September 2014 CE, and contains within its ranks the current Prime Minister Haider al-Abadi. It was one of the component parties of the State of Law Coalition, which came second in the 2010 CE elections with

89 of the 328 available seats, and subsequently dominated the 2014 CE elections, winning 94 seats.

The Sadrist Movement: a political and religious movement headed by the Shia cleric Muqtada al-Sadr, and indirectly representing the militia groups Mahdi Army, the Promised Day Brigade and the Peace Companies. The al-Ahrar Bloc, a Shia coalition of which the movement was part, took 33 seats in the 2014 CE elections.

The Patriotic Union of Kurdistan (PUK): a liberal, secular party led by former president Jalal Talabani. The party describes its goals as self-determination, human rights, democracy and peace for the Kurdish people of Kurdistan and Iraq. In the 2010 elections, PUK and the Kurdistan Democratic Party (KDP) formed the Kurdistan Alliance, coming in fourth place with 43 seats. In the 2014 CE elections, PUK, running independently of the KDP, obtained 19 seats.

Kurdistan Democratic Party: has a wide presence among the Kurdish clans, and is led by Masoud Barzani, the president of Iraqi Kurdistan. The party seeks to secure the right of the Kurds to self-determination, to develop a federal-parliamentary system and to guarantee the participation of Kurds in political decision-making through representation in federal institutions. The KDP won 19 seats in the 2014 CE elections.

The Judiciary

The Judiciary is made up of the Higher Judicial Council, the Supreme Court, the Court of Cassation, the Public Prosecution Department, the Judiciary Oversight Commission, the Central Criminal Court, and other federal courts, each with their own powers.

The legal system is based on a mixture of civil and Islamic law. In practice, the functioning of the political system, which came into being after 2003 CE, is far from perfect. In fact, in many respects Iraq might be termed a dysfunctional state.

The Military

Introduction

Despite defeating Islamic State militants, with assistance from Western powers and military advice from Iran's elite al-Quds brigade, peace continues to elude the oil-rich nation of Iraq. Post-conflict, questions remain about the long-term shape of the country's armed forces, particularly the Shia-dominated Popular Mobilization Units and the role of Kurdish forces.

In 2019 CE, Iraq ranked 53 out of 137 countries included in the annual GFP review. That year, the number of people who reached military age was estimated at 664 169 personnel, while military expenditure was estimated at $6.1 billion. In 2018 CE, military expenditure accounted for 2.7 % of GDP, compared with 3.8 % in 2017 CE and 3.5 % in 2016 CE, according to the Stockholm International Peace Research Institute.

In May 2003 CE, the Coalition Provisional Authority dismantled the Iraqi military and sent home its personnel, a move widely considered unwise. With time to spare and with their military expertise the disbanded military provided a large pool of insurgents.

In place of the armed forces that had fought for Saddam Hussein against Iran, the American-led coalitions, and against large parts of the Iraqi population, a politically neutral military was envisioned.

From 2003 CE American advisers, mostly private contractors, trained the Iraqi armed forces from scratch, until 2011 CE, when the last American troops left the country. According to the British International Institute of Strategic Studies (IISS), the army alone has nearly 300 000 troops under its command, augmented by more than half a million police and government militia.

These troops had their baptism of fire in 2008 CE. The year before, the British occupation forces had left the southern city of Basra, leaving a power vacuum that was quickly filled by radical Shiite militia groups, such as the Iranian-influenced Mahdi Army of cleric Muqtada Sadr, and by lawlessness in general. With British and American air and artillery support and provided with ample intelligence on Mahdi Army positions, in particular, Iraqi forces subdued the armed opposition and restored order within weeks.

The Collapse

The collapse of the Iraqi armed forces in Mosul in 2014 CE against combatants of the Islamic State (IS) is in stark contrast with the relatively muscular image the regular troops had built up previously. It was reported that the personnel of two Iraqi divisions, some 15 000 men, changed into civilian clothes and fled, when confronted with some 800 IS men. Hundreds were captured by IS and summarily executed. The Iraqi Army left equipment and supplies behind.

The main reason for this collapse is generally considered to have been poor leadership, the lack of training and glaring deficiencies in equipment, such as lack of artillery and air support, but especially the army's low morale. Sunni units just did not want to fight for the Shiite-dominated government, and Shiites did not want to fight for Sunni towns. Corruption is rife. Although a large amount of Gulf War-era materiel was kept in service, a large-scale modernization plan was initiated.

T-72 Tanks were bought from Hungary, and armoured personnel carriers were provided by Switzerland and Ukraine.

The United States provided the most equipment, some of it sold to the Iraqi government, and other materiel was left behind by withdrawing American occupation forces, such as 'up-armoured' Humvees and assorted Mine Resistant Ambush Protected (MRAP) vehicles.

One of the most notable 'big ticket' items was the U.S. M1 Abrams tank, of which the Iraqi Army was supposed to receive a total of 320. In October 2014 CE, fewer than two hundred have been delivered, and it is doubtful whether the rest of the order will materialize, given the shaky morale of the government troops. IS has paraded and used captured Abrams tanks.

The Iraqi air force was once a large and capable organization equipped with relatively modern Russian and French fighter-bombers. After more than a hundred aircraft fled the allied onslaught in the first Gulf War in 1991, seeking refuge in Iran, it became a hollow force with little flying equipment and even less operational training.

After the American-led invasion of 2003 the remaining fighters, such as MiG-25s, were found to have been buried in the sand in quiet corners of their airbases, waiting for better times.

During the American occupation, Iraqi air space was defended by U.S. aircraft based in the country to give air support to ground operations against insurgents.

When the American troops left the country, the air component of the Iraqi armed forces consisted only of helicopters, mostly Russian, and some U.S.-made Cessna Caravans armed with Hellfire missiles.

There is interest in acquiring additional, more capable aircraft and helicopters, such as the South-Korean KAI T-50 light-attack jet, of which two dozen were ordered, Serbian Utva Lasta turboprop trainer/light attack aircraft, and Russian Mil Mi-35 gunships. A deal for Boeing AH-64 Apache helicopters fell through after the Iraqi government apparently ordered Mil Mi-28 Havoc helicopter gunships from Russia instead. The first Havocs have already been delivered.

In June 2014 CE the first of an order of 36 F-16 fighter-bombers was handed over to the Iraqi air force. In the following November the date for initial operational capability remains unclear.

Another curious chapter was opened when then-prime minister Nuri al-Maliki declared in June 2014 that his country had bought Su-25 ground-attack aircraft from Belarus and the Russian Federation in order to stop IS convoys on their way to Baghdad and the Shiite south of Iraq. Also, Iranian Su-25 planes were seen on an Iraqi air base near the capital, Baghdad. Ironically, these could have originated in Iraq, when some of these had sought refuge in neighbouring Iran in 1991.

The Iraqi navy, the smallest of the armed services, has also seen some modernization, after most of the equipment was lost or damaged between 1991 CE and 2003 CE. The navy had always been modest, as the Iraqi coastline measures only some sixty kilometres. In 2014 CE the single Iraqi naval base at Umm Qasr is being modernized under the supervision of the U.S Army Corps of Engineers, with the construction of, among other things, a pier and seawall.

The inventory of vessels is being upgraded as well, after the onslaught of 2003 CE and preceding allied bombardments that turned most vessels into sunken hulks. The Iraqi navy currently operates four Italian-made 54-metre patrol vessels, five Chinese-built Predator-class patrol boats, and some thirty small U.S-built Defender rigid-hull inflatable boats (RHIBs). The Iraqi navy also took delivery of a dozen American new-built Swiftship patrol boats, the last in 2014 CE.

Language

The major language in Iraq is Mesopotamian Arabic; the secondary language is Kurdish. There are a range of other languages, English is important.

Religion

The constitution of Iraq recognizes Islam as the official religion in the country, and states that no law may be enacted that contradicts the provisions of the Islamic religion. However, it guarantees freedom of religious beliefs and practices of other non-Muslim groups.

Although the government recognizes these rights, there are conditions that prevent the government from ensuring the freedom of religion from the insurgency, sectarian violence, and terrorism. Since the fall of Saddam Hussein in 2003 CE, the government has been calling for tolerance and acceptance of religious minorities. Despite the efforts, some government institutions have continued discriminatory practices against religious minorities, such as the Bahai Faith and the Wahhabi Sunni Muslims. In 2006 CE there was an attack on one of the most significant Shia mosque, the Al-Askari Mosque, which contains the mausoleums of the Tenth and the Eleventh Imams.

Shia Islam

Shia Islam in Iraq dates back to the fourth Caliph of Sunni Islam. In 15th and 16th Centuries CE, the Marsh Arabs converted from Sunnism to Shiism. In the 18th Century CE, Banu Khazal converted into Shiism. A massive conversion of Iraq's Sunni Arab to Shiism took place in the 19th Century CE and continued into the 20th Century CE. Today, Shia Islam stands as a dominant religion in Iraq. The Shiite Muslims believe that after the death of the Prophet Muhammad (pbuh), his successor was his cousin and son-in-law, Ali. They believe in the school of thought known as 'Twelvers' or 'fivers' which refers to the number of imams that they recognize. More than half of the population of Iraq are Shiite Muslims. Iraq holds the major religious cities of the Shiite Muslims Najar and Karbala. Najar is the tomb site of the first Shia Imam, Ali Ibn Abi Talib, and Karbala the tomb site of Hussein Ibn Ali, the grandson of the Prophet Muhammad (pbuh).

Sunni Islam

Sunni Islam emerged as an opposing group to Shia Islam. After the death of Prophet Muhammad (pbuh), they felt that the most appropriate person to succeed Prophet Muhammad (pbuh) was his closest friend, Abu Bakar. They believe that after the death of Prophet Muhammad (pbuh) any able, pious male of the Quraysh clan needed to succeed him instead of his cousin and son-in-law. They have several Imams and religious leaders as opposed to their Shiite compatriots. They comprise of approximately 20% of the population of Iraq. Many of them converted to Shia Islam in the 19th and 20th Centuries CE. Some of them do not even consider the Shiite Muslims to be true Muslims.

Chaldean Catholic Christian Church

The Chaldean Catholic Church began as the Assyrian Church of the East. It was founded in 1552 by Yohannan Sulaqa. A group of Assyrian bishops elected him as a priest. He travelled to Rome, and the pope consecrated him as a patriarch. He ordained five other bishops thus beginning what was finally called the Chaldean Catholic Church. believe in God as the creator of Heaven and Earth and his only son Jesus Christ. God sent his son Jesus to die for the sin of humankind and reconcile them to God. The Christians of this church are very few as they endured persecution and massacres in the hands of the Muslims. Their indigenous heritage dating back to bronze age and iron age was desecrated.

Yazidism

The origins of the Yazidi faith were a complex process of *syncretism*, or a mingling of various beliefs. The religious beliefs of a local faith influenced the Adawiyya people who lived in the mountains causing them to deviate from the Muslim faith. They believe that God created the world and entrusted it to seven angels. Melek Taus was the leader of the angels and is the central figure in their belief system. They do not believe that hell exists. To them, all people have the innate good and evil, and they make their choices without being tempted. They pray facing the sun in the morning, at the moon, and in the evening. The Muslims greatly denounce Yazidism, and many followers have suffered persecution at the hands of the terrorist groups ISIS, Al-Qaeda, and other radical Islamic jihadists.

Persecution Of Non-Muslims

Islam is the principal religion in Iraq, and has a following constituting 97% of the national population. Christianity and other religions consist of only 3% of the people. Islam exists in two sects; Sunni and Shia. Many cities in Iraq are of religious importance to the Sunni and Shiite Muslims. Only a small portion of the country is inhabited by the Christians and other religions thus Iraq exists as an Islamic state. The schism of Sunni and Shia Islam is the largest and oldest in the history of Islam. The two sects share many beliefs and practices but differ in doctrine, rituals, law and religious organization. One opinion that is shared by both of them is the Pilgrimage to Mecca, the Holy City. Other religions found in Iraq include the Nestorian Christians, Jacobite Christians, Mandaeans, Shabakis, Kakais, and atheists. These minor religions have suffered great persecution at the hands of certain intolerant groups of radical Muslims. This persecution has forced them to exist in subtle populations largely confined to the mountainous regions of Iraq.

Economy

The economy of Iraq is dominated by the oil sector, which has provided about 99.7% of foreign exchange earnings in modern times. Iraq's hitherto agrarian economy underwent rapid development following the 14[th]July Revolution overthrowing the Hashemite Iraqi monarchy, becoming the third-largest economy in the Middle East by 1980 CE. This occurred in part because of the Iraqi government's successful industrialization and infrastructure development initiatives in the 1970's, which included irrigation projects, railway and highway construction, and rural electrification.

In the 1980s CE, financial problems caused by massive expenditures in the Iran-Iraq War and damage to oil export facilities by Iran led the Ba'athist government to implement austerity measures, borrow heavily, and later reschedule foreign debt payments; Iraq suffered economic losses of at least $80 billion from the war. After the end of hostilities, in 1988 CE, oil exports gradually increased with the construction of new pipelines and restoration of damaged facilities, but again underwent a sharp decline after the Persian Gulf War, dropping to one-fourth of its 1980 gross domestic product and continuing to decline under post-war international sanctions until receiving aid from the UN Oil-for-Food Programme in 1997 CE.

Despite the efforts of the Coalition Provisional Authority to modernize Iraq's economy after the 2003 CE U.S.-led invasion through privatization and reducing its foreign debt, its economy continued to decline due to continued violence, economic mismanagement, and oil shortages caused by outdated technology. Since mid-2009 CE, oil export earnings have returned to levels seen before Operation New Dawn and government revenues have rebounded, along with global oil prices. In 2011 CE Baghdad probably increased oil exports above the current level of 1 900 000 bbl (300 000 m^3) per day as a result of new contracts with international oil companies but is likely to fall short of the 2 400 000 barrels (380 000 m^3) per day it is forecasting in its budget. Iraq's recent contracts with major oil companies have the potential to greatly expand oil revenues, but Iraq will need to upgrade its oil processing, pipeline, and export infrastructure to enable these deals to reach their potential.

An improved security environment and an initial wave of foreign investment are helping to spur economic activity, particularly in the energy, construction, and retail sectors. Broader economic improvement, long-term fiscal health, and sustained increases in the standard of living still depend on the government passing major policy reforms and on continued development of Iraq's massive oil reserves. Although foreign investors viewed Iraq with increasing interest in 2010

CE, most are still hampered by difficulties in acquiring land for projects and by other regulatory impediments.

Inflation has decreased consistently since 2006 CE as the security situation has improved. However, Iraqi leaders remain hard pressed to translate macroeconomic gains into improved lives for ordinary Iraqis. Unemployment remains a problem throughout the country.

CHAPTER 12:
THE LEVANT

Jordan

Jordan, officially the Hashemite Kingdom of Jordan, is an Arab country in Western Asia, on the East Bank of the Jordan River. Jordan is bordered by Saudi Arabia to the south and the east, Iraq to the north-east, Syria to the north and Israel to the west. The Dead Sea is located along its western borders and the country has a 26-kilometre coastline on the Red Sea in its extreme south-west. Jordan is strategically located at the crossroads of Asia, Africa and Europe. The capital, Amman, is Jordan's most populous city as well as the country's economic, political and cultural centre.

General Geography and Topography

The country consists mainly of a plateau between 700 m and 1 200 m, divided into ridges by valleys and gorges, and a few mountainous areas. West of the plateau, land descends to form the East Bank of the Jordan Rift Valley. The valley is part of the north-south Great Rift Valley, and its successive depressions are Lake Tiberias (Sea of Galilee; its bottom is about −258 m below the Jordan Valley, the Dead Sea (its bottom is about −730 m) Arabah, and the Gulf of Aqaba at the Red Sea. Jordan's western border follows the bottom of the rift. Although an earthquake-prone region, no severe shocks have been recorded for several centuries.

By far the greatest part of the East Bank is desert, displaying the landforms and other features associated with great aridity. Most of this land is part of the Syrian Desert and northern Arabian Desert. There are broad expanses of sand and dunes, particularly in the south and southeast, together with salt flats. Occasional jumbles of sandstone hills or low mountains support only meagre and stunted vegetation that thrives for a short period after the scanty winter rains. These areas support little life and are the least populated regions of Jordan.

The drainage network is coarse and incised. In many areas the relief provides no eventual outlet to the sea, so that sedimentary deposits accumulate in basins where moisture evaporates or is absorbed in the ground. Toward the depression in the western part of the East Bank, the desert rises gradually into the Jordanian Highlands—a steppe country of high, deeply cut limestone plateaus with an average elevation of about 900 m. Occasional summits in this region reach 1 200 m in the northern part and exceed 1 700 m in the southern part; the highest peak is Jabal Ramm at 1 754 m (though the highest peak in all of Jordan is Jabal Umm al Dami at 1854 m. It is located in a remote part of southern Jordan). These highlands are an area of long-settled villages.

The western edge of this plateau country forms an escarpment along the eastern side of the Jordan River-Dead Sea depression and its continuation south of the Dead Sea. Most of the wadis- that provide drainage from the plateau country into the depression carry water only during the short season of winter rains. Sharply incised with deep, canyon-like walls, whether flowing or dry the wadis can be formidable obstacles to travel.

The Jordan River is short, but from its mountain headwaters (approximately 160 kms north of the river's mouth at the Dead Sea) the riverbed drops from an elevation of about 3 000 m above sea level to more than 400 m below sea level. Before reaching Jordanian territory the river forms the Sea of Galilee, the surface of which is 212 meters below sea level. The Jordan River's principal tributary is the Yarmouk River. Near the junction of the two rivers, the Yarmouk forms the boundary between Israel on the northwest, Syria on the northeast, and Jordan on the south. The Zarqa River, the second main tributary of the Jordan River, flows and empties entirely within the East Bank.

A 380 km long rift valley runs from the Yarmouk River in the north to Al Aqaba in the south. The northern part, from the Yarmouk River to the Dead Sea, is commonly known as the Jordan Valley. It is divided into eastern and western parts by the Jordan River. Bordered by a steep escarpment on both the eastern and the western side, the valley reaches a maximum width of twenty-two kms at some points. The valley is properly known as *Al Ghawr* or *Al Ghor* (the depression, or valley).

The Rift Valley on the southern side of the Dead Sea is known as the Southern *Ghawr* and the Wadi al Jayb (popularly known as the Wadi al Arabah). The Southern Ghawr runs from Wadi al Hammah, on the south side of the Dead Sea, to Ghawr Faya, about twenty-five kilometers south of the Dead Sea. Wadi al Jayb is 180 km long, from the southern shore of the Dead Sea to Al Aqaba in the south. The valley floor varies in level. In the south, it reaches its lowest level at the Dead Sea (more than 400 m below sea level), rising in the north to just above sea level. Evaporation from the sea is extreme due to year-round high temperatures. The water contains about 250 g of dissolved salts per liter at the surface and reaches the saturation point at 110 m.

The Dead Sea occupies the deepest depression on the land surface of the earth. The depth of the depression is accentuated by the surrounding mountains and highlands that rise to elevations of 800 to 1 200 m above sea level. The sea's greatest depth is about 430 m, and it thus reaches a point more than 825 m below sea level. A drop in the level of the sea has caused the former Lisan Peninsula to become a land bridge dividing the sea into separate northern and southern basins.

Climate

The major characteristic of the climate is the contrast between a relatively rainy season from November to April and very dry weather for the rest of the year. With hot, dry, uniform summers and cool, variable winters during which practically all of the precipitation occurs, the country has a Mediterranean-style climate.

In general, the farther inland from the Mediterranean Sea a given part of the country lies, the greater are the seasonal contrasts in temperature and the less rainfall. Atmospheric pressures during the summer months are relatively uniform, whereas the winter months bring a succession of marked low pressure areas and accompanying cold fronts. These cyclonic disturbances generally move eastward from over the Mediterranean Sea several times a month and result in sporadic precipitation.

Most of the East Bank receives less than 120 mm of rain a year and may be classified as a dry desert or steppe region. Where the ground rises to form the highlands east of the Jordan Valley, precipitation increases to around 300 mm in the south and 500 mm or more in the north. The Jordan Valley, lying in the lee of high ground on the West Bank, forms a narrow climatic zone that annually receives up to 300 mm of rain in the northern reaches; rain dwindles to less than 120 mm at the head of the Dead Sea.

The country's long summer reaches a peak during August. January is usually the coolest month. The wide ranges of temperature during a twenty-four-hour period are greatest during the summer months and have a tendency to increase with higher elevation and distance from the Mediterranean seacoast. Daytime temperatures during the summer months frequently exceed 36 °C and average about 32 °C. In contrast, the winter months, November to April, bring moderately cool and sometimes cold weather, averaging about 13 °C. Except in the rift depression, frost is fairly common during the winter, it may take the form of snow at the higher elevations of the northwestern highlands. Usually, it snows a couple of times a year in western Amman.

For a month or so before and after the summer dry season, hot, dry air from the desert, drawn by low pressure, produces strong winds from the south or southeast that sometimes reach gale force. Known in the Middle East by various names, including the *'Khamsin'*, this dry, *'Scirocco'* style wind is usually accompanied by great dust clouds. Its onset is heralded by a hazy sky, a falling barometer, and a drop in relative humidity to about 10%. Within a few hours there may be a 5.6 °C to 8.3 °C rise in temperature. These windstorms ordinarily last a day or so, cause much discomfort, and destroy crops by desiccating them.

The *'Shamal'*, another wind of some significance, comes from the north or north west, generally at intervals between June and September. Remarkably steady during daytime hours but becoming a breeze at night, the *'Shamal'* may blow for as long as nine days out of ten and then repeat the process. It originates as a dry continental mass of polar air that is warmed as it passes over the Eurasian landmass. The dryness allows intense heating of the Earth's surface by the sun, resulting in high daytime temperatures that moderate after sunset.

Soils

The distribution of soils in Jordan follows closely the climate and topography. Specific soil orders can be found within the dry and hot subtropical, subhumid-semiarid, semiarid-arid, and arid regions. The soils of the dry and hot subtropical Jordan Valley are dominated by the soil orders Inceptisols and Entisols. The main Great Groups are: Ustochrepts (the suborder Ochrepts is now obsolete; these soils are mainly part of the Ustepts and Udepts soil suborders in the 11th edition), and Ustifluvents north of the area which receives more than 250 mm of annual rainfall, while the area with less than 250 mm rainfall and north of the Dead Sea is dominated by Torrifluvents. The area south of the Dead Sea to Aqaba is dominated by Torripsamments and Torrifluvents.

Minerals and Natural Resources

Oil Shale

Another primary natural resource in Jordan is oil shale. Geological evidence indicates that oil shale could be found in more than 70% of Jordan's territory and the country had more than 30 billion tonnes of oil shale. Jordan's most vital oil shale reserves were situated in the country's western region, and they are situated close to the surface where infrastructure had been developed. The country's oil shale was initially explored before the World War I; however, large scale exploration took place during the 1970s CE as a result of higher prices for oil shale and the development of new technology that made it easier to extract the oil shale. The government of Jordan signed several agreements with foreign corporations to allow them to extract the oil and convert it to energy. Some of the companies that undertook Jordan's oil shale exploration include Royal Dutch Shell and Petrobras. The government of Jordan planned to utilize its oil shale reserves for power generation to meet the country's energy requirements. The government of Jordan also signed an agreement with a local company to allow the company to use the country's oil shale in the production of cement.

Minerals

Jordan has several minerals such as potash and phosphates which are vital to the country's economy. According to the Jordanian government, in 2003 CE the country produced roughly 2 million tonnes of potash which were mostly exported to other nations. In that year, potash exports earned the country more than $192 million. In 2004 CE, Jordan's potash production declined slightly as the country only produced 1.9 million tonnes of potash. In 2004 CE, Jordan's phosphate mines produced roughly 6.75 million tonnes of phosphates which were exported to other countries earning the country roughly $135 million. In 2005 CE, the country's phosphate production decreased to 6.4 million tonnes; however, Jordan was ranked as the third largest producer of phosphate in the world.

Uranium

By 2015 CE, Jordan had roughly 47,700 tonnes of uranium which are crucial to the country's economic development. The Jordanian government planned to use the country's significant uranium resources to generate nuclear power. The Jordanian government granted Areva Group S.A. the exclusive rights to utilize the country's uranium deposits in the country's central region. The agreement gives the company exclusive rights to exploit the uranium in the central region of the country for roughly 25 years. The Jordanian government also signed an agreement with Rio Tinto Alcan allowing the organization to search for uranium in the country.

Food, Agriculture, Flora and Fauna

Arable Land

Data from the World Bank indicated that in 2015 CE, approximately 11.9% of Jordan's land was considered arable. From 2004 CE to 2015 CE, the size of arable land in Jordan fluctuated significantly, and it reached its lowest levels in 2007 CE when it accounted for only 10.9% of the country's land area. Arable land has been vital to the Jordanian people for much of their history as they relied on agriculture as one of their crucial economic activities. By the time Jordan became an independent nation, agriculture was one of the most important industries; however, its significance declined in later years. During the 1950s CE, the agricultural sector contributed roughly 40% of the country's gross domestic product, and in 2015 the industry contributed only 4% of the gross domestic product. The sector declined as an important contributor to the country's national income because of several factors such as Jordan losing control of the West Bank and the increasing importance of other sectors of the economy. Jordanian farmers grow a wide variety of crops such as wheat, tobacco, and barley. The Jordanian government estimated that in 1999 CE, the country's farmers produced more than 12 000 tonnes of wheat as well as 5 000 tonnes of barley. The Jordanian government has implemented several policies to grow the country's agricultural sector with one of the main ones being the introduction of irrigation schemes such as the East Ghor Canal which covers a length of 48 miles. The Jordanian government has also encouraged the formation of cooperatives which have been vital in assisting the local farmers by providing loans and advice on modern farming practices.

Livestock

Jordanian farmers keep significant numbers of livestock, and they are part of the most critical natural resources in the country. During the 1980s CE, Jordan had roughly 35 000 cattle and more than 1.5 million goats and sheep. The government adopted several measures to try and increase the number of animals in the country. At the time, the Jordanian livestock industry could only meet 33% of the local demand and the country was forced to import livestock from other nations. The major challenge that limited the growth of Jordan's livestock industry was the high price of imported feeds.

Population

Jordan has a population of approximately 9 531 712 inhabitants (Female: 47%; Males: 53%) as of 2015 CE. Jordanians are the citizens of Jordan, who share a common Levantine Semitic ancestry. Some 98% percent of Jordanians are Arabs, while the remaining 2% are other ethnic minorities. Around 2.9 million were non-citizens, a figure including refugees, legal and illegal immigrants. Jordan's annual population growth rate stood at

2.05% in 2017, with an average of three children per woman. More than half the population is under 30.

Politics

The politics of Jordan takes place in a framework of a parliamentary monarchy, whereby the Prime Minister of Jordan is head of government, and of a multi-party system. Jordan is a constitutional monarchy based on the constitution promulgated on 8 January 1952 CE. The king exercises his power through the government he appoints which is responsible before the Parliament.

King Abdullah II of Jordan has been sovereign since the death of his father King Hussein, in 1999 CE.

Language

Jordan's language is Arabic. Modern Standard Arabic is the base although Jordanian Arabic is also common, a dialect. English is a second language.

Religion

Sunni Islam is the dominant religion in Jordan. Muslims make up about 95% of the country's population. There are also a small number of Ahmadi Muslims, and some Shia. Many Shia are Iraqi and Lebanese refugees.

Economy (Snapshot)

Jordan is an emerging knowledge economy. The main obstacles to Jordan's economy are scarce water supplies, complete reliance on oil imports for energy, and regional instability. Just over 10% of its land is arable and the water supply is limited. Rainfall is low and highly variable, and much of Jordan's available ground water is not renewable.

  · GDP: $42.291 billion (nominal; 2018); $93.404 billion (PPP 2018). (UK: GDP: $2.64 trillion (nominal, 2020 CE est.); $2.98 trillion (PPP, 2020 CE).

- GDP per capita: $4 270 (nominal; 2018 est.); $9 431 (PPP 2018 est.).

- GDP by sector: Agriculture: 4.5% · Industry: 28.8% · Services: 66.6% (2017 CE est.).

- Population below poverty line: 14.4% (2010 World Bank CE est.); 18.1% on less than $5.50/day (2010 CE est.).

- Labour force: 2 631 115 (2019 CE); 32.1% employment rate (2014 CE).

Syria

Syria, or the Syrian Arab Republic, is a country in Western Asia, bordering Lebanon to the southwest, the Mediterranean Sea to the west, Turkey to the north, Iraq to the east, Jordan to the south, and Israel to the southwest. A country of fertile plains, high mountains, and deserts, Syria is home to diverse ethnic and religious groups, including the majority Syrian Arabs, Kurds, Turkmens, Assyrians, Armenians, Circassians, Mandeans, and Greeks.

Religious Groups

Religious groups include Sunnis, Christians, Alawites, Ismailis, Mandeans, Shiites, Salafis and Yazidis. Arabs are the largest ethnic group, and Sunnis the largest religious group.

Syria is a unitary republic consisting of 14 governorates and is the only country that politically espouses Ba'athism. It is a member of one international organization other than the United Nations, the Non-Aligned Movement; it was suspended from the Arab League in November 2011 CE and the Organisation of Islamic Cooperation, and self-suspended from the Union for the Mediterranean.

General Geography and Topography

The topography consists of a narrow coastal plain in the west which rises up to the Syrian Coastal Mountain Range which runs parallel with the coast. South of this is the Homs Gap, beyond which are Mount Lebanon and the Anti-Lebanon Mountains which separate Syria from Lebanon. Further east is a large area of steppe or Badia in the centre of the country. This is divided by the River Euphrates, on which a dam was built in 1973 CE creating a reservoir, Lake Assad, which is the largest lake in Syria. In the east and south of the country is the Syrian Desert and in the far south is the Jabal al-Druze Mountain Range.

Climate

The coastal mountains and the coast have a Mediterranean climate. Here the winter is mild and wet, with up to 1 000 mm of annual precipitation, and the summer, from May to October, hot and dry. Further inland, the rainfall levels decrease rapidly, being 250 to 500 mm on the steppes and less than 130 mm in the desert. There is also a much greater variation between maximum and minimum temperature inland, with frosts sometimes occurring at night and temperatures rising as high as 45 °C by day in summer.

Soils

The most important soils in Syria are summarized as follows: Dry soils: This soil covers 50% of Syrian land. Soils not well developed: This soil covers 25% of the total area. Soil rich in organic matter: This soil covers 2% of the total area of the country. Undeveloped soil: This soil covers 2% of the total area of the country.

Minerals and Natural Resources

Syria accounted for about 2% of the world's supply of phosphate rock in 2010 CE. It ranked ninth in the world in phosphate rock production.

The mining sector also produced cement, marble, natural crude asphalt, nitrogen fertilizer, phosphate fertilizer, salt, steel, gypsum, and industrial sand.

Metals

Syria's net imports of steel products amounted to 2.2 mt and consisted of crude, semi-finished, and finished steel in 2010 CE. Most of the imports were from Ukraine and Russia.

In that year, Hmisho Steel produced low and medium grade carbon-content rebar from its newly constructed mill in Latakia. The company was also involved in construction of a new billet plant at Adra Industrial City.

Industrial Minerals

Syria's cement production was about 10 million mt/yr at the end of 2010.

In 2010 CE, General Organization for Cement and Building Materials (GOCBM) operated eight state-owned cement plants in Syria and produced more than 5 Mt of cement. Likewise, a cement plant operated by Military Housing Establishment of the Ministry of Defense produced 293 000 Mt of cement.

GOCBM was also involved in upgrading and expanding operations in 2010 CE at its Tartus plant. Saudi Arabia's Pharon Commercial Investment Group provided $50 million for the expansion in exchange for 400,000 t/yr of the plant's production.

In 2010 CE, a $164 million flat-glass plant operated by First Glass, a subsidiary of Kaveh Glass Industry Group of Iran, was designed with the capacity to produce 10,000 t/yr of glass.

Syria's phosphate rock production amounted to about 3.8 mt in 2010. This was a 70% increase compared to 2009 CE production of 2.1 Mt. The increase was attributed to the increase in global demand for phosphate rock. In the same year, Syria struck a deal with India to start a joint-venture company aimed at developing phosphate rock production facilities.

Fossil Fuels

Syria's total natural gas production in 2010 CE saw an increase of 37% to 7.8 billion m^3 from 5.7 billion m^3 in 2009 CE. The increased output from Ebla Petroleum Co., Oudeh Petroleum Co., Abu Kamal Petroleum, and Syria-Sino Alkawkab Oil Co. was the reason behind the overall increase. The entire production was used for domestic consumption, and some more was imported from Egypt.

In 2010 CE, the government opened the Ebla gas plant at Al-Freqlus. The 2.5 million m^3/d capacity plant was jointly operated by Suncor Energy Inc. of Canada and Petrofac Co. Ltd. of UK.

By the end of 2010, it was estimated that Syria's proven petroleum reserves amounted to about 2.5 billion bbl

Food, Agriculture, Flora and Fauna

Despite crisis in Syria, agriculture remains a key part of the economy. The sector still accounts for an estimated 26 percent of gross domestic product (GDP) and represents a critical safety net for the 6.7 million Syrians, including those internally displaced, who still remain in rural areas. However, agriculture and the livelihoods that depend on it have suffered massive loss. Today, food production is at a record low and around half the population remaining in Syria is unable to meet their daily food needs.

By the mid-1980s CE, the Syrian government had taken measures to revitalize agriculture. The 1985 CE investment budget saw a sharp rise in allocations for agriculture, including land reclamation and irrigation. The government's renewed commitment to agricultural development in the 1980s CE, by expanding cultivation and extending irrigation, promised brighter prospects for Syrian agriculture in the 1990s CE.

During the Syrian Civil War, the agricultural sector has witnessed a drop in producing all kinds of commodities such as wheat, cotton and olives, due to the lack of security and emigration of agricultural workforce,

Around 3 100 species of flowering plant have been recorded in Syria as well as about 112 gymnosperms. The country can be considered to be at a crossroads between various vegetation zones and the flora shows influences from three continents, Europe, Asia and Africa. The ice ages pushed Palearctic species further south, and when the climate ameliorated, some species clung on in mountainous regions of Turkey, Syria and Lebanon. The prevailing westerly winds bring greater precipitation near the coast and the vegetation on the western side of the coastal mountain ranges differs from that on the eastern side, which differs again from inland mountain ranges and once again from the drought-resistant plants that grow on the eastern plateau.

Syria has a diverse fauna with 125 species of mammal, 394 of bird, 127 of reptiles, 16 of amphibian and 157 species of freshwater fishes recorded in the country. Human activities have affected the biodiversity of the fauna. The Asiatic lion and cheetah, Caspian tiger and leopard used to be present, but they have died out in the country, and so the brown bear and the gray wolf are the largest carnivores remaining. Also present are the red fox, striped hyena, golden jackal, Egyptian mongoose, least weasel, marbled polecat, honey badger, European badger and European otter. The cat family are represented by the caracal, jungle cat, sand cat and wildcat. Grazing animals include the mountain gazelle and the goitered gazelle, the roe deer, wild goat, Nubian ibex and Arabian oryx. There are also rock hyrax, hedgehogs, hares, shrews and bats. The many species of rodents include squirrels, dormice, jerboas, gerbils, hamsters, mole-rats, jirds, voles, rats, mice and spiny mice.

Ten species of whale have been recorded off the coast as well as the endangered Mediterranean monk seal. Four species of turtle are sometimes seen, the most common being the loggerhead sea turtle, and about 295 species of marine fish have been recorded in Syria.

Of the nearly 400 species of bird recorded in the country, many are migrants, particularly visiting the coastal mountain range, the Euphrates valley and seasonal salt lakes that form in arid regions. Sabkhat al-Jabbul is a nature reserve at one of these salt lakes and is visited by migrating greater flamingos. Endangered breeding birds include a few pairs of northern bald ibis in the north of the country, the lesser kestrel and the great bustard. Rare visiting species include the corn crake, Dalmatian pelican, white-headed duck and eastern imperial eagle

Population

The population of Syria is estimated as 10 - 15 million. It is difficult to be precise as the civil war continues. It reached a high point of around 20 million. More than half were under 30.

Politics

Politics in the Syrian Arab Republic takes place in the framework of a semi-presidential republic with multiparty representation. President Bashar al-Assad's family and his Arab Socialist Ba'ath Party have remained dominant forces in the country's politics since the 1970 CE *'coup d'état'*.

Until the early stages of the Syrian uprising, the president had broad and unchecked decree authority under a long-standing state of emergency. The end of this emergency was a key demand of the uprising, and decrees are now subject to approval by the People's Council, the country's legislature. The Ba'ath Party is Syria's ruling party and the previous Syrian constitution of 1973 CE stated that the Arab Socialist Ba'ath Party leads society and the state. At least 167 seats of the 250-member parliament were guaranteed for the National Progressive Front, which is a coalition of the Ba'ath Party and several other much smaller allied parties. The new Syrian constitution of 2012 CE introduced multi-party system based on the principle of political pluralism without guaranteed leadership of any political party. The continuing civil strife has re-concentrated power in the hands of the President and the party. The

Syrian army and security services maintained a considerable presence in the neighbouring Lebanese Republic from 1975 CE until 24 April 2005 CE.

Language

Arabic is the official language of Syria and is the most widely spoken language in the country. Several modern Arabic dialects are used in everyday life, most notably Levantine in the west and Mesopotamian in the northeast. According to The Encyclopedia of Arabic Language and Linguistics, in addition to Arabic, the following languages are spoken in the country, in order of the number of speakers: Kurdish, Turkish, Neo-Aramaic, Circassian, Chechen, Armenian, and finally Greek. None of these languages has official status.

Religion

Religion in Syria refers to the range of religions practiced by the citizens of Syria. Historically, the region has been a mosaic of diverse faiths with a range of different sects within each of these religious communities. The majority of Syrians are Muslims, of which the Sunnis are the most numerous, followed by the Shia groups, and Druzes. In addition, there are several Christian minorities. There is also a small Jewish community.

Economy (Snapshot)

Syria's economic history has been turbulent and has deteriorated considerably since the beginning of the Syrian Civil War. The Arab Socialist Ba'ath Party came to power in 1963, and adopted socialist policies involving nationalizations and land reform. After General Hafez al-Assad took power in 1970 CE, restrictions on private enterprise were relaxed, though a substantial part of the economy was still under government control. By the 1980s CE, Syria was politically and economically isolated, and in the midst of a deep economic crisis. Real per capita GDP fell 22% between 1982 CE and 1989 CE. In 1990 CE, the Assad government instituted a series of economic reforms, although the economy remained highly regulated. The Syrian economy experienced strong growth throughout the 1990s CE, and into the 2000s CE. Syria's per capita GDP was U.S.$4 058 in 2010 CE. There is no authoritative GDP data available after 2012 CE, due to Syria's civil war.

- GDP: $27.26 billion (2021 CE est.); $56.28 billion (PPP 2015 CE est.). (UK: GDP: $2.64 trillion (nominal, 2020 CE est.); $2.98 trillion (PPP, 2020 CE).

- GDP by sector: Agriculture: 10.49%; Industry: 26.51%; Services: 63.0% (2017 CE est.).

- Labour force by occupation: Agriculture: 19%; Industry: 15%; Services: 66% (2008 CE est.).

- Main export partners: Saudi Arabia 15.0%; Lebanon 13.1%; Turkey 9.97%; Spain 8.92%; United Arab Emirates 5.66%; Kuwait 4.3%; Serbia 3.1%.

- Main import partners: China 20.5%; Turkey 20.0%; United Arab Emirates 19.2%; Egypt 3.67%; Russia 3.67%; Lebanon 3.3% (2018 CE).

Lebanon

Lebanon officially known as the Lebanese Republic, is a country in the Levant region of Western Asia, and the transcontinental region of the Middle East. It is bordered by Syria to the north and east and Israel to the south, while Cyprus lies west across the Mediterranean Sea. Lebanon's location at the crossroads of the Mediterranean Basin and the Arabian hinterland has contributed to its rich history and shaped a cultural identity of religious and ethnic diversity. At just 10 452 sq.km it is one of the smallest recognized sovereign states in the Asian continent. The official language, Arabic, is the most common language spoken by the citizens of Lebanon.

General Geography and Topography

Lebanon is a small country in the Middle East, located at approximately 34 ° N, 35 ° E. It stretches along the eastern shore of the Mediterranean Sea and its length is almost three times its width. From north to south, the width of its terrain becomes narrower. Lebanon's mountainous terrain, and the economic and religious movements that either originated in the region or crossed through to leave an imprint upon Lebanese society, give form to the country's history. The country's role in the region, as indeed in the world at large, was shaped by trade. Lebanon is named '*the Pearl of the Middle East*'. It serves as a link between the Mediterranean world and India and East Asia. The merchants of the region exported oil, grain, textiles, metal work, and pottery through the port cities to Western markets. The hilly Mediterranean geography has influenced the history, cuisine, and culture of Lebanon.

Climate

Lebanon has a Mediterranean climate characterized by a long, semi-hot, and dry summer, and a cold, rainy and snowy winter. Autumn is a transitional season with a lowering of temperature and little rain; spring occurs when the winter rains cause the vegetation to revive. Topographical variation creates local modifications of the basic climatic pattern. Along the coast, summers are warm and humid, with little or no rain. Heavy dews form, which are beneficial to agriculture. The daily range of temperature is not wide. A west wind provides relief during the afternoon and evening; at night the wind direction is reversed, blowing from the land out to sea.

Winter is the rainy and snowy season, with major precipitation falling after December. Rainfall is generous but is concentrated during only a few days of the rainy season, falling in heavy cloudbursts. The amount of rainfall varies greatly from one year to another. Snow is common in inland areas and mountains, with temperatures reaching an average of -1 °C in December, -5 °C in January, and -7 °C in February. A hot wind blowing from the Egyptian desert called the Khamsin may cause sudden increase in temperatures, mostly in spring. Bitterly cold winds often come from Southern Europe. Along the coast the proximity to the sea provides a moderating influence on the climate, making the range of temperatures narrower than it is inland, but the temperatures are cooler in the northern parts of the coast where there is also more rain.

Soils

Soil quality and makeup in Lebanon vary by region. The shallow limestone soil of the mountains provides a relatively poor topsoil. The lower and middle slopes, however, are intensively cultivated, the terraced hills standing as a scenic relic of the ingenious tillers of the past. On the coast and in the northern mountains, reddish topsoils with a high clay content retain moisture and provide fertile land for agriculture, although they are subject to considerable erosion.

Minerals and Natural Resources

The mining sector of Lebanon produces industrial mineral commodities such as cement, gypsum, aluminium sulphate, lime, limestone, phosphate fertilizer, phosphoric acid, sulfuric acid, and salt. However, it did not produce any metals or mineral fuels. The leading mineral commodity was limestone that was used for cement.

Pearls and precious and semiprecious gemstones were exported and accounted for 26% of the country's total exports, while exports of base metals and chemical products accounted for 11% and 7% of the total export value, respectively.

Food, Agriculture, Flora and Fauna

Arable land is scarce, but the climate and the relatively abundant water supply from springs favour the intensive cultivation of a variety of crops on mountain slopes and in the coastal region. On the irrigated coastal plain, market vege-tables, bananas, and citrus crops are grown. In the foothills the principal crops are olives, grapes, tobacco, figs, and almonds. At higher elevations, 460 m, peaches, apricots, plums, and cherries are planted, while apples and pears thrive at an eleva-tion of about 900 m. Sugar beets, cereals, and vegetables are the main crops cultivated in Al-Biqa. Poultry is a major source of agricultural income, and goats, sheep, and cattle are also raised.

Lebanon is rich in flora, with over 3 000 species. Olive and fig trees and grapevines are abundant on lower ground, while cedar, maple, juniper, fir, cypress, valonia oak, and Aleppo pine trees occupy higher altitudes. Vegetation types range from subtropical and desert to alpine. Although hunting has killed off most wild mammals, jackals are still found in the wilder rural regions, and gazelles and rabbits are numerous in the south. Many varieties of rodents, including mice, squirrels, and gerbils, and many types of reptiles, including lizards and snakes (some of them poisonous), may be found. Thrushes, nightingales, and other songbirds are native to Lebanon; there are also partridges, pigeons, vultures, and eagles.

Population

Population of Lebanon is 6.8 million, of which 80% are urban. Over 50% of the population is under 30.

Politics

Lebanon is a parliamentary democratic republic within the overall framework of confessionalism, a form of consociation-alism in which the highest offices are proportionately reserved for representatives from certain religious communities. The constitution of Lebanon grants the people the right to change their government. Article 7 of Lebanon's Constitution also states that all Lebanese are equal before the law and are *'equally bound by public obligations and duties without any distinction'.* Meaning that all Lebanese citizens- politicians included- are to be held to the same standards of the law, and yet this is not the case. However, from the mid-1970s CE until the parliamentary elections in 1992 CE, the Lebanese Civil War (1975–1990 CE) precluded the exercise of political rights.

According to the constitution, direct elections must be held for the parliament every 4 years but after the parliamentary election in 2009 CE another election was not held until 2018 CE. The Parliament, in turn, elects a President every 6 years to a single term. The President is not eligible for re-election. The last presidential election was in 2016 CE. The president and parliament choose the Prime Minister. Political parties may be formed; most are based on sectarian interests. 2008 CE saw a new twist to Lebanese politics when the Doha Agreement set a new trend where the opposition is allowed a veto power in the Lebanese Council of Ministers and confirmed religious Confessionalism in the distribution of political power. The Economist Intelligence Unit classified Lebanon as a hybrid regime in 2016 CE. Currently, 2021 CE, the Government is in disarray.

Language

Modern Standard Arabic is the language of Lebanon.

Religion

Lebanon is an eastern Mediterranean country that is composed of mostly Muslims and Christians. The main two religions are Islam with 53% of the citizens (Sunni, Shia, and a small number of Alawites and Ismailis) and Christianity with 40.7% of the citizens (the Maronite Church, the Greek Orthodox Church, the Melkite Greek Catholic Church, Protestantism, the Armenian Apostolic Church). The Druzeare about 7% of the citizens. The country has the most religiously diverse society of all states within the Middle East.

Economy

The economy of Lebanon is classified as a developing, upper-middle income economy. The nominal GDP was estimated $54.1 billion in 2018 CE, with a per capita GDP amounting to $12 000. Government spending amounted to $15.9 billion in 2018, or 23% of GDP.

The Lebanese economy significantly expanded after the war of 2006 CE, with growth averaging 9.1% between 2007 CE and 2010 CE. After 2011 CE the local economy was affected by the Syrian civil war, growing by a yearly average of 1.7% on the 2011–2016 CE period and by 1.5% in 2017 CE. In 2018 CE, the size of the GDP was estimated to be $54.1 billion. Lebanon is the third-highest indebted country in the world in terms of the ratio of debt-to-GDP. As a consequence, interest payments consumed 48% of domestic government revenues in 2016 CE, thus limiting the government's ability to make needed investments in infrastructure and other public goods. By 2021 CE the economy had collapsed.

The Lebanese economy is service-oriented. Lebanon has a strong tradition of laissez-faire, with the country's constitution stating that 'the economic system is free and ensures private initiative and the right to private property'. The major economic sectors include metal products, banking, agriculture, chemicals, and transport equipment. Main growth sectors include banking and tourism. There are no restrictions on foreign exchange or capital movement.

- GDP: $56.372 billion (nominal, 2018 CE est.) $84.288 billion (PPP 2019 CE est.). (UK: GDP: $2.64 trillion (nominal, 2020 CE est.); $2.98 trillion (PPP, 2020 CE)).

- GDP Growth: −1.9% (2018 CE); −5.6% (2019 CE e); −10.9% (2020 CE f); −6.3% (2021 CE f).

- GDP Per Capita: $9 251 (nominal, 2018 CE est.); $14 689

(PPP 2018 CE est.).

- GDP By Sector: Agriculture: 3.9%; Industry: 13.1%; Services: 83% (2017 CE est.).

- Inflation (CPI) 17.0% (2020 CE est.).

Israel

Israel, officially known as the State of Israel, is a country in Western Asia, located on the southeastern shore of the Mediterranean Sea and the northern shore of the Red Sea. It has land borders with Lebanon to the north, Syria to the northeast, Jordan on the east, the Palestinian territories of the West Bank and the Gaza Strip to the east and west, respectively, and Egypt to the southwest.

Israel's economic and technological centre is Tel Aviv, while its seat of government and proclaimed capital is Jerusalem, although international recognition of the state's sovereignty over Jerusalem is limited.

General Geography and Topography

The geography of Israel is very diverse, with desert conditions in the south, and snow-capped mountains in the north. Israel is located at the eastern end of the Mediterranean Sea in Western Asia. It is bounded to the north by Lebanon, the northeast by Syria, the east by Jordan and the West Bank, and to the southwest by Egypt. To the west of Israel is the Mediterranean Sea, which makes up the majority of Israel's 273 km coastline, and the Gaza Strip. Israel has a small coastline on the Red Sea in the south.

Israel's area is approximately 20 770 sq.km which includes 445 sq.km of inland water. Israel stretches 424 km from north to south, and its width ranges from 114 km to, at its narrowest point, 15 km It has an Exclusive Economic Zone of 26 352 sq.km.

The Israeli-occupied territories include the West Bank, 5 879 sq.km, East Jerusalem, 70 sq.km and the Golan Heights, 1 150 sq.km. Of these areas, Israel has annexed East Jerusalem and the Golan Heights, an act not universally recognized by the international community.

Southern Israel is dominated by the Negev desert, covering some 16 000 sq.km, more than half of the country's total land area. The north of the Negev contains the Judean Desert, which, at its border with Jordan, contains the Dead Sea which, at -417 m is the lowest point on Earth. The inland area of central Israel is dominated by the Judean Hills of the West Bank, whilst the central and northern coastline consists of the flat and fertile Israeli coastal plain. Inland, the northern region contains the Mount Carmel mountain range, which is followed inland by the fertile Jezreel Valley, and then the hilly Galilee region. The Sea of Galilee is located beyond this region and is bordered to the east by the Golan Heights, a plateau bordered to the north by the Israeli-occupied part of the Mount Hermon massif, which includes the highest point under Israel's control, a peak of 2 224 m The highest point in territory internationally recognized as Israeli is Mount Meron at 1 208 m.

Climate

Israel has a wide variety of climatic conditions, caused mainly by the country's diverse topography. There are two distinct seasons: a cool, rainy winter (October–April) and a dry, hot summer (May–September). Along the coast, sea breezes have a moderating influence in summer, and the Mediterranean beaches are popular. Precipitation is light in the south, amounting to about 25 mm per year in the Arava Valley south of the Dead Sea, while in the north it is relatively heavy, up to 1 120 mm a year in the Upper Galilee region. In the large cities, along the coastal plain, annual rainfall averages about 508 mm per year. Precipitation occurs on about 60 days during the year, spread over the rainy season. Severe summer water shortages ensue in years when the rains come late or rainfall totals are less than normal.

Average annual temperatures vary throughout Israel based on elevation and location, with the coastal areas adjacent to the Mediterranean Sea having milder temperatures—ranging from about 29 °C in August to about 16 °C in January—and higher rates of humidity than areas inland, especially during the winter. Likewise, higher elevations, such as Upper Galilee, have cool nights, even in summer, and occasional snows in the winter. However, the coastal city of Eilat, in the south, despite its proximity to the Red Sea, is closer to the climate of the Jordan and Arava valleys and the Negev, which are hotter and drier than the northern coast; there, daytime temperatures reach about 21 °C in January and may rise as high as 46 °C in August, when the average high is 40 °C.

Soils

The coastal plain is covered mainly by alluvial soils. Parts of the arid northern Negev, where soil development would not be expected, have windblown loess soils because of proximity to the coastal plain. The soils of Galilee change from calcareous rock in the coastal plain, to Cenomanian and Turonian limestone (deposited from about 99 to 89 million years ago) in Upper Galilee, and to Eocene formations (those dating from about 55 to 35 million years ago) in the lower part of the region. Rock salt and gypsum are abundant in the Great Rift Valley. The southern Negev is mainly sandstone rock with veins of granite.

Minerals and Natural Resources

Minerals

The Dead Sea is an important source of potash, materials containing potassium. Potash is used throughout the world in fertilizers. The Dead Sea is also a source of magnesium bromide, which is used in both sedatives and anti-convulsant medications. Israel also produces phosphate rocks, which are mined for a variety of uses in industry and agriculture.

Wood and Metal

The CIA World Fact Book lists timber as one of Israel's natural resources, though Israel cannot tap its lumber resources extensively because trees are a limited resource in this desert region. The land is also a source of some copper ore.

Natural Gas

Currently, Israel produces relatively small amounts of natural gas, but its natural gas industry has grown substantially since it was first developed in 1986 CE. In 2009 CE Israel produced 54.74 billion cubic feet of dry natural gas, almost half of its annual consumption. Since then the Tamar and Leviathan fields off Haifa not only mean Israel is self-sufficient in gas for the next 40 years but that Turkey, Cyprus, Lebanon, Egypt have rights in adjoining and spillover reservoirs; Russian Gazprom and U.S companies have development contracts. The fields are potentially reorganising the East Mediterranean diplomatic map.

Crude Oil

It is a myth that Israel produces no oil at all, but its reserves are so small that they often are not worth drilling for. In 2009 CE, the country produced an average of only 10 barrels per day. As a point of comparison, the same year Syria produced 368 thousand barrels per day

Food, Agriculture, Flora and Fauna

Agriculture in Israel is a highly developed industry. Israel is a major exporter of fresh produce and a world-leader in agricultural technologies despite the fact that the geography of the country is not naturally conducive to agriculture. More than half of the land area is desert, and the climate and lack of water resources do not favour farming. Only 20% of the land area is naturally arable. In 2008 CE agriculture represented 2.5% of total GDP and 3.6% of exports. While farmworkers made up only 3.7% of the work force, Israel produced 95% of its own food requirements, supplementing this with imports of grain, oilseeds, meat, coffee, cocoa and sugar.

Israel is home to two unique types of agricultural communities, the kibbutz and moshav, which developed as Jews from all over the world made 'Aliyah' (immigration) to the country and embarked on rural settlement.

Natural vegetation is highly varied, and more than 2 800 plant species have been identified. The original evergreen forests, the legendary "cedars of Lebanon," have largely disappeared after many centuries of timber cutting for shipbuilding and to clear land for cultivation and goat herding; they have been replaced by second-growth oak and smaller evergreen conifers. The hills are mostly covered by maquis, and wildflowers bloom profusely in the rainy season. Only wild desert scrub grows in the Negev and on the sand dunes of the coastal plain. North of Beersheba, most of the country is under cultivation or is used for hill grazing. Where irrigation is available, citrus groves, orchards of subtropical fruit, and food crops flourish. Millions of trees have been planted through a government reforestation program.

Population

The State of Israel has a population of approximately 9 227 700 inhabitants as of July 2020 CE. Some 74.24% are Jews of all backgrounds (about 6 829 000 individuals), 20.95% are Arab of any religion other than Jewish (about 1 890 000 individuals), while the remaining 4.81% (about 434 000 individuals) are defined as 'others', including persons of Jewish ancestry deemed non-Jewish by religious law and persons of non-Jewish ancestry who are family members of Jewish immigrants (neither of which are registered at the Ministry of Interior as Jews), Christian non-Arabs, Muslim non-Arabs and all other residents who have neither an ethnic nor religious classification.

Israel's annual population growth rate stood at 2.0% in 2015, more than three times faster than the OECD average of around 0.6%. With an average of three children per woman, Israel also has the highest fertility rate in the OECD by a considerable margin and much higher than the OECD average.

Politics

Politics in Israel is dominated by Zionist parties. They traditionally fall into three camps, the first two being the largest: Labor Zionism, Revisionist Zionism and Religious Zionism. There are also several non-Zionist Orthodox religious parties, non-Zionist secular left-wing groups as well as non-Zionist and anti-Zionist Israeli Arab parties.

Compared to other countries, the number of parties contesting Knesset elections is relatively high considering the population size. This has resulted in a fragmented legislature where smaller parties have representation in the Knesset and no party has the 60+ seat majority needed to form a government on its own.

This system also allows fringe parties which hold views outside of the mainstream political and public consensus to have representation in the Knesset. Examples of these are the Haredi religious parties, parties that represent the national religious or limited agenda parties such as Gil, which represented pensioners in the 2006 CE elections.

Language

•   Hebrew. Hebrew is the everyday speaking language of Israel. This language was revived after 150 years of neglect.

•   Arabic. Arabic is the second official language of Israel. It is spoken by 20% of the total population of Israel.

- Russian. Although Russian is not the official language of Israel but owing to the immigration of Russian Jews it is spoken widely.

- English. English is one of the important languages of Israel.

Religion

Jews constitute about 75% of the total population of Israel. Almost all the rest are Palestinian Arabs, of whom most (roughly 75%) are Muslim; the remaining Arabs are Christians and Druze, who each make up only a small fraction of the total population. Arabs are the overwhelming majority in the Gaza Strip and the occupied territory of the West Bank.

Economy

The economy of Israel is a developed free-market economy. Israel ranks 35th on the World Bank's ease of doing business index. It has the second-largest number of start-up companies in the world after the United States, and the third-largest number of NASDAQ-listed companies after the U.S. and China. American companies such as Intel, Microsoft, and Apple built their first overseas research and development facilities in Israel, and other high-tech multi-national corporations, such as IBM, Google, HP, Cisco Systems, Facebook and Motorola have opened R&D centres in the country.

The country's major economic sectors are technology and industrial manufacturing; the Israeli diamond industry is one of the world's centres for diamond cutting and polishing, amounting to 23.2% of all exports. Relatively poor in natural resources, Israel depends on imports of petroleum, raw materials, wheat, motor vehicles, uncut diamonds, and production inputs, though the country's nearly total reliance on energy imports may change in the future with recent discoveries of natural gas reserves off its coast on the one hand and the leading role of the Israeli solar energy industry on the other.

GDP: $387.717 billion (nominal, 2019 CE est.) $334.675 billion (PPP 2020 CE est.). (UK: GDP: $2.64 trillion (nominal, 2020 CE est.); $2.98 trillion (PPP, 2020 CE)).

GDP Growth: 3.4% (2018 CE); 3.5% (2019 CE); −6.3% (2020 CE e); 5.0% (2021 CE e)

GDP Per Capita: $42,823 (nominal, 2019 CE est.) $39,121 (PPP 2019 CE est.)

GDP By Sector: Agriculture: 2.4%; Industry: 26.5%; Services: 69.5% (2017 CE est.)

Population below the poverty line 28%

Palestine

Palestine officially recognized as the State of Palestine by the United Nations and other entities, is allegedly a *de jure* sovereign state in Western Asia officially governed by the Palestine Liberation Organization (PLO) and claiming the West Bank and Gaza Strip with Jerusalem as the designated capital; in practice, however, only partial administrative control is held over the 167 'islands' in the West Bank, and Gaza is ruled by a rival government (Hamas). The entirety of territory claimed by the State of Palestine was, after the end of the Palestine mandate in 1948 CE, Egyptian (Gaza Strip) and Jordanian (West Bank) and was then occupied by Israel after the Six-Day War in 1967 CE. Palestine has a population of 5 051 953 as of February 2020 CE, ranked 121st in the world. It is in many ways an artificial state created after the 1967 CE Six-Day War by the Palestine Liberation Organisation as supported by the USSR's KGB.

After World War II, in 1947 CE, the UN adopted a Partition

Plan for Mandatory Palestine recommending the creation of independent Arab and Jewish states and an internationalized Jerusalem. This partition plan was accepted by the Jews but rejected by the Arabs. The day after the establishment of a Jewish state in Eretz Israel, to be known as the State of Israel on 14 May 1948 CE, neighbouring Arab armies invaded the former British mandate and fought the Israeli forces. Later, the All-Palestine Government was established by the Arab League on 22 September 1948 CE to govern the Egyptian-controlled enclave in Gaza. It was soon recognized by all Arab League members except Transjordan. Though jurisdiction of the Government was declared to cover the whole of the former Mandatory Palestine, its effective jurisdiction was limited to the Gaza Strip. Israel later captured the Gaza Strip and the Sinai Peninsula from Egypt, the West Bank (including East Jerusalem) from Jordan, and the Golan Heights from Syria in June 1967 CE during the Six-Day War.

On 15 November 1988 CE in Algiers, Yasser Arafat, Chairman of the PLO, proclaimed the establishment of the State of Palestine. A year after the signing of the Oslo Accords in 1993 CE, the Palestinian National Authority was formed to govern (in varying degrees) areas A and B in the West Bank, comprising 165 'islands', and the Gaza Strip. After Hamas became the PNA parliament's leading party in the most recent elections (2006 CE), a conflict broke out between it and the Fatah party, leading to Gaza being taken over by Hamas in 2007 CE (two years after the Israeli disengagement).

The State of Palestine has been recognized by 138 of the 193 UN members and since 2012 CE has had a status of a non-member observer state in the United Nations. Palestine is a member of the Arab League, the Organisation of Islamic Cooperation, the G77, the International Olympic Committee, and other international bodies. From its inception it has been bound up in the proxy war (s) between the USSR and the U.S.A.

General Geography and Topography, Climate

Soils

The location of Palestine is at the eastern coast of the Mediterranean Sea. Palestine is located to the south of Lebanon and to the west of Jordan. Palestine Geography consists of four regions in the country. The four regions of Palestine Geography are Jordan valley and Ghawr, coastal and inner plains, Mountain and Hills and Southern Desert.

The coastal plains of Palestine are divided by Saruunah plain, Mount Carmel plain and the Acre plain. In the category of the geography of Palestine the location of Jordan Valley is below the sea level and Ghawr. It results in the quality of the soil to be of very high standard but the resource of water is very limited.

The climate of Palestine results in the growing of such types of vegetables in the last phase of winter season, which usually are grown in the summer season. The hills and the mountains of Palestine have rocky features and terraces are made in the mountains so that the tress can grow.

The geography in Palestine supports the growth of olive trees to a large extent. In some of the parts of Palestine patches of plain land are found which helps in the growth of barley, wheat, lentils. There are many rivers in Palestine and the weather of Palestine remains pleasant for the maximum part of the year.

Minerals and Natural Resources

Key natural resources within Palestine areas include oil in the West Bank and gas off the coast of Gaza. These are effectively controlled by Israel.

Water is limited.

Other resources exist but are not abundant.

Food Agriculture Flora and Fauna

There is 27 000 sq. km of agricultural land of which 10 000 are cultivable.

Agriculture remains a dominant sector of the Palestinian economy. It represents a major component of the economy's GDP and employs a large fraction of the population. Furthermore, the agricultural sector is a major earner of foreign exchange and supplies the basic needs of the majority of the local population. In times of difficulty, the agricultural sector has acted as a buffer that absorbs large scores of unemployed people who lost their jobs in Israel or other local sectors of the economy.

Palestinian agriculture is constrained by available land and water, as well as access to markets. These constraints have been the object of political conflict, as Israeli authorities have limited available land, water and markets. It is widely recognized that resolution of these conflicts is essential to the establishment of peace in the region. Since Palestinian agriculture is a major potential user of land and water, it is important to establish its needs for these resources. Typically, models for the allocation of water in the region have used a simple derived demand function for water, in which the elasticity of demand is the key parameter.

Over 2 800 species of plants have been identified here on a comparatively small area. In the last century there were still large wooded areas. Today, fruit trees (olive, almond, orange, apricot ...) dominate the countryside while wild species such as pine, cypress, carob, acacia and turpentine trees are limited to certain regions (in the Galilee and on Mt. Carmel), on the edges of villages and in wadis.

The vast wild desert or semi-desert mountainous spaces are a refuge for various wildlife species of which some can be observed in the wadis in the early morning or at dusk. The Nubian ibex (Capra ibex nubiana) and the Dorcas gazelle (Gazella dorcas) are common on the hills of the West Bank. In Wadi Araba, another gazelle (Gazella gazella) and the rock daman (Procavia capensis), a member of the marmot family, are amongst the most numerous and accessible animals. Predators also exist here: wolves (Canis lupus) are common in uninhabited areas, panthers (Panthera pardus) make their home in the arid mountains of the South Hebron Hills, and striped hyaena (Hyaena hyaena) live near remote villages where one sometimes hears their laughing cry.

Land based fauna is similarly quite diverse unique and rich with over 730 species including mammals, reptiles, amphibians and birds. Furthermore, because of its unique position between Africa, Asia and Europe, Palestine is considered as a major grassroots for Migratory birds such as Storks and Pelicans. The Jordan Valley – Jericho and Jerusalem mountains routes are major pathways during the migration times as well as important spots for resident and breeding birds. Over 520 species of birds have been recorded in Palestine by the Wildlife Society.

Population

The population of Palestine is just under 5.5 million.

Politics

The 1948 CE Israeli War of Independence was between the neighbouring Arab countries and the newly formed state of Israel. The Arab countries did not send troops to help the people that are today known as *'Palestinians'* but rather they sent troops to drive the Jews into the sea. Most of the *'Palestinian Arabs'* fled to avoid the fighting. Note, in 1948 CE they were not referred to as *'Palestinians'*. This name was created by the Soviet disinformation masters in 1964 when they created the *Palestine Liberation Organization (PLO)*. The term *'Palestinian People'* as a description of Arabs in Palestine appeared for the first time in the preamble of the 1964 CE PLO Charter, drafted in Moscow. The Charter was affirmed by the first 422 members of the Palestinian National Council, handpicked by the KGB. This term was formally used by newspapers around the world after 1967 CE.

The complicated politics of Palestine is summarised by the list of political parties:

- Palestinian National Liberation Movement (Al-Fatah).
- Popular Front for the Liberation of Palestine.
- Popular Front for the Liberation of Palestine – General Command.
- Democratic Front for the Liberation of Palestine.
- Vanguard for the Popular Liberation War.
- Arab Liberation Front.
- Palestinian Popular Struggle Front.
- Front for the Liberation of Palestine.
- Palestinian Democratic Union.
- Palestinian People's Party.
- Third Way Party.
- Palestinian National Initiative.
- Islamic Resistance Movement (Hamas).
- Islamic Jihad Movement.

Language

Palestinians speak Standard Arabic.

Religion

Palestinians are generally Sunni Muslims

Economy

- GDP (PPP) 2018 CE estimate: Total $26.479 billion (–); Per capita $5 795 (–). (UK: GDP: $2.64 trillion (nominal, 2020 CE est.); $2.98 trillion (PPP, 2020 CE)).

- GDP (nominal) 2018 CE estimate: Total $14.616 billion (–); Per capita $3 199 (–).

CHAPTER 13: TURKEY AND NORTHERN CYPRUS

Turkey, officially the Republic of Turkey is a transcontinental country straddling southeastern Europe and Western Asia. It is bordered on its northwest by Greece and Bulgaria; north by the Black Sea; northeast by Georgia; east by Armenia, Azerbaijan, and Iran; southeast by Iraq; south by Syria and the Mediterranean Sea; and west by the Aegean Sea. Istanbul, which straddles Europe and Asia, is the country's largest city, while Ankara is the capital. Approximately 70 to 80% of the country's citizens are ethnic Turks, while the largest minority are Kurds at 20%.

Cyprus and Northern Cyprus

Cyprus officially called the Republic of Cyprus, is an island nation in the eastern Mediterranean Sea. It is the third largest and third most populous island in the Mediterranean and is located south of Turkey; west of Syria; northwest of Lebanon, Israel and Palestine; north of Egypt; and southeast of Greece. Nicosia is the country's capital and largest city.

The island was invaded by Turkey in 1974 and effectively split in two. This remains the case today.

General Geography and Topography

Geographically, Turkey forms a natural land bridge between the old-world continents of Asia, Africa and Europe. The Anatolian peninsula is the westernmost point of Asia, divided from Europe by the Bosphorus and Dardanelles-straits. Thrace is the western part of Turkey on the European continent.

Examination of Turkey's topographic structure on a physical map of the world shows clearly the country's high elevation in comparison to its neighbours, half of the land area being higher than 1000 m and two thirds higher than 800 m. Mountain ranges extend in an east-west direction parallel to the north and south coasts, and these are a principal factor in determining ecological conditions. This also means that apart from the Asi river in Anatolia and the Meriç in Thracian Turkey, all Turkey's rivers have their sources within its borders and flow into the sea, into neighbouring countries or into interior drainages. Turkey has seven river basins. The principal rivers in the Black Sea basin being the Sakarya, Kizilirmak Yesilirmak and Çoruh. There are also several rivers with short courses but high water flows in the Eastern Black Sea region, such as the Ikizdere, Hursit Cayi and Firtina.

The Marmara basin has fewer rivers, the longest being the Kocaçay (whose upper and middle reaches are called the Simav and Susurluk respective) which rises on Mount Murat and flows into the Marmara Sea from the south.

The Kuçuk Menderes, Büyük Menderes and Gediz rivers in the Aegean basin lend their names to the plains which they water.

In the Mediterranean basin the principal rivers are the Aksu, Kopruçay, Manavgat, Goksu, Ceyhan and Seyhan.

Two major rivers flow from Turkey into the Caspian Sea basin; the Aras and Kura. Water from Turkey flows into the Indian Ocean through the Gulf of Basra via the famous Euphrates and Tigris rivers.

Turkey also has two inland drainage basins. The first is the Central Anatolia basin which contains the Tuz Golu (salt lake) in Konya, and the Yay, Seyfe, Kulu and several other satellite lakes. The major river in this basin is the Çarsamba which is outflow of Beysehir Lake and contributes a large volume of water for irrigation of the fertile Konya Plain, and is linked by a canal to Tuz Golu. The Karasu, Incesu, Deliçay and Bendimahi rivers flow into the interior drainage basin of Van. There are waterfalls on the Bendimahi.

Another significant aspect of Turkey's topography is its continental character, preserved in the ancient name of Asia Minor. This land mass is indeed a small scale continent in many respects, above all with respect to the climate of the interior. In some provinces the temperature difference over 24 hours can be as much as 20 °C. During the spring months it is not unusual to find weather typical of two or even three seasons at different locations around Turkey in a single day. The Mediterranean coast may be enjoying summer heat while the temperate Black Sea region gets as much as 2 000 mm of precipitation in some places, there are parts of Central Anatolia with an average precipitation only one eighth of this total.

Geological and topographic structure are among the main factors affecting diversity of species in terrestrial ecosystems. While the mountain ranges running parallel to the Black Sea and Mediterranean create a barrier for rain clouds moving inland, they cause abundant rainfall on the mountain slopes facing the coast. On the Aegean the mountain ranges run perpendicularly towards the coast, divided by broad valleys which allow the maritime climate to prevail several hundred kilometres inland. Alluvion carried by the rivers has created fertile plains in this Aegean region. Eastwards these mountain ranges move closer together in Central Entail, spreading apart once more in northeast and southeast Turkey. The height of plains and plateaus in Central Anatolia varies from 700 to 1 100 m, while in Eastern Anatolia this rises to 1 100-1 900 m, and drops to 700-500 in Southeast Anatolia. Despite the existence of broad plains and plateaus, the topography is largely hilly and mountainous across Turkey as a whole.

Climate

The coastal areas of Turkey bordering the Aegean Sea and the Mediterranean Sea have a hot-summer Mediterranean climate, with hot, dry summers and mild to cool, wet winters. The coastal areas of Turkey bordering the Black Sea have a temperate Oceanic climate with warm, wet summers and cool to cold, wet winters. The Turkish Black Sea coast receives the greatest amount of precipitation and is the only region of Turkey that receives high precipitation throughout the year. The eastern part of that coast averages 2 500 mm annually which is the highest precipitation in the country.

The coastal areas of Turkey bordering the Sea of Marmara (including Istanbul), which connects the Aegean Sea and the Black Sea, have a transitional climate between a temperate Mediterranean climate and a temperate Oceanic climate with warm to hot, moderately dry summers and cool to cold, wet winters. Snow does occur on the coastal areas of the Sea of Marmara and the Black Sea almost every winter, but it usually lies no more than a few days. On the other hand, it is rare in the coastal areas of the Aegean Sea and very rare in the coastal areas of the Mediterranean Sea.

Conditions can be much harsher in the more arid interior. Mountains close to the coast prevent maritime influences from extending inland, giving the central Anatolian plateau of the interior of Turkey a humid continental climate with sharply contrasting seasons.

Winters on the plateau are especially severe. Temperatures of -30 °C to -40 °C do occur in northeastern Anatolia, and snow may lie on the ground at least 120 days of the year and in the mountains almost the entire year. In central Anatolia the temperatures can drop below -20 °C with the mountains being even colder. Summers are hot and dry, with temperatures generally around or above 30 °C in the day. Annual precipitation averages about 400 mm with actual amounts determined by elevation. The driest regions are the Konya Plain and the Malatya Plain, where annual rainfall frequently is less than 300 mm (12 in). May is generally the wettest month, whereas July and August are the driest.

Soils

Turkey's soils match the varied topographical nature of the country. The Leptosols are the dominant soils followed by the Calcisols, Fluvisols, Cambisols, Vertisols, Kastonozems, Regosols, Arenosols and Acrisols.

Minerals and Natural Resources

Natural Gas

Turkey consumes a significant amount of natural gas, much of which is imported. However, it also has the potential to increase its level of domestic production, namely through shale gas and its share of the gas resources in the Eastern Mediterranean (a cause of friction between Turkey and Greece, and other nations). Turkey's strategic location makes it a natural 'Energy Bridge' between major oil and gas producing regions and major consumer markets. Natural gas consumption in Turkey has increased over time to 48.6 billion cubic meters in 2014 CE, but the country only produced 0.5 billion cubic meters of natural gas during that same year. Current gas production meets about 3% of domestic consumption requirements, but Turkey has approximately 675 billion cubic meters of shale gas reserves, especially in the southeastern region of Anatolia and Trace. Additionally, 650 billion cubic meters of these reserves can be drilled in the first stage. Currently, Turkey's Ministry of Energy and Natural Resources is exploring other potential reserve areas throughout the country, especially in Central and Eastern Anatolia, which is suspected to have shale gas potential. The giant Tuna gas field was discovered in 2020 CE in the

Black Sea, and as noted Turkey may have additional discoveries in the Mediterranean. Turkey is therefore likely to become self-sufficient in energy resources.

Coal

Turkey produces more coal than oil and gas, and this coal is primarily used for power generation. In fact, the country produced approximately 1.5 million tons of hard coal, which accounted for about 40% of Turkey's total energy production. Major hard coal deposits are located in the Zonguldak basin and Amasra, on the coast of the Black Sea in northwestern Turkey. The basin is estimated to hold 1.3 billion tonnes of hard coal and is the only region in the country where hard coal is extracted. However, the basin has a complex geological structure, making mechanized coal production nearly impossible. The state-owned Turkey Hard Coal Enterprise (TTK) has the sole monopoly of hard coal production, processing, and distribution. TTK has five operational deep mines in the Zonguldak basin that produced 1.5 million tonnes of coal in 2015 CE.

Lignite

Lignite is one of Turkey's local energy sources, with a proven reserve of 15.6 billion tonnes. Lignite, together with coal, was responsible for 27% of the country's primary energy supply in 2015 CE. Lignite deposits are spread throughout the country, but the most significant deposit is located in the Afsin-Elbistan basin. The basin is located southeast of Anatolia and has reserves estimated at roughly 7 billion tonnes. Other major mining areas include the Soma basin, Yenikoy, and the South Aegean lignite facility. The quality of lignite produced in Turkey is generally poor, and only 5.1% of existing reserves have a heat content that exceeds 3 000 Kcal/kg. In Turkey, lignite is produced at a relatively low cost, making it more competitive than other energy sources. Most of its production comes from opencast mines, while a small is mined underground.

Iron Ore

Turkey contains approximately 80 million tonnes of iron ore reserves, which are distributed throughout the country, especially in Anatolia, Erzincan, Malatya, and Sivas. Production levels have not changed much over the years due to the insufficient reserves. One of the largest iron ore reserves in Turkey is the Avnik mine, which is located in Bingol Province, about 452 miles east of Ankara. Avnik has an estimated reserve of 105 million tonnes of ore grading 42% iron, and contains 44 million tonnes of iron metal. In 2008, Turkey produced about 4.7 million tonnes of iron ore. Due to low levels of iron ore production, Turkey relies on imports, mainly from Brazil, Russia, Sweden, and Ukraine.

Copper

Turkey has several copper mines spread across the county. One of the largest copper mines in the country is the Cayeli mine, located in Rize Province, about 470 km east of Ankara. The mine has an estimated reserve of 20 million tonnes of ore, which contain about 500 000 million tonnes of copper metal. The Murgul mine located in Artvin Province, about 465 km from Ankara. The reserve has an estimated 40 million tonnes of ore grading 1.25% copper. Other copper mines in Turkey include the Damar mine, Cakmakkaya mine, Tirebolu mine, and Cevizlidere mine.

Gold

Gold is mined on a small scale in several parts of Turkey. In 2012 CE, a total of 29.5 tonnes of gold were mined throughout the country, making Turkey a major gold producer. The largest gold mine in the country is the Kısladag mine, which located in Usak Province, and is owned and operated by the Canadian-based Eldorado Gold Company. The Copler mine is also one of the largest gold mines in Turkey and the world, with an estimated reserve of 6 million ounces of gold. The mine is located in Erzincan Province and is operated by U.S.-owned Alacer Gold Corporation

Food, Agriculture, Flora and Fauna

Agriculture in Turkey has an important role in the economic activity in Turkey, as the total area of arable agricultural land is 23.2 million hectares, exports reach about $ 18 billion, while imports are about $ 13 billion, with a total trade surplus of $ 5 billion.

The agricultural sector in Turkey employs about 5.3 million workers, and the GDP from the agricultural sector reaches about $ 50 billion.

Agriculture income in Turkey increased by 77.7% between 2002 CE and 2018 CE.

Turkey Agricultural Products

The crops cultivated in Turkey vary between grains, fruits, vegetables, and medicinal and aromatic plants.

Grains Crops Grown in Turkey

Cereal production in Turkey increases greatly, due to the suitable climate in addition to the use of appropriate agricultural technology and the development of modern types of seeds.

The grains grown in Turkey vary between wheat, barley, oats, corn, and rice.

Wheat

Wheat is one of the most important agricultural products in Turkey that is used domestically and exported abroad.

Wheat is mostly grown in the Central Anatolia region of Turkey. Agriculture is also widespread in the regions of Marmara, the Mediterranean and Southeastern Anatolia. The harvest of wheat grown in the Mediterranean region takes place in May, while the harvest takes place in July for Central Anatolia and August in Eastern Anatolia.

Turkey is one of the largest producers of wheat and flour in the world, with total production in 2019 CE reaching about 20 million tonnes of wheat.

Barley

Barley grows in a shorter period of time than wheat, which drives many farmers and investors to cultivate it instead of wheat, as Turkey produced, according to the latest statistics in 2020 CE, about 7 million tonnes of barley, to be one of the largest producing countries in the world.

Barley is produced in Central Anatolia. İt's used in food products, beverages and animal feed.

Rye and oats

Turkey ranks seventh in the world in the cultivation of oats, and the grown oats are used in the food industry and can be grown in cold and high places in Turkey.

Maize (Corn)

Turkey produces about 6 million tonnes of corn annually. Maize production is grown naturally in the Black Sea and Marmara regions, and in other regions, most notably Central Anatolia, through irrigation.

In recent years the states of the Mediterranean region have begun to expand the production of maize.

Rice

Rice is produced in Turkey in the states of Samsun, Sinop, Corum, Cankiri, Bursa, Balikesir, Canakkale, Tekirdag, Edirne and Kirklareli.

Turkey's rice production is about 550 000 tonnes per year, while the consumption reaches about 750 000 tonnes, and accordingly, Turkey imports about a quarter of a million tonnes of rice annually.

Industrial Crops Grown in Turkey

Industrial crops are one of the most important agricultural

crops in Turkey, which are not used directly after their production and harvest, as they must be processed in different industrial facilities.

Industrial crops in Turkey range from tea, tobacco, cotton, sunflower, sugar beet, flax, hashish for medicinal purposes, and poppy.

Tobacco

Tobacco cultivation is done in Turkey with the legal permission of the state, as cultivating tobacco in Turkey without permission is illegal and punishable.

İt's is produced in different regions according to the climate and soil conditions in Turkey, where the following states produce tobacco in Turkey:

Manisa, Izmir, Denizli, Aydin, Ushak, Mugla, Balikesir, Bursa, Samsun, Bitlis, Mus, Malatya, Adiyaman, Hatay.

Tobacco needs moisture and temperature during its growing period. It is used as a raw material in the cigarette, cigar and chemical industries. as the tobacco is dried and cured.

Cotton

Cotton requires a lot of water during the growing period, as cotton grows more easily in alluvial soil. it is mainly produced in the far southeast of Anatolia. The fibres, seeds and pulp extracted from cotton are used in industrial activities. Oil is produced from cotton pulp in Turkey.

Turkey's cotton production, according to the latest statistics, is about 750 000 tonnes per year.

Sugar Beet

Turkey is one of the largest producers of sugar beet in the world, as it ranks fifth among the countries producing beets.

Sugar beet is produced in most regions of Central Anatolia in Turkey and is also grown in the regions of Inland Western Anatolia, Central and Western Black Sea, Marmara regions and Eastern Anatolia.

Turkey's production of sugar beet, according to the latest statistics, is about 2.25 million tonnes per year.

Tea

Tea is a very famous product for agriculture in Turkey as it's in the cities of Rize, Trabzon, Giresun and Artvin, on eastern Black Sea. Tea leaves are fermented (dried) in the factories of the city of Rize.

Turkey gained momentum in the forties of the last century after the production and export of Turkish tea to various countries of the world, which is famous for its high quality and popularity.

Turkey's production of tea, according to the latest statistics, is about 200 000 tonnes per year.

Poppy

Poppies are grown in hot summer and moderate rain regions, and their cultivation requires a permit from the state.

The drug called opium is obtained from a poppy capsule, oil from its seeds, and animal fodder from its pulp.

Poppy has been produced in Turkey for many years, with 90% of the poppy produced for medicinal purposes that are exported.

Hemp "Weed"

Cannabis cultivation in Turkey requires a permit from the state in addition to periodic follow-up to ensure that hemp is not used illegally.

Hemp is produced in Turkey in the states of Sinop, Kastamonu and Zonguldak in addition to Sakarya, for medical purposes.

Oil Crops Grown in Turkey

Many oil crops are produced in Turkey, the most important of which are olives, sunflower, soybeans, peanuts, anise, rose and sesame.

Olives

Olives in Turkey are generally produced in the Aegean region, south of Marmara, and the coasts of the Mediterranean and Kilis are also places where olive growing is widespread.

With the growing interest in healthy living and nutrition in the world in recent years, the importance of production and consumption of olive oil has increased.

Turkey's olive production, according to the latest statistics, is about 160 000 tonnes per year, and olive trees in Turkey give a high agricultural production of about 27 kg per tree per year.

Sunflower

Sunflower cultivation in Turkey requires rainfall during the growing period in addition to warm weather conditions during the ripening period.

Sunflower oil in Turkey is one of the most used agricultural products in Turkey. 70% of sunflower production is produced in the provinces of Edirne, Tekirdag, Kırklareli, Bursa and Balikesir.

Central Anatolia and the Central Black Sea region are other regions where sunflowers are produced.

Turkey's production of sunflowers, according to the latest statistics, is about 2 million tonnes per year.

Soybean

Due to the short cultivation period of soybeans, it is grown as a by-product in the coasts of Cukurova, the Antalya Plain and the Aegean Sea, and is also grown in the Central and Eastern Black Sea region.

Peanuts and Sesame

Peanuts grow in loose soil for hot and humid climates. It is used in all the nuts and oil industries.

About 90% of Turkey's peanut production is grown in the Mediterranean region.

The states of Osmaniye and Adana are among the prominent states in the cultivation of peanuts.

Sesame is mostly produced in Marmara, Aegean, Mediterranean and Southeastern Anatolia. While the oil is obtained from sesame seeds, it is also used in making tahini, cake, biscuits, and bread.

Legumes Grown in Turkey

Turkey is famous for the production of many legumes, most notably beans, kidney beans, chickpeas, lentils, and peas. Turkey has gained momentum with pulses production since the 1980s CE.

Lentils

Since lentils are high in protein, they are consumed in a high proportion in Turkey.

Lentil production in Turkey is divided into green lentils and red lentils, as red lentils are grown in Turkey in the southeastern Anatolia region, while green lentils are cultivated in central Anatolia.

Turkey is the third largest country in the world in producing lentils

Turkey's agricultural production of lentils, according to the latest statistics, is about 480 000 tonnes per year.

Chickpeas

Chickpeas are grown in Turkey in the regions of Central Anatolia, the Aegean Sea and southeastern Anatolia.

Turkey's agricultural production of chickpeas, according to the latest statistics, is about 500 000 tonnes per year, and the productivity of each hectare is about 120 kg.

Beans

The beans are grown in areas not higher than 1500 m and can be watered in summer. Beans are also known as a warm-climate vegetable. The temperature drop of two or three degrees in the areas where it is grown is detrimental to the beans.

The beans are grown in the coastal region of Turkey and along rivers.

Fruit Grown in Turkey

The fruits grown in Turkey vary between hazelnuts and figs, citrus fruits, walnuts, grapes, apples, figs, apricots, and kiwi in addition to many other fruits.

Pistachios

Turkey is famous for growing the finest types of pistachios in the states of Gaziantep, Sirt, and Sanliurfa, where Turkey is considered one of the most important producers of pistachios in the world, as the number of pistachio trees in Turkey is about 40 million trees.

Hazelnut

Hazelnut are one of the most important agricultural products in Turkey, as Turkey is the largest producer of hazelnuts in the world, out of every 10 hazelnuts consumed 8 of them were cultivated in Turkey.

İt is one of the most important agricultural crops in Turkey, as about 4 million people are connected to the cultivation of Hazelnut, directly and indirectly. The area of plantation in Turkey is about 500 to 600 000 hectares.

Hazelnuts grow in cold regions with heavy rain. The winter temperature ranges between 5 and 6 °C, while the summer temperature ranges between 20 and 25 °C. It grows to a height of between 0 and 500 m. It is mostly grown in the central and eastern regions of the coastal regions of the Black Sea in Turkey. In these regions, hazelnut production is adversely affected when the winter temperature drops below zero.

Citrus

Citrus fruits that are grown in Turkey are tangerines, oranges, grapefruit, and lemons. İt can be grown, in places where the winter temperature does not fall below zero degrees Celsius.

It is famous for the coastal regions of the Mediterranean and the Aegean. With its very high production of citrus fruits, in addition to the cities of Mersin, Adana, Antalya and Hatay.

Fig

Turkey is one of the world's largest producers of figs, as it is grown on the Aegean coast.

Figs are grown mainly in the cities of Izmir and Aydin, because figs need a high temperature of not less than 0 °C in winter.

Apples

Most of Turkey's apple production is grown in the Inner Anatolia Region of Turkey. At the city level, production in Nigde, Nevsehir and Konya is high.

The city of Amasya in the Central Black Sea region is prominent in apple production, some cultivated apples are exported.

Walnut

Walnut cultivation in Turkey is spread in the Western Anatolia region, where Turkey ranks fourth in the world most producing walnut countries.

In 2019 CE, Turkey produced about 225 000 tonnes of walnuts. The largest production of walnuts was in Hakkari state, at about 12 000 tonnes. After Hakari, Kahramanmaraş is followed by 11 000 tonnes, and Mercenelles with 11 000 tonnes.

Peach

The peach fruit is one of the most important fruits grown in Turkey, and Bursa is famous for growing high-quality peaches.

Vegetables grown in Turkey

Turkey grows many vegetables, the most important of which are tomatoes, peppers, cucumbers and zucchini, in addition to potatoes, garlic and onions.

Central Anatolia Region is one of the most important regions in the production and cultivation of vegetables in Turkey.

Turkey is famous for producing tomatoes, a large proportion of which are exported abroad, especially to Russia.

Agricultural regions in Turkey

Agriculture in Turkey varies according to the region, as it is divided between the Marmara region, the Aegean region, the Mediterranean region, the Central Anatolia region, the Black Sea region, the eastern Anatolia region, and the southeastern Anatolia region.

Agriculture in the Eastern Anatolia Region

Due to the rugged topography of the eastern Anatolia region in Turkey, in addition to the height above sea level, the short summer and long winter, agriculture is limited to the plains between the mountains only.

Livestock has developed as an alternative to agriculture in eastern Anatolia, where local people herd sheep and cattle.

Agriculture in Central Anatolia

Crops of wheat, barley, corn, sunflower, sugar beets, garlic, onions, cherries, and potatoes are famous for cultivation in central Anatolia, and Eskişehir, the capital, Ankara, Çorum, Konya, Çankarı, Niğde, and many other states are famous for agriculture in Central Anatolia.

Agriculture in the Aegean and Mediterranean region

The Aegean region and the Mediterranean Sea is famous for being one of the most important agricultural areas in Turkey due to the mild climate in the winter, where all kinds of vegetables and fruits are grown, such as wheat, barley, tobacco, poppy, and cotton, in addition to walnuts, grapes, olives and citrus fruits.

Agriculture in the Marmara region

The crops cultivated in western Anatolia vary from vegetables such as tomatoes, cucumbers and zucchini to fruits, including cherries and grapes, and the states of Bilecik , Balkasir, Bursa, Chanakkala, Istanbul and Kriklari are considered.

Agriculture in the Black Sea region

The Black Sea region in Turkey produces many agricultural products in Turkey, the most important of which are tea in Rize, hazelnuts and vegetables, in addition to various fruits.

Governmental Support For Agriculture In Turkey

The Turkish government offers many incentives to Turkish and foreign investors to help with agriculture in Turkey, the most important of which is financial incentives in the form of payments to producers.

The state provides support to producers who use licensed seedlings, and the Turkish government also sets a number of conditions for granting subsidies that must be met before obtaining payments.

Ziraat Bank is responsible for supporting and financing Turkish farmers, in addition to many other government banks.

Hazelnuts, pistachios, wheat, barley and tomatoes are the most important Turkish agricultural products.

Agriculture in Turkey is characterized by the diversity of crops and the fertility of the lands, as it is possible to grow many diverse products in different regions due to the different climatic regions in Turkey.

Arable Land

Turkey is the 37th largest country in the world, with a total land area of approximately 780 000 sq.km. Of this total, 50.1%, or sq.km is considered suitable for agriculture. However, arable land accounts for only 27% of the country's total land area, which is equal to 20.6 million hectares. The Food and Agricultural Organization of the United Nations (FAO) defines arable land as land under temporary crops, pasture, kitchen garden, or temporarily fallow. Approximately 66% of Turkey's arable land is under crops at any given time, while the remainder is fallow. About 90% of the cultivated area is under cereals, especially wheat, which accounts for about 40% of annual grain production. Other agricultural products include maize, sunflower, cotton, oranges, and tobacco. The majority of arable land in Turkey is located in the Aegean Region.

Flora of Turkey

The rich Turkish flora includes more than 9 000 varieties of plants. About 3 000 of them are endemic to Turkey and grow in nature nowhere else in the world.

Turkey is the only country in the world under the influence of 3 botanical, geographical and climatic regions.

Turkey is the centre of origin for more than 30 species of fruits, and also a centre for world's most important plant genetic sources especially for grains and legumes.

Endemic Species

Turkey's average altitude is over 1100 m. Fed by hundreds of streams, over 10 large rivers, including Euphrates and Tigris, originate from Anatolia mountains and flow to five seas. Special climates and habitats exist also in and around numerous wetlands and lakes. Around Tuz Lake, more than 30 endemic species of plants grow. As grounds become saltier, attention given to salt resistant plants are becoming more pronounced.

Turkey is also endowed with a diverse richness of medical and aromatic plants. Istanbul supports a remarkably high diversity of plant species with approximately 2 000 species. Forests cover 26% of the homeland. Totally 564 species of trees, 76 of them being endemic. The ratio of natural forests to total forest area is 93% in Turkey.

Fauna of Turkey

Turkey's fauna is so rich, different types of animals, beautiful birds, fish. 40.000 animal species found in Turkey are estimated to represent over 80% of the ones found in the whole continent of Europe.

The diversity of fauna in Turkey is even greater than that of wild plants. While the number of species throughout Europe as a whole is around 60 000, in Turkey they number over 80 000. If subspecies are also counted, then this number rises to over a hundred thousand.

Turkey's Wildlife

Anatolia is the original homeland of several species. E, g., the red deer comes from the foothills of the Taurus Mountains between Antalya and Adana; the pheasant from Samsun on Turkey's Black Sea coast; and the rare Anatolian Leopard.

Turkey is one of the most important bird migration routes in the world. The total number of migratory and local bird species are 456 in Turkey. Today, the mountains and national parks still abound with wildlife, such as brown bears, wild boar, lynx, wolves, mountain goats, water buffalo, the occasional leopard and over 400 species of birds, several of them endangered.

Population

In 2020 CE, the population of Turkey was 83.6 million with a growth rate of 1.39% per annum. Turkish people are the largest ethnic group, followed by Kurdish people.

The population is relatively young, with 22.8% falling in the 0–14 age bracket. According to OECD/World Bank population statistics, from 1990 CE to 2008 CE the population growth in Turkey was 16 million or 29%,

Politics

The politics of Turkey take place in the framework of a presidential republic as defined by the Constitution of Turkey. The President of Turkey is both the head of state and head of government.

Turkey's political system is based on a separation of powers. Executive power is exercised by the Council of Ministers, which is appointed and headed by the President. Legislative power is vested in the Grand National Assembly. The judiciary is independent of the executive and the legislature. Its current constitution was adopted on 7 November 1982 CE after a constitutional referendum.

Major constitutional reforms were passed by the National Assembly on 21 January 2017 CE and approved by referendum on 16 April 2017 CE. The reforms, among other measures, abolished the position of Prime Minister and designated the President as both head of state and government, effectively transforming Turkey from a parliamentary regime into a presidential one.

Turkey is effectively a dictatorship.

Language

The main language of Turkey is Turkish.

Religion

Islam is the largest religion in Turkey according to the state, with 99.8% of the population being initially registered by the state as Muslim, for anyone whose parents are not of any other officially recognised religion and the remaining 0.2% are Christians or adherents of other officially recognised religions like Judaism. Due to the nature of this method, the official number of Muslims include people with no religion; converted people and anyone who is of a different religion from their Muslim parents but has not applied for a change of their individual records. The records can be changed or even blanked on the request of citizen, by filing an e-government application since May 2020 CE, using a valid electronic signature to sign the electronic application. Any change in religion records additionally results in a new ID card being issued. Any change in religion record also leaves a permanent trail in the census record, however, record of change of religion is not accessible except for the citizen in question, next-of-kin of the citizen in question, the citizenship administration and courts.

Over 70% of the country is Sunni Muslim with a further 20% Shia.

Economy

The economy of Turkey is an emerging market economy as defined by the International Monetary Fund. Turkey is among the world's developed countries according to the CIA World Factbook. Turkey is also defined by economists and political scientists as one of the world's newly industrialized countries. With a population of 82.6 million as of 2020 CE, Turkey has the world's 20th-largest nominal GDP, and 13th-largest GDP by PPP. The country is among the world's leading producers of agricultural products; textiles; motor vehicles, transportation equipment; construction materials; consumer electronics and home appliances.

- GDP: $720 billion (2020). (UK: GDP: $2.64 trillion (nominal, 2020 CE est.); $2.98 trillion (PPP, 2020 CE)

- GDP per capita: $8 599 (nominal, 2020 CE); $29 293 (PPP 2020 CE est.).

- GDP by sector: Agriculture: 3.8%; Industry: 32.3%; Services; 60.7% (2017 est.).

- Population below poverty line: 8.4% (2018 CE), 11.7% at risk of poverty or social exclusion (AROPE · 2019 CE); 2.3% on less than $5.50/day (2020 CE f).

- Labour force: 41 817 015 (2020 CE); 42. 9% employment rate (September 2020) · about 3.2 million Turks work abroad.

- Labour force by occupation: Agriculture: 16.7%; Industry/Construction: 27.1%; Service: 56.2%. (November 2020 CE).

Northern Cyprus

Northern Cyprus, officially the Turkish Republic of Northern Cyprus is a *de facto* state that comprises the north eastern portion of the island of Cyprus. Recognised only by Turkey, Northern Cyprus is considered by all other states to be part of the Republic of Cyprus.

Northern Cyprus extends from the tip of the Karpass Peninsula in the northeast to Morphou Bay, Cape Kormakitis and its westernmost point, the Kokkina exclave in the west. Its southernmost point is the village of Louroujina. A buffer zone under the control of the United Nations stretches between Northern

Cyprus and the rest of the island and divides Nicosia, the island's largest city and capital of both sides.

A *'coup d'état'* in 1974 CE, performed as part of an attempt to annex the island to Greece, prompted the Turkish invasion of Cyprus. This resulted in the eviction of much of the north's Greek Cypriot population, the flight of Turkish Cypriots from the south, and the partitioning of the island, leading to a unilateral declaration of independence by the north in 1983 CE. Due to its lack of recognition, Northern Cyprus is heavily dependent on Turkey for economic, political and military support.

Attempts to reach a solution to the Cyprus dispute have been unsuccessful. The Turkish Army maintains a large force in Northern Cyprus. While its presence is supported and approved by the TRNC government, the Republic of Cyprus, the European Union as a whole, and the international community regard it as an occupation force, and its presence has been denounced in several United Nations Security Council resolutions.

Northern Cyprus is a semi-presidential, democratic republic with a cultural heritage incorporating various influences and an economy that is dominated by the services sector. The economy has seen growth through the 2000s CE and 2010s CE, with the GNP per capita more than tripling in the 2000s but is held back by an international embargo due to the official closure of the ports in Northern Cyprus by the Republic of Cyprus. The official language is Turkish, with a distinct local dialect being spoken. Most of the population consists of Sunni Muslims, while religious attitudes are mostly moderate and secular. Northern Cyprus is an observer state of ECO and OIC under the title 'Turkish Cypriot State', and of PACE under the title 'Turkish Cypriot Community'.

CHAPTER 14: GLOBAL POSITION, REGIONAL POSITION, NATIONAL POSITIONS AND PROSPECTS

North West Africa

In this Chapter each country in the Middle East is looked at through the lenses of their global position, their regional (Middle East) position, and their national position.

There is always focus on how the U.S. in particular orchestrates events in the Middle East but, these days, threatening vectors appear from many different parts of the world compass. Additionally, each country will be affected differently by the top trends likely to reshape the world over the next twenty years or so.

Libya

International relations with Libya are coloured
by the move to a united Government.

In 2011 CE China had nearly one hundred companies operating in Libya, 36 000 and took 10% of Libya's oil. As it has done elsewhere in the Middle East China has not taken sides preferring 'to do business'. It was neutral in the 2020 CE agreements to try and build a new unified state; where Russia, Turkey, U.S.A., and other Middle Eastern States were not.

The U.S. supported the Government of National Accord, as do most western countries, Turkey, Qatar and Italy.

The self-styled Libya National Army is supported by Russia, Egypt, France and the UAE.

The country is a primary human trafficking route from Africa south of the Sahel to Europe. This is difficult to control, is itself partly controlled by ISIS, and will remain so for the foreseeable future.

Nationally the key challenges are a stable government and reconstruction in a divided human and cultural environment.

Egypt

Egypt's foreign policy operates along non-aligned lines. Factors such as population size, historical events, military strength, diplomatic expertise and a strategic geographical position give Egypt extensive political influence in the Middle East, Africa, and within the Non-Aligned Movement as a whole. Cairo has been a crossroads of the Arab world's commerce and culture for centuries, and its intellectual and Islamic institutions are at the centre of the region's social and cultural landmarks.

The relationship between China and Egypt is strong, but not as deep as elsewhere. Aircraft and military hardware have been exchanged over the last 25 years, Beijing and Cairo have university exchanges; there are about 50 Chinese financial institutions in Egypt and Egypt has supported China over both Hong Kong and the Uighurs. As may be expected, given the road and belt initiative, China has a strong interest in the 'North West Suez Economic Zone'.

Relations with the U.S. have been up and down post 1945 CE. The U.S. helped to keep Nasser in power during Suez in 1956 CE and has spent around $1.5 billion in military aid per annum since. It has a bi-lateral economic arrangement which gives Egyptians tariff free access to the U.S. market for all goods with at least 10.5% Israeli content. Peace discussions with Israel were brokered and are kept in place by aid. Egypt is the second largest recipient of U.S. aid after Israel in the Middle East. Egypt did not agree to send troops to either Afghanistan or Iraq. Recent relationships have been tense especially since ant-U.S. demonstrations during and after the Arab Spring.

Egyptian Russian relations go back centuries; with long term support given to Egyptian Christians by Russia over equally long periods of time. More recently Egypt's Nasser had huge support from the USSR. The USSR financed the Nasser Dam on the Nile and also threatened the use of nuclear weapons if the West's attack on Suez Canal was not called off. In the intervening 60 years relations have gone up and down; often up, and as of the start of President Sisi's term there has been huge co-operation including large scale weapon sales such as the Su-35 – against which the U.S. has threatened sanctions.

Regionally Egypt is seen as a strong military power. That said it has been reluctant to get involved in a number of conflicts ranging from Afghanistan to Yemen. It has been proactive in trying to resolve the Palestinian question. However, this does not extend to wholesale support, and borders have frequently been closed to Palestinians particularly under Hamas' Palestinian leadership. Close relations are kept with Saudi Arabia and many educated Egyptians have found work in Saudi Arabia. However, that is changing with increasing Saudi nationalisation of jobs. Good relations are kept with Sudan, Egypt being in favour of a united Sudan. Egypt has supported the eastern rebel army in Libya. The UAE was active in bringing down Morsi and elevating Sisi by way of financial support to the Tamarod movement and through them support to the coup plotters in the Army. Turkey released the evidence of this. As another strong regional power Turkey has been variously supportive and not of Egypt. Current relations are improving after a downturn caused by Turkey's support of Morsi. Some Mediterranean energy resources are shared between Egypt and Turkey.

The Ethiopian Grand Ethiopian Renaissance Dam on the Blue Nile continues to cause friction between Egypt, Ethiopia and Sudan fifty years after the building of the Aswan Dam. The lessons from that clearly have not been fully learned at regional level. As of 2021 the tension is increasing, the matter referred to the UN, and may result in war.

Nationally the country is run by an effective dictatorship; and has to control continuing unrest and dissent in the younger population who have seen little improvement in their standard of living. This is the biggest threat to Egyptian stability. In 2020 the leadership shut down an embryonic election competitor 'The Plan for Hope' group.

Sudan

Sudan and China have a significant relationship with much of the Sudanese oil business run by China, significant development loans from China to Sudan, and infrastructure and labour support to development projects. Both support each other against accusations of human rights abuses.

The U.S. has been critical of Sudan's human rights record and has sent support to the UN Peacekeeping Mission in Darfur.

Russia has had an up and down relationship with Sudan over the last fifty years. However, it has been generally positive with most arms supplies to Sudan coming from Russia, bi-lateral support in the UN, and support from Russia for operations in Darfur.

Regionally Sudan has some issues with its neighbours.

Egypt may be a problem in the future regarding the Nile and other resources. See Egypt above.

Nationally a stable Government is required. It is not quite stable currently. Sudan probably needs a strong leader.

The GCC and Yemen

Yemen

Yemen is still in a civil war. China keeps ties with both sides. It has trodden a basically neutral path but emphasised that it stands ready to assist with development once the war is over. In the 1950s CE and 1960s CE China lent Yemen money but there have been no major loans recently.

Relations between the Government of Yemen and the U.S. are good, with the U.S. supporting the Government alongside Saudi Arabia in the civil war. Iran supports the rebels; it is a Sunni versus Shia contest. Recent collapses in ceasefires are blamed on the rebels. Since the 26 March 2015 CE invasion of Yemen by Saudi Arabia in what was initially thought to be a quick campaign matters have not gone well for the U.S. or the Saudis.

Russia has maintained contact with both sides of the civil war. Recently it has entertained the Southern Transitional Council, backed by the UAE, which along with the Saudi backed Government is fighting the Houthi rebels. This triangle plays into the hands of Russia as it seeks a base close to the Red Sea.

Regionally the triangle of powers competing for success in Yemen is divisive and unhelpful to Saudi's aim of unifying the peninsula.

Nationally there have been numerous attempts to unify the Sunni sides of the conflict, so far with little success. Meantime the country as a whole is possibly the greatest humanitarian disaster in the world.

Saudi Arabia

Saudi Arabia's relationship with China is developing. Already China is the biggest importer of Saudi oil; quite a reverse from even 2010 CE. There is therefore a very strong trading relationship. However, the two do not share the same view on Iran. Until recently Huawei equipment was banned from Saudi oilfields. Over the last few years Huawei equipment has begun to displace both U.S. and European equipment. In a secret deal with China in the 1980s CE the Saudis bought an air defence system from China. This infuriated the U.S. and almost caused a war with Israel. The relationship is probably best described as functional. China's key strategy is business first.

Since the discovery of oil there has been a very close relationship between the U.S. and Saudi Arabia. which began in 1933 CE when full diplomatic relations were established and became formalized in the 1951 CE Mutual Defence Assistance Agreement. Despite the differences between the two countries, an ultraconservative Islamic absolute monarchy, and a secular constitutional republic, the two countries have been allies. Former Presidents George W. Bush and Barack Obama have close and strong relations with senior members of the Saudi Royal Family.

Ever since the modern U.S.–Saudi relationship began in 1945 CE, the United States has been willing to overlook many of the kingdom's more controversial aspects as long as it maintained oil production and supported U.S. national security policies. Since World War II, the two countries have been allied in opposition to Communism, in support of stable oil prices, stability in the oil fields and oil shipping of the Persian Gulf, and stability in the economies of Western countries where Saudis have invested. In particular the two countries were allies against the Soviets in Afghanistan and in the expulsion of Iraq from Kuwait in 1991 CE.

The two countries have been in disagreement with regard to the State of Israel, as well as the embargo of the U.S. and its allies by Saudi Arabia and other Middle East oil exporters during the 1973 CE oil crisis (which raised oil prices considerably), the 2003 CE U.S.-led invasion of Iraq (which Saudi Arabia opposed), aspects of the 'War on Terror', and what many in the U.S. see as the pernicious influence of Saudi Arabia after the September 11 attacks. In recent years, particularly the Barack Obama administration, the relationship between the two countries became strained and witnessed major decline. However, the relationship was strengthened by President Donald Trump's trip to Saudi Arabia in May 2017 CE, which was his first overseas trip after becoming President of the United States. The October 2018 assassination of Saudi dissident and *Washington Post* journalist Jamal Khashoggi in a Saudi consulate in Turkey caused a serious rift between the countries. The United States sanctioned some Saudi nationals and Congress unsuccessfully attempted to cut off U.S. weapons sales to Saudi related to the war in Yemen due to opposition from the Trump administration. Turkish authorities and U.S. intelligence agencies concluded the killing was done on the order of Mohammed bin Salman, the Crown Prince of Saudi Arabia.

Saudi Arabia subsidized its oil exports to the U.S. until President George W. Bush proposed the overthrow of the Iraqi government in 2002 CE. The shale oil boom enabled the United States to become a net exporter of petroleum products in 2019 CE, making the U.S. economy significantly less dependent on Saudi oil. Arms sales to Saudi Arabia remain an important U.S. export. The U.S. Department of Defense acts as an intermediary charging 7% of such sales, allowing it to fund training activities in other countries such as Bolivia.

During the shale boom in the U.S. relations between the U.S. and Saudi Arabia took a distinct turn for the worse.

Relations between Saudi Arabia and Russia have been distant since the 1930s CE. As two oil producing superpowers, they have co-operated on controlling the market. They have also co-operated on allowing Russian Muslims to undertake the Hajj (more since the Russian Federation than under the Soviet Union). Saudi Arabia backed the Mujaheddin against the Soviet invasion of Afghanistan; and have been on opposite sides of the Syrian civil war. However, both support Sisi in Egypt and the LNA in Libya.

Regionally Saudi Arabia is the major player in the GCC, the Sunni community, as a financial backer of Egypt, invader of Yemen, scourge of Qatar, and, until very recently, an implacable foe of both Israel and Iran. The Israeli situation ameliorated under the Abraham Accords and some less strident rhetoric has been evident in regard to Iran. This said its relationship with the UAE is now under strain with differing approaches to the oil production regime of OPEC, Saudi favouring cuts, and to Qatar towards whom the UAE is more hawkish. As Saudi diversifies it is encroaching on previously UAE-led initiatives such as ease of doing business and tourism.

Nationally Saudi Arabia has huge problems of diversification away from oil, loss of oil revenue, poor management particularly at middle management level, a population skewed to the under 30s with not enough jobs, difficulties with the emancipation of women from conservative religious groups, human rights issues ranging from the Khashoggi affair to the imprisonment of women, the disaster of the Yemen war, the disaster of the attempted takeover of Qatar – all of which are issues that the de facto leader MBS would rather have been successes than the failures they clearly are. A rapprochement with Israel as a consequence of the Abraham accords, a true victory for Trump, may help.

Future prospects: an increasingly large mountain to climb to deliver a diverse economy and satisfy a young population. On the death of King Salman there may be political changes.

Oman

Oman exports too much of its crude oil to China, while the Asian powerhouse invests too little in the sultanate's non-oil industries. The imbalanced nature of this economic relationship places Oman in a weak position to address mounting economic challenges.
Despite decades of economic diversification initiatives, Oman's oil and gas sector accounts for approximately 72% of government revenue. China consumes the vast majority of exported Omani crude oil. In April and May, China imported nearly 90% of Oman's crude oil exports. This was not always the case. Between 2000 CE and 2017 CE, China's share of Oman's crude oil exports increased from 35.2% to 82.5%.

The growth in Chinese imports of Omani crude oil coincided with a decrease in the relative importance of other Asian importers. Prior to 2012 CE, Oman maintained a more diverse group of crude oil trading partners, including Japan, India, South Korea, and Thailand. Japan actually imported more Omani crude oil than China in the early 2000s CE.

In Duqm, a fishing village along Oman's southern coast, the foundations of the Gulf's next boomtown are being laid.

Eager to wean its economy off hydrocarbons, Oman opened its doors to Chinese investment last year in a major step towards transitioning to a knowledge-based economy. Oman Wanfang, a consortium of six private Chinese firms, plans to build a $10.7bn industrial city in Duqm, situated 550 km south of of the capital, Muscat.

For perspective, Oman Wanfang's $10.7bn investment is the equivalent of more than half of Oman's stock of foreign direct investment. The Chinese consortium has promised to develop at least 30% of the project area within five years, with financing and construction firms to be sourced from China.

Dubbed the Sino-Oman Industrial City, China's endeavour along Oman's Arabian Sea coast will transform an idle seaport into a vital nerve centre of global trade and manufacturing. According to a BMI Research forecast, the Sino-Oman Industrial City will be a major stimulus for Oman's construction sector and double its growth rate from 2.4% to 4.9 % by 2019 CE.

The U.S. involvement in Oman is largely about trade and a military co-operation agreement. To support the Fleet in Bahrain and bases elsewhere a new railway from Salalah to Dubai has frequently been mooted. So far, the resources have not been found. This railway would clearly be a means of bypassing the Straits of Hormuz. The UK is building a small naval base in Duqm.

For many years Oman and Russia were antagonists, particularly in the 1970s when Russia supported the Popular Front for the Liberation of Oman. Neutral relations followed in much of the 1980s CE and 1990s CE. When Oman and Russia both became members of OPEC then a more friendly alliance based on oil was formed through OPEC.

Oman faces billions of dollars in looming loan repayments, including to China, and needs even more money as its youthful population seeks jobs and its government is unable to afford the cradle-to-grave benefits given in other Gulf Arab nations. The new Sultan faced his first unrest in 2021 CE in the town of Sohar where protesters gathered to complain about lack of jobs.

UAE

The global interests of Abu Dhabi are centred around its sovereign wealth fund and the aspirations of its *de facto* ruler the Crown Price, known as MBZ.

The UAE is the second largest Chinese trading partner in the Middle East. This is a consequence of its international entrepot status and the Port of Jebel Ali being important to the shipment of Chinese goods into other parts of the Middle East and Africa. There is competition between the UAE's ports conglomerate DP World and China's ports conglomerate China Merchants Port Holdings. This is particular to Djibouti where China has tried to oust DP with a resultant Hong Kong court case. More generally DP challenges part of China's Belt and Road Initiative and they compete elsewhere in the world too.

Relations with the U.S. are both straightforward and complicated. Sitting on the seventh largest reserves of oil in the world the UAE has large reserves of mineral wealth. It has hosted a U.S. presence since at least 1974 CE and there are a number of U.S. military and intelligence stations in the UAE. The UAE is a significant buyer of U.S. arms. The UAE lobbies hard in the U.S. – and supported the campaigns of both Hillary Clinton and Donald Trump with large donations. The U.S. has praised some military operations of the UAE; especially the recapture of the Port of Mukalla in Yemen from the Al Qaeda in the Arab Peninsula Group in 2016 CE. There is also a bi-lateral nuclear agreement, with a nuclear power station coming on stream.

On the other hand, the U.S. has been irritated by the UAE's recognition of Syria and by several financial transactions regarding Iran discovered on UAE soil. Additionally, the UAE and the U.S. do not always find themselves on the same side in other places other than Syria, Libya for example.

A decade on from the 2011 CE Arab revolutions, the United Arab Emirates has emerged as the most powerful counter-revolutionary force and Russia's most trusted ally in the region. At the same time the United States is in a process of transforming its regional engagement from direct relationships to more remote control. The intensifying partnership between the Kremlin and the Crown Prince is neither coincidental nor based on geopolitics; it is founded on growing ideological synergies that fill a void left by America's increasing absence. Both Putin and MBZ are 'strongmen', both work together, and Putin describes MBZ as an 'old friend'. In various different spheres they act on the same side, if not together. An issue remains criminal activity. Russian criminals launder cash through the UAE and are partly responsible for trafficking prostitutes through and to the country.

Regionally the UAE holds great influence. MBZ is regarded by some as the leading Middle Eastern ruler. He has/does mentor MBS in Saudi Arabia and he is a driving force in many regional initiatives not least in Libya, Egypt, Yemen, Sudan, Djibouti, Bahrain, Kuwait, Oman, Israel and Palestine. He supports the Government in Syria, is close to Putin. However, relations with Turkey are not good and MBZ has warned Turkey to stay out of Arab affairs. Recently, MBZ's close relationship with MBS has come under strain through oil, regional business competition, tourism competition, aviation and differing views on a number of different countries and initiatives.

The UAE promoted itself as a broker between Israel and Palestine following the conflict between Israel and Palestine of May 2021 CE. The UAE was a founding signatory along with Bahrain and Israel of the Abraham Accords. It has been buying land in Israel around Jerusalem; and is reported by some to have had a recent hand, perhaps with Saudi Arabia, in Jordan's recent leadership hiatus.

Qatar

Qatar especially through Qatar's sovereign wealth fund, is a major world player.
Relations with China are centred around trade and development. Trade includes the building of new ships for Qatar's LNG fleet; and the construction of football stadia in readiness for the 2022 CE World Cup. There has been support in this respect

from China throughout the COVID pandemic. China has also provided clean water technology and, during the pandemic, PPE to Qatar. Both are active in the WHO.

Qatar hosts the U.S.'s CENTCOM Forward headquarters, was an and is an important base and ally in the Gulf and has participated in a number of U.S. led operations not least the two Gulf Wars and attacks on ISIS/ISIL. Trade relations are robust with major arms deals, over 120 companies represented in Qatar, extensive support for the oil and gas sector and a source of many imports. Relations became a little tense after the expulsion of Qatar from the GCC in 2017 CE. However, the U.S. dissuaded Saudi Arabia from actually invading Qatar in response to allegations that it had become a financial hub for the finance of terrorism regionally (and elsewhere). Qatar rejoined the GCC in 2021 CE. This was probably a defeat for MBS in Saudi as Qatar survived an embargo, allowed Turkish troops onto the Saudi Peninsula for the first time since the Ottomans left and developed a relationship with Iran – all anathema to MBS.

Russia and Qatar stood on opposite sides of the Syrian conflict. Russia did not take a side over the embargo of Qatar. Relations between Putin and the Al Thanis are cordial.

As noted above the major regional issue has been the embargo placed on Qatar in 2017 CE. At a summit in January 2021 CE, some GCC countries including the UAE who had stopped trade and travel links with Qatar agreed to restore diplomatic ties with Qatar. A joint declaration brokered by Kuwait and the United States pledged to 'restore collaboration' among the six members of the GCC, (although notably, the declaration didn't include any specific timelines).

Emirati Minister of State for Foreign Affairs Anwar Gargash (since succeeded by Sheikh Shakhbout bin Nayan) has said that the UAE was "*behind this deal, and positive about the prospect of re-establishing relations with Qatar*" adding that "*The return of movement [of people] and trade between the two countries... will be within a week of the signing*". Qatar Airways started flights to Dubai and Abu Dhabi from 27 January 2021 CE.

The normalisation of these regional relationships is potentially promising on various fronts, for both businesses and individuals. The FIFA World Cup is set to be held in Qatar in 2022 CE, in what is a milestone for the region. FIFA themselves have noted that Qatar is the first west Asian nation and also the smallest country to host a FIFA World Cup. This is the first World Cup ever to be held in the Arab world. The normalising of relations will (amongst other things) present opportunities for the increased exploitation of media rights in the region. Broadcasters will benefit from the reconciliation, as well as those servicing and advising broadcasters.

In a sign of progress, it is understood that Qatar's Al Jazeera and Saudi Arabia's Al Arabiya are exploring reunifying their news content following the reconciliation. This raises the possibility of them coordinating their news coverage. Al Hudood has suggested that the first phase of this "*will remind Gulf citizens of the things they have in common with their neighbours, like history, religion, language... etc*". It is yet to be seen if similar co-operation brings a conclusion to the ongoing media war between the two countries media outlets.

Media financing could also benefit from the revised political situation. In 2017 CE, the Doha Film Institute (a leading source of financing for Arab films) was stopped from providing grants to projects coming from Emirati, Saudi and Egyptian filmmakers. It is expected that in light of the changing political landscape, the Doha Film Institute will be able to provide funding to a broader range of Arab beneficiaries again. While there are other sources of funding available such as the Jeddah based Red Sea Film Festival fund, the return of the Doha Film Institute's benefaction can only be seen as an additional benefit to the Middle Eastern creative industry.

Fully restoring diplomatic ties will take time as parties on both sides work to rebuild trust. As part of this rebuilding there will be a number of opportunities across the GCC. It is undoubtedly good news for the Middle East's media, entertainment and creative landscape. Reconciliation should increase distribution opportunities for broadcasters and media agencies as well as increasing options relating to content, financing and territory. Qatar 2022 is expected to be greatly boosted by the change in political circumstances; and should bring additional revenues to the whole of the GCC.

However, there is some continued disunity as Qatar has refused, so far, to surrender new contacts made with those that helped it overcome the embargo. This is a defeat for MBS. In the particular case of Turkey ideology, business and bad neighbours have encouraged an unlikely alliance.

Nationally Qatar has emerged from the embargo with stronger international ties. It has managed to circumvent restraints on imports, export and travel. Qatar remains a small country within the Arab world; but its power is based on its sovereign wealth fund and its huge oil and gas reserves. The sovereign wealth fund deploys over $300 billion of assets in property in London, banks such as Credit Suisse, Barclays, Volkswagen, numerous U.S. companies and start-ups worldwide including Russia.

Recently (May 2021) the Finance Minister, who led the discussions with Turkey, has been fired for corruption. The immediate consequence of this is some tightening of rules by the Qatar Finance Centre Regulatory Authority.

Bahrain

Bahrain has strategic geopolitical value for the Belt and Road Initiative strategy in comparison to other GCC states. First, the Kingdom is a gateway to the Gulf and one of the key Gulf countries along the new Silk Road route, enabling it to serve as a transportation hub for the region The island is surrounded by several of the Middle East's large oil fields and commands a strategic position amid the Persian Gulf's shipping lanes, which is the access route for much of the Western world's oil to the open ocean. Bahrain stands at the crossroads of China's new Silk Road strategy and is an important nexus for trade, investment, science, and cultural exchanges between the Arab and Chinese and the greater Asian, African, and European worlds.

Second, the country benefits from a strategic geographical location on the crossroads of African, Asian, and European markets at the heart of the GCC market, which is currently valued at approximately \$2.2 trillion. China has already become the GCC region's largest trading partner; bilateral trade now exceeds \$260 billion per year and is projected to reach \$350 billion in the next decade.

Third, Bahrain, known as 'the Pearl of the Gulf', is an important port on the ancient maritime Silk Road. The relationship is deeply rooted in shared history, geography, culture, and economic exchanges.

Fourth, Bahrain is also one of the most modern and dynamic countries within the top-ranking business environment in the Middle East open and liberal lifestyle, unique market access, world-class regulatory environment, and highly competitive taxation system, combined with the lowest operating costs in the region, high quality of life, and a technologically literate population make the Kingdom an ideal access point for Chinese companies to this \$1.5 trillion GCC. For Chinese investors seeking business opportunities in the Gulf countries and Africa, Bahrain can be a commercial hub of operations. Bahrain ranks first among the Gulf states in '*Doing Business 2020*', including with the highest number of regulatory reforms. The low cost of doing business in Bahrain is a significant incentive for Chinese and foreign investors seeking a competitive advantage and gateway to large regional markets, stated the World Bank Group in 2019 CE.

Through its strong support for Bahrain's sovereignty and political stability, the PRC has conveyed an indirect message to Iran that it does not support any instability in the Persian Gulf region. This stance appears to be much appreciated by both

Bahrain and Saudi Arabia.

A practical example of Bahrain's importance to China is the size of the Huawei office in Seef, Bahrain. In a country which is the size of Birmingham in the UK the Huawei office in Bahrain is suited to a country many times the size.

Bahrain is the headquarters of the U.S. 5th Fleet and an important base and resource during the Gulf Wars. This arrangement is embedded in a defence agreement. The American Mission Hospital has been in place for over 100 years. There is a free trade agreement. Bahrain became a signatory to the second Abraham Accords, thereby paving the way for Saudi Arabian acceptance of the same.

Bahrain's relationship with Russia is complicated by Russia's support and friendship with Iran. As Bahrain is relatively small and a client state of Saudi Arabia in many ways then the importance of Bahrain to Russia is less than, say, to China which sees Bahrain, as noted, as a key component of the Belt and Road Initiative.

Regionally Bahrain is a client state of Saudi Arabia. It is a state with a large Shia majority ruled by a Sunni King. Saudi Arabia showed during the Arab Spring of 2011 that it would not hesitate to intervene in support of the monarchy if it were threatened. Bahrain was, historically, part of Iran so there is always a tension based on history, but the key issue is that Iran sees the population of Bahrain as a proxy to destabilise the state and Saudi Arabia. It is also a conduit to the Shia population in the eastern province of Saudi Arabia which Iran also tries to use as a proxy to destabilise Saudi Arabia.

Nationally the key issue is the Shia majority. Despite the efforts of the Crown Prince in regard to reconciliation this remains a difficulty. Further national issues surround the slow progress regarding the development of a Gulf financial and cyber hub, overtaken by Dubai in most respects. Foreign tourism has suffered because of the damage to beaches and corals from overfishing and the reclaiming of land from the sea. Tourism is principally the up to 250 000 Saudis who visit every weekend.

Kuwait

Recently Kuwait and China discussed promoting the digital economy during a virtual forum, with the aim of enhancing cooperation in several fields to achieve the interests of the two countries and meet aspirations of their peoples. Based on the intent to diversify its economy, Kuwait sees a digital economy as one of the most important applications in which to further invest.

Based mainly on oil, the Kuwait economy is suffering due to the drastic decrease in oil prices that was witnessed during the past period, which led to a deficit in its budget. Diversification of the economy will reduce dependency on oil and contribute to enhance its economy and therefore increase its revenue through developing more projects providing more jobs for Kuwaitis. For China, the move will boost cooperation with Kuwait and expand its business in the Gulf countries.

During the forum, a number of senior officials from Kuwait and China focused on the Belt and Road Initiative (BRI) project based on international standards for globalization through economic development and artificial intelligence.

The BRI is a transcontinental, long-term policy and investment program aimed at developing infrastructure and accelerating economic integration among countries along the route of the historic Silk Road. The initiative, which was disclosed in 2013 by China's president, Xi Jinping, targets boosting the connectivity of Asian, European and African continents and their adjacent seas, founding and strengthening partnerships among the countries along the Belt and Road.

Speaking at the forum, the deputy chairperson of the Kuwait Chamber of Commerce and Industry, Abdulwahab Al-Wazzan, said that in light of the digital economy and the era of global economic transformation, Kuwait has responded to China's

BRI as the first Gulf country to sign deals with the Chinese side on this matter.

He said Kuwait believes that reviving the historic Silk Road would change the pattern and shape of international relations by offering great economic, political and cultural benefits to the Chinese and Kuwaiti nations and to all peoples of the entire region.

He noted the initiative includes several vital sectors and fields that are compatible with Kuwait Vision 2035 CE and the country's development priorities in terms of stimulating economic growth and industrialization and increasing intra-trade and financial integration to achieve sustainable development.

The United States and Kuwait are working collectively towards the common goal of a stable, secure, and prosperous Middle East. Kuwait is also a vital U.S. partner on a wide range of regional security issues and a leader in the Global Coalition to Defeat ISIS. The United States works with Kuwait and other members of the Gulf Cooperation Council to increase cooperation on border security, maritime security, arms transfers, cybersecurity, and counterterrorism. The access, basing, and overflight privileges granted by Kuwait facilitate U.S. and Global Coalition partners in the fight against the Islamic State of Iraq and Syria (ISIS), as well as operations against Al Qaeda, and their regional and global affiliates.

In 1991 CE, as part of Operation Desert Shield/Desert Storm, U.S. military forces led a multinational coalition to expel the forces of the former Iraqi regime from Kuwait. Kuwait subsequently served as the major logistics base for U.S. and Coalition operations in Iraq during Operation Iraqi Freedom, providing up to 60 percent of its territory for coalition use. Kuwait also assisted with the drawdown of U.S. combat forces and equipment from Iraq that was completed in 2011 CE.

Kuwait and the United States have a formal Defence Cooperation Agreement (DCA). Approximately 13 500 U.S. forces are based in Kuwait, primarily at Camp Arifjan and Ali al Salem Air Base. Only Germany, Japan, and South Korea host more U.S. forces than Kuwait does. The United States currently maintains 2 200 Mine Resistant Ambush Protected vehicles in Kuwait. The majority of these vehicles are prepositioned for any necessary U.S. Army operations, and the remainder are contracted for distribution to partners throughout the region.

During the peak of Soviet influence, the Gulf region was an arena of Soviet-American confrontation. The general atmosphere of the Cold War influenced the formation of Soviet strategic goals in the Gulf region. The U.SSR had traditionally considered its foremost task in the region as one of assisting governments predisposed to the path of 'non-capitalist' development, with Iraq as a central ally. This allegiance meant that the U.SSR gave Iraq unconditional support, something that was demonstrated during the 1961 CE Kuwaiti crisis when the Soviet Union took Iraq's side, even when its leader, Abdul Karim Qasim, demanded the annexation of Kuwait as an integral part of Iraq's territory. On two occasions, the Soviet Union used its veto power as a permanent member of the UN Security Council in favour of Iraq. Relations improved in the 1960s CE to an extent as Kuwait hoped to find in Russia an ally against Iraqi aggression and invasion; deteriorated in the 1970s CE, and improved again after the U.S. refused to sell Kuwait 'Stinger' missiles. Matters deteriorated again when Russia sided with Iraq over the Gulf War.

Regionally Kuwait has come to the fore recently in regard to brokering the return of Qatar to the GCC fold. This is reasonably important to Kuwait because Qatar can help the balance against both the UAE and Saudi Arabia in the GCC power stakes. Kuwait has had up and down relationship with Saudi, cannot abide Iraq, and distrusts Iran. The division between Saudi and Kuwait regarding the divided zone on their mutual border from 2009 – 2019 CE was resolved in 2019 CE and has worked well so far. This border dispute was essentially about two things: oil and the smuggling of bombs and guns, often from Iraq. The management of the oil resources has now been resolved.

Nationally Kuwait still suffers from the aftereffects of the

Gulf Wars despite massive reconstruction, rehabilitation and finance. There are still roaming groups of stateless persons who can be seen on the streets and are sometimes a threat to locals and visitors. Kidnaps still take place in the desert areas. There is an element of lawlessness about part of the country. Some Iraqi insurgent groups take advantage of this to cause difficulties in both Kuwait and Saudi Arabia.

Iran

In Spring 2021 CE Iran and China signed a long-gestating 25-year cooperation accord as both countries remain under Unites States sanctions. The agreement was signed in Tehran by Iran's Foreign Minister Mohammad Javad Zarif and China's Foreign Minister Wang Yi. Wang also met with President Hassan Rouhani, and Ali Larijani, a representative of the Supreme Leader Ali Hosseini Khamenei who is said to have been the point person on the 25-year accord.

On the surface the deal seems meaningful; in exchange for a steady supply of oil, Beijing has agreed to invest $400 billion in Iran. But there's scepticism among Middle East experts about whether it actually signals a significant new phase in Tehran-Beijing relations. There is continuing debate about the threat this poses to the U.S., the JCPOA and Iran itself. There is stilla question over whether it is real. Proponents of the deal say Iran will benefit from turning east as the U.S and the West adopt an increasingly hostile approach, while critics say Iran may be giving up too much in its quest to boost ties with China.

Relations with the U.S., and Europe, were damaged by the revolution and hostage crisis (quite rightly from an Iranian perspective). U.S. and European sanctions over nuclear enhancement have damaged the country. The U.S. leaving the nuclear agreement has further damaged relationships although, hopefully, the Biden administration's decision to re-join the nuclear accord will see some improvement in relations all round.

Regionally, the Sunni/Shia split is enhanced by the rhetoric be-tween Saudi Arabia and Iran to the detriment of both. As noted MBS has reduced the volume of his rhetoric and this may pave the way for better relationships.

Internally there remains much resistance to the governing class and there is always an insurrection threat.

Further, in 2021 CE Iran saw the beginnings of a shift in U.S policy towards the Iran Nuclear Deal from which the U.S. had withdrawn under Trump. This deal was basically about re-stricting the ability of Iran to develop nuclear weapons.

Iran's relationship with the U.S is coloured by much history, The present Iranian regime, dating from 1979 CE, is a theocracy that displaced the U.S. backed Shah. The later hostage situation complicated matters further as has the interference of both in the internal affairs of the other. Add to this the support by the U.S. of Israel, Saudi Arabia and the issues around the nuclear deal and Iran feels at least threatened. It is not surprising Iran keeps close to its old ally Russia and its newer ally China.

Russia is an old ally of Iran. But as with other country relationships across the region this has been up and down. Iran supported the Russians in Afghanistan for the most part, for example. Iran belongs to the Russian led Collective Security Treaty Organisation military alliance and the Russian led EuroAsian Economic Zone.

Regionally Iran is the Shia powerhouse. It is a theocracy, so this drives everything from a policy perspective. It is politically anti Sunni Saudi, Sunni UAE, decries the Sunni Egyptians for making peace with Israel, questions Sunni Turkey and has supported Shia terrorists in Afghanistan against Sunni Pakistan; but also supported the Taliban etc. It is an implacable foe of ISIS and Al Qaeda and has occasionally supported the U.S. against both. It blames Saudi Arabia for their financing and Pakistan for giving them cover.

Nationally the ruling regime is not without its critics. To 1979 CE Iran was a fairly open, western oriented and dressed, regional technological leader. It can still muster an internal technological expertise which is much more independent than any other Middle East country with the exception of Turkey. It could feed itself, it does not at the moment. Unrest comes from the sometimes brutal repression of the regime and the focus on religion. These have damaged independent thought and the advancement of science to the country's cost. Living standards continue to fall, poverty is rampant, literacy rates are falling but it is still a powerful and capable country (official figures deny these trends). After the stalemate of the Iran-Iraq conflicts in the 1980s CE the Revolutionary National Guard was formed and they are now recognised as a powerful military force in their own right, capable of international engagement. Elections are planned for the autumn of 2021 and it is expected that it will be business as usual as the theocracy has final say on most things including elections.

Ruhollah Zam was a critic of the regime. His social media channel had a following greater than the BBC's Persia Service. He was in exile in Paris when lured to Iraq, kidnapped and sentenced to death for sedition and hanged four days later in 2020. There is a parallel here with Jamal Khashoggi, killed in the Saudi Embassy in Turkey.

In mid-2021 Iran claimed to be enriching Uranium once again.

Iraq

Globally Iraq remains a major source of oil. As oil passes the $70 mark (2021), and with luck stays there, there is some hope that Iraq can benefit from increased oil revenues to stave off poverty reinforced by COVID and by a lack of oil revenue. Iraq remains dependent on global imports as it seeks to restructure after the worst decline in GDP since 2003 CE.

There is little doubt that Iraq plays a diplomatic game, playing off China, Russia and the U.S. against each other. Early in 2021 CE it put on hold an advance payment of $2 billion plus from China for petroleum, just as Trump lost and Biden won. This is presumably the first act in a round of effort to obtain more money from the U.S. and/or Russia. In the meantime, it continues to import electricity and gas from Iran, with U.S. waivers of sanctions given every few months.

Today, the U.S. and Iraq still consider themselves as strategic partners, given the American political and military involvement after the invasion of Iraq and their mutual, deep-rooted relationship that followed. The U.S. provides the Iraqi security forces millions of dollars of military aid and training annually as well as uses its military bases.

However, in 2020 CE, Iraq voted to ask the U.S. and its coalition members to withdraw all of their troops from the country, with U.S. President Trump asserting that sanctions would be imposed against Iraq if the United States' troops were forced to exit Iraq. Meanwhile, Iraq has prepared a mechanism for the withdrawal of coalition troops from the country and begun discussing it with coalition members. According to the office of Iraq's Prime Minister, the United States has promised to follow up on unauthorized use of Iraqi airspace and violations of its sovereignty.

Before and during the 2003 CE invasion of Iraq, Russian government provided intelligence to Saddam Hussein about the location of U.S forces and their plans. In 2018 CE, Iraq received T-90 tanks from Russia. In 2020 CE, Iraq is reportedly considering the purchase of S-400 missile system from Russia.

Regionally Iraq falls between the Sunni and Shia powerhouses. Saudi supports the Sunnis, Iran supports the Shias. The Kurds have some support from the U.S., but not from Turkey which views them as terrorists, and little from elsewhere.

The Levant

Jordan

China and Jordan have good relations with, in particular, investment by China in Jordan's potash business. During the COVID pandemic the Belt and Road News stated that relations were good and there had been mutual assistance with regard to medical supplies.

Jordan recognises the state of Israel and has housed millions of refugees. As a consequence it is a large recipient of U.S. aid. The United States is Jordan's single largest provider of bilateral assistance, providing more than $1.5 billion in 2020 CE, including $1.082 billion appropriated by the U.S. Congress to Jordan through U.S, AID in the 2020 CE fiscal year budget, and $425 million in State Department Foreign Military Financing funds. The United States has also provided nearly $1.7 billion in humanitarian assistance to support Syrian refugees in Jordan since the start of the Syria crisis. In 2018 CE, the U.S. and Jordan signed a non-binding Memorandum of Understanding (MOU) to provide $6.375 billion in bilateral foreign assistance to Jordan over a 5-year period, pending the availability of funds. The MOU reinforces the U.S. commitment to broaden cooperation and dialogue between the two countries in a variety of areas. Assistance programs contribute to a strong bilateral relationship centred on a stable, reform-oriented Jordan. Development assistance has resulted in improved health indicators, road and water networks, hundreds of schools built, thousands of Jordanians in various fields educated and trained in the United States, grants and loans for U.S. agricultural commodities, and assistance for Jordanian communities hosting refugees from Syria. Current focus areas include macroeconomic policy, competitiveness, private sector development, energy, water security, governance, education, health, and women and youth empowerment. A strong U.S. military assistance program is designed to meet Jordan's legitimate defence needs, including preservation of border integrity and regional stability through the provision of materiel and training.

U.S. assistance for Jordan's COVID-19 response has totalled almost $35.4 million, including nearly $20.8 million in humanitarian assistance to support vulnerable individuals in Jordan, including refugees and members of host communities. It also includes $13.1 million in humanitarian assistance to provide emergency food assistance, and $1.5 million in health assistance to support efforts to stop the spread of the disease, as well as strengthening laboratories for large-scale COVID-19 testing

Jordan's relationship with Russia has been historically somewhat distant, given close ties with Britain, initially, and later the U.S. However, recently they have co-operated over Syria both militarily and from a refugee perspective, much to the U.S.'s irritation (many refugees are in a U.S. military base in Jordan). Jordan needs money, Russia might help. Many Russian tourists visit Jordan, and Russia may want its own military base in Jordan.

Jordan's regional position is complicated by its border with Israel, the large number of Palestinian refugees it houses, the number of Syrian refugees it houses, its financial dependence on the U.S. and its developing relationship with Russia. These mean that it wants to become more like Egypt but does not quite have the independence to do so. Jordan has over 4 million refugees; more than half of them Palestinian and many of the rest Syrian. It has an acute and chronic shortage of water.

Nationally the alleged recent coup, for which the King's half-brother was placed under house arrest and two senior figures jailed has complicated issues within the royal family. Externally the same event has caused issues between Saudi Arabia,

MBS, and the King.

Syria

Syria's global position is defined by the civil war; with Russia and the U.S. on opposing sides, each seeking a long-term advantage. China supports the Government. Other players line up behind the key powers.

In practice, China's diplomatic engagement in Syria has been reactive, cautious, and pragmatic. China has displayed an unwavering commitment to promoting and supporting peace talks. Yet, the overriding aim of China's Syria policy has been to maintain a stable and friendly government in power in Damascus. This has been enhanced since 2016 CE by military support, admittedly low key. Further since 2018 CE. The U.S. government has imposed a series of economic sanctions on Syria. The chief form of sanctioning results in Syria's inclusion on the list of state sponsors of terrorism. These include legislatively mandated penalties, including export sanctions and ineligibility to receive most forms of U.S. aid or to purchase U.S. military equipment. There has been increasing interest by China in taking a lead in rebuilding the country, with some obvious assistance from Iran. This has been complicated by some issues around Huawei, which seem to have been overcome.

U.S. supports the rebels in the Syrian civil war.

Russia supports the Syrian Government and hopes to gain trade, resources and a military presence in the long-term, probably for its Black Sea fleet.

Regionally Syria has had support from Iran but few other countries support the regime.

Nationally the country faces a huge physical, economic and human reconstruction task.

Lebanon

As a former French protectorate, Lebanon is a historically Western-orientated country. However, China has lately worked to establish itself as a viable alternative to Western partnership. As COVID-19 took hold, China rushed to contribute supplies to Lebanon, a move repeated globally that attracted the tag of 'donation diplomacy'. After the Beirut port explosion in 2020, China sent a group of its Lebanon-based U.N. peacekeepers to assist Beirut with medical expertise.

Trade ties are already strong, with 40 percent of Lebanese imports coming from China. Chinese businessmen have offered to invest in Lebanon's faltering electricity grid, which sees regular blackouts for the country's citizens. The northern port of Tripoli has been identified by China as an important link for Beijing's Belt and Road Initiative (BRI) and revival of the Beirut-Tripoli railway in Lebanon has been reported as a Chinese business target. Not only would a Chinese presence in this area assist with Eurasian trade, but it would provide ample opportunity for China to invest in the reconstruction of post-conflict Iraq and Syria. The devastation of Beirut port will provide the opportunity for Chinese investment in its reconstruction, which will be a necessity if China wants Lebanon to be a successful BRI hub.

Even before the explosion, Lebanon was positioning itself to seek assistance from China in defiance of the U.S. In a recent interview, the head of Hezbollah, a powerful Shiite political party and militant group, blamed the U.S. for causing the economic crisis in Lebanon through restricting dollar deposits. Furthermore, he advocated that Lebanon should divest from its reliance on the U.S. dollar, stating that *"Chinese companies are ready to inject money into this country."* These comments made Hezbollah the subject of criticism in a subsequent interview given by U.S. Ambassador Dorothy Shea, who claimed that Hezbollah were jeopardizing the prospect of Lebanese economic recovery. That interview in turn earned Shea a sharp rebuke from the Chinese Embassy in Lebanon, which expressed displeasure with the U.S. portrayal of Chinese involvement in Lebanon. *"Chinese loans have no political strings,"* the embassy insisted, while dismissing the risk of *"Chinese debt traps"* for developing countries. Soon after the Hezbollah leader's comments about pivoting to Chinese investment, the Lebanese prime minister met with the Chinese ambassador to discuss strengthening ties.

But now, that comfortable relationship with the political establishment could prove detrimental to Chinese efforts in the country.

Lebanon's history since independence in 1943 CE has been marked by periods of political turmoil interspersed with prosperity built on its position as a regional centre for finance and trade. The country's 1975-90 CE civil war was followed by years of social and political instability. Sectarianism is a key element of Lebanese political life. Neighbouring Syria long influenced Lebanon's foreign policy and internal policies, and its military forces were in Lebanon from 1976 CE until 2005 CE. After the Syrian military withdrew, the Lebanon-based terrorist group Hezbollah and Israel continued to engage in attacks and counterattacks against each other, fighting a brief war in 2006 CE and engaging in cross-border skirmishes in 2019 CE and 2020 CE. Lebanon's borders with both Syria and Israel are still to be resolved.

The United States seeks to help Lebanon preserve its independence, sovereignty, national unity, stability, and territorial integrity. The U.S. along with the international community, supports full implementation of UN Security Council Resolutions (UNSCRs) 1559, 1680, and 1701, including the disarming of all militias, the delineation of the Lebanese-Syrian border, and the deployment of the Lebanese Armed Forces (LAF) throughout Lebanon. The U.S. believes that a peaceful, prosperous, and stable Lebanon can make an important contribution to comprehensive peace in the Middle East.

Russia perceives Lebanon as part of its Syrian track, so Moscow will strive to continue playing in this field to capitalize on its influence after intervening in the Syrian conflict. One of Russia's main goals in the Middle East is to expand its influence in the region and control the energy resources in the eastern Mediterranean. In the last few years, Russia started playing a larger role in Lebanon following the defeat of ISIS and growing civil unrest in Syria. Russia is important in helping solve the Syrian refugee crisis since Lebanon hosts around 1.5 million Syrian refugees. For some Lebanese, Russia is seen as a force that can provide stability. Russia has also offered security and military coordination and investments in Lebanon's underdeveloped energy sector. Russia has recently been showing greater interest in Lebanon's domestic affairs, specifically when it comes to breaking the political deadlock between President Michel Aoun and Prime Minister-designate Saad Hariri.

Lebanon has remained resilient throughout the seven-year conflict in neighbouring Syria. However, the country once again finds itself caught in the winds of dangerous regional rivalries, not least that between Israel and Iran.

Iran's Lebanese ally, Hezbollah, now has the strongest domestic military force in Lebanon, holding effective veto power over political developments there. The group's active role in the conflict in Syria has been costly in lives and international standing, but beneficial in military experience and capability. Thus, Hezbollah has a fighting force that is more effective than ever before. Viewing Hezbollah as its front-line deterrent against the perceived Israeli threat, Tehran prioritises efforts to secure and expand the group's access routes into Lebanon from Syria. Hezbollah is an important force in Lebanon but has little formal responsibility. This seems to suit it well.

These efforts have considerably raised the stakes for an Israel that has perceived Hezbollah as unfinished business since

2006, when the sides engaged in an indecisive war in Lebanon. Israel believes that Hezbollah is pointing thousands of Iranian-supplied missiles its way, and that Iran intends to further strengthen the group through the provision of more powerful and accurate missiles and the establishment of a military presence in Syria, particularly in the Golan. This could allow Hezbollah to open a second front against Israel if it engages in another war in Lebanon.

But Israel is not the only regional state with increasing ambitions to diminish Iranian influence in Lebanon. In November 2017, Saudi Crown Prince Mohammed bin Salman seemed to orchestrate a failed bid to force the resignation of the Lebanese Prime Minister Saad Hariri. This was an apparent attempt to highlight Hezbollah's ascendancy over the Lebanese state, by removing the perceived veneer of political legitimacy provided by the Hariri premiership and thereby provoking a crisis that could force Israel and the United States to harden their line. It may even have been an effort to provoke another war in Lebanon. Ultimately, the move turned Lebanon's citizens against Riyadh and enabled Hezbollah to present itself as the most responsible actor in the country.

Saudi Arabia eventually backed down under strong international pressure. But the incident provided a reminder of how regional rivalries might unfold to worrying effect in Lebanon. It also highlighted Israeli unwillingness to be drawn into a war in Lebanon on Riyadh's behalf.

Paradoxically, the pressure on Lebanon is likely to intensify now that the Syrian civil war appears to be approaching its military end game. Local and regional actors have long hedged their bets in Lebanon, waiting to see how the conflict in Syria would unfold. Now that the Assad regime and Iran are in the ascendant, domestic and regional actors are likely to recalibrate their positions in Lebanon. For now, Hezbollah and Israel appear to be engaged in a careful dance based on strong mutual deterrence. This allows them to avoid full confrontation with one another, even as they engage in periodic clashes.

The current situation in Lebanon is absolutely chaotic. For nearly 18 months now, Lebanon has been assailed by compounded crises—specifically, an economic and financial crisis, followed by COVID-19 and, lastly, the explosion at the Port of Beirut on 4 August 2020 CE.

Of the three, the economic crisis has had by far the largest (and most persistent) negative impact. Lebanon is enduring a severe, prolonged economic depression: real GDP growth contracted by 20.3% in 2020 CE and inflation reached triple digits, while the exchange rate keeps losing value. Poverty is rising sharply.

The banking sector, which informally adopted strict capital controls, has ceased lending and does not attract deposits. Instead, it endures in a segmented payment system that distinguishes between older (pre-October 2019 CE) dollar deposits and minimum new inflows of 'fresh dollars'. The former is subject to sharp deleveraging through de facto lirafication and haircuts (up to 70% on dollar deposits). The burden of the ongoing adjustment and deleveraging is highly regressive, falling hardest on smaller depositors and Small and Medium Enterprises (SMEs). Inflationary effects are highly regressive factors, disproportionately affecting the poor and middle class. The social impact, already dire, could become catastrophic; more than half the country's population is likely below the poverty line; a higher share of households is facing challenges in accessing food, healthcare and basic services; like poverty, unemployment is on the rise.

Meanwhile, Lebanon is dealing with the COVID pandemic through intermittent lockdowns and other measures that mitigate the impact of the virus both on people and the already weak health system. Vaccination, launched on 14 February 2021 CE with initial financing from the World Bank, is progressing according to the National COVID-19 Deployment and Vaccination Plan. This aims to vaccinate 70% of the total population, citizens and non-citizens in a multi-phase rollout by the end of 2022 CE. Efforts are underway to speed up the campaign through the procurement of vaccines via additional sources, including the private sector.

Israel

The State of Israel was declared in 1948, after Britain withdrew from its mandate of Palestine. The UN proposed partitioning the area into Arab and Jewish states, and Arab armies that rejected the UN plan were defeated. Israel was admitted as a member of the UN in 1949 and saw rapid population growth, primarily due to migration from Europe and the Middle East, over the following years. Israel fought wars against its Arab neighbours in 1967 CE and 1973 CE, followed by peace treaties with Egypt in 1979 CE and Jordan in 1994 CE. Israel took control of the West Bank and Gaza Strip in the 1967 CE war, and subsequently administered those territories through military authorities. Israel and Palestinian officials signed a number of interim agreements in the 1990s CE that created an interim period of Palestinian self-rule in the West Bank and Gaza. Israel withdrew from Gaza in 2005 CE. While the most recent formal efforts to negotiate final status issues occurred in 2013-2014 CE, the U.S continues its efforts to advance peace. Immigration to Israel continues, with 28,600 new immigrants, mostly Jewish, in 2016 CE. The Israeli economy has undergone a dramatic transformation in the last 25 years, led by cutting-edge, high-tech sectors. Offshore gas discoveries in the Mediterranean, most notably in the Tamar and Leviathan gas fields, place Israel at the center of a potential regional natural gas market. However, longer-term structural issues such as low labor force participation among minority populations, low workforce productivity, high costs for housing and consumer staples, and a lack of competition, remain a concern for many Israelis and an important consideration for Israeli politicians. Prime Minister Benjamin Netanyahu has led the Israeli Government since 2009; he formed a centre-right coalition following the 2015 CE elections. Three Knesset elections held in April and September 2019 CE and March 2020 CE all failed to form a new government. The political stalemate was finally resolved in April 2020 when Netanyahu and Blue and White party leader Benny Gantz signed an agreement to form a coalition government. Under the terms of the agreement, Netanyahu would remain as prime minister until October 2021 when Gantz would succeed him. Israel signed normalization agreements, the Abraham Accords, brokered by the U.S, with Bahrain, the United Arab Emirates, and Morocco in late 2020 and with Sudan in early 2021

Relations with the Chinese are cordial with the Chinese State commenting as follows:

"In 1950, Israel was the first country in the Middle East to recognize the PRC as the legitimate government of China. However, China did not establish normal diplomatic relations with Israel until 1992. Since then, Israel and China have developed increasingly close strategic economic, military and technological links with each other. Israel maintains an embassy in Beijing and is planning to open a new consulate in Chengdu, its third in Mainland China. China is Israel's third largest trading partner globally and largest trading partner in East Asia. Trade volume increased from $50 million in 1992 to $15 billion in 2013. Shared commonalities and similarities between the cultures and values of the two nations with ancient roots dating back thousands of years as well as convergence of interests have made the two countries natural partners. In addition, China is one of the few countries in the world to concurrently maintain warm relations with Israel, Palestine, and the Muslim world at large."

Israel–United States relations refer to the bilateral relationship between Israel and the U.S. Since the 1960s CE, the United

States has been a very strong supporter of Israel. It has played a key role in the promotion of good relations between Israel and its neighbouring Arab states, namely Jordan, Lebanon and Egypt, along with several others in the 2020 CE Abraham Accords, while also holding off hostilities from other Middle Eastern nations such as Syria and Iran. Relations with Israel are a very important factor in the U.S. government's overall foreign policy in the Middle East, and Congress has likewise placed considerable importance on the maintenance of a close and supportive relationship.

Since 1985 CE, the U.S. has provided nearly U.S. $3 billion in annual grants to Israel, which has been the largest recipient of annual American aid from 1976 CE to 2004 CE and the largest cumulative recipient of aid ($146 billion, not inflation-adjusted) since World War II; approximately 74 percent of these funds are spent on the purchases of American goods and services. More recently, in fiscal year 2019 CE, the U.S. provided Israel with $3.8 billion in military aid. Israel also benefits from around $8 billion in American loan guarantees. While the U.S. has disbursed significant financial aid for Israel in the past, the primary form of American aid for Israel at present is military-oriented (see Israel–United States military relations) rather than economic.

In addition to financial and military aid, the United States also provides large political support to Israel, having used its UN Security Council veto power 42 times against resolutions condemning Israel, out of a total 83 times in which its veto has ever been used. Between 1991 CE and 2011 CE, out of the 24 vetos invoked by the U.S., 15 were used to protect Israel.

Putin has pursued improved ties with Israel since he came into office in March 2000 CE and the two countries have significantly improved ties on a number of fronts. Russian and Israeli officials hold meetings and telephone conversations on a regular basis and maintain multiple open channels of communication. The two countries have an agreement on visa-free tourist travel for their citizens. Israel is home to over a million immigrants from the former Soviet Union, which bolsters Russia's ties to Israel. Russian is the third most popular language in Israel after Hebrew and English. Economic relations between the two countries have especially improved, exceeding $3 billion in 2014 CE, a figure slightly higher than Russia's trade with Egypt the same year. Military relations improved as well. Indeed, in late 2015 CE, according to press reports, Israel sold ten search drones to Russia, despite Israel's concerns about Russia's military and political ties to Iran.

Yet complexities remain. Putin wants to be seen as a key player throughout the Middle East, and Israel matters in the region. Putin's regional policy, however, is primarily driven by zero-sum anti-Westernism to position Russia as a counterweight to the West in the region and, more broadly, to divide and weaken Western institutions. Israel, unlike Russia, is a pro-Western democracy. Moscow's growing aggression in the former Soviet Union, especially in Ukraine, and increasing influence in the Middle East in the context of Western retreat from the region, complicates Russia-Israeli relations.

Israel maintains full diplomatic relations with two of its Arab neighbours, Egypt and Jordan, after signing peace treaties in 1979 CE and 1994 CE respectively. In 2020 CE, Israel signed agreements establishing diplomatic relations with four Arab League countries, Bahrain, the United Arab Emirates, Sudan and Morocco following the agreement of the Abraham Accords.

After a continuous period of 12 years Benjamin Netanyahu was forced out of the office of Prime Minister in 2021 shortly after the latest of a number of elections and the last of a number of Israeli-Palestinian conflicts. His departure probably means a new direction for Israel; which has become a much more diverse country ethnically and politically than it was fifty years ago. The new leader is Naftali Bennett a right-wing settler advocate who believes Israel should keep all its existing boundaries and take a tougher line with Palestine. He has had a tough baptism.

By mid-2021 the key issue emerging in Israel is the balance between Jews and no-Jews. The number of the latter may prove to be the key 'existential' threat.

Palestine

China-Palestine relations encompass the long bi-lateral relationship between China and Palestine dating back from the early years of the Cold War. During the era of Mao Zedong, China's foreign policy was in support of Third World national liberation movements. In the post-Mao era, China continued to support the Palestinian Liberation Organization in international forums. China recognized the State of Palestine in 1988 CE. Since 1992 CE, China also established formal diplomatic relations with Israel and has since maintained a cordial relationship with both entities.

Palestinian leaders Yasser Arafat and Mahmoud Abbas have both visited China in official capacities, and relations between the two countries have been considered as cordial. China does not consider Hamas ruling the Gaza Strip as a terrorist organization, and officially supports the creation of a 'sovereign and independent Palestinian state' based on the 1967 CE borders with East Jerusalem as its capital.

Relations between the U.S. and Palestinians are complex and strained. The U.S. does not recognize the State of Palestine, but accepts the Palestine Liberation Organization (PLO) as a representative of the Palestinian people and the Palestinian National Authority as the authority legitimately governing the Palestinian territories under the Oslo Accords.

The U.S. does not officially maintain any diplomatic office

in the Palestinian territories nor provide consular services to Palestinians, and since the closure of the PLO mission in Washington D.C. in October 2018 CE, the Palestinians have had no diplomatic representation in the U.S.. The United States has designated a Palestinian Affairs Unit within the U.S Embassy in Jerusalem to handle relations with the Palestinian Authority but Palestine is presently maintaining a public policy of non-cooperation with the office and with the U.S. in general.

Since 2011 CE at least, the PLO's diplomatic effort has focused on the Palestine 194 campaign, which aims to gain full membership for Palestine in the UN. It seeks to effectively gain international recognition of the State of Palestine based on the 1967 CE borders, with East Jerusalem as its capital. The U.S. minimal conditions for relations with the Palestinians were Palestinian acceptance of UN Security Council Resolutions 242 and 338, the recognition of Israel's right to exist, and renunciation of terrorism.

As commented upon elsewhere Arafat was offered anything he wanted bar Israel itself in 1993 CE. Relations went up and down until Trump lashed out at Abbas calling him a liar and a murderer. Following this the U.S. Embassy was moved to Jerusalem and U.S. economic aid stopped. The Abraham Accords followed these events. It is to be seen what Biden now does, as he has, historically, been a 'dove' as far as Palestine is concerned.

The PLO under Arafat was viewed by the USSR as part of its own ant-U.S. proxy war policy. Later this was challenged because of the PLO's support for Chechen soldiers. These days Russia is broadly neutral on the question of Palestine. It has asked Israel to stop killing Palestinians and sent Palestinians aid. At the same time Russsia has been critical of the Palestinian split following the 2007 CE civil war, *"we want the Jewish and Arab peoples to live in peace and accord. We're ready to facilitate the peace process at the bilateral level and within in-*

ternational organizations". Amid the ground operation in Gaza the logic of events prevails over political expediency. In Gaza there are different groups that do not maintain contacts. The situation is not controlled by a single centre. This complicates attempts to find a political solution.

Although Palestine has sought to be recognised as a single state the de facto position is that it is two. Following the civil war in 2007 CE Abbas has led the West Bank Palestinians and Hammas has led Gaza, although Gaza itself is split into numerous factions. This, of course, means that a solution to the internal Palestinian conflict and the wider Palestine – Israel conflict becomes even more distant.

Turkey and Cyprus

China and Turkey have maintained relations, despite China's conflicts with Turkic Uyghurs in Xinjiang and a Uyghur diaspora population residing in Turkey. According to a recent study, although Uyghur issue and Turkey's affiliation with the NATO alliance have created rigid boundaries between China-Turkey, Belt and Road economic cooperation has heralded a new era in bilateral relations. Economic cooperation between the two countries has also been growing in recent years.

Erdogan's consolidation of power and corresponding suppression of journalists, academics, civil society organizations, and minorities contradicts the underlying principles of American society and Turkey's own North Atlantic Treaty Organization (NATO) membership. Diverging policies and perspectives— such as Turkey's incursion into northern Syria, its intention to purchase an advanced air defence system from Russia, and the arrest of more than a dozen Americans and three Turks employed by the U.S. embassy, have further widened the chasm between the United States and Turkey.

Turkey has its own list of grievances against the U.S., including tariffs on Turkish steel and aluminium after an agreement on the release of Pastor Andrew Brunson fell through in the summer of 2018 CE; U.S. military coordination with the People's Protection Units (YPG), which the Turkish government claims is part of the Kurdistan Workers' Party (PKK), long designated as a terrorist group by Turkey; and the refusal of the U.S. to extradite Fethullah Gulen, whom Ankara blames for the failed July 2016 *coup d'état* that killed 249 people.

It is not clear that even with enough diplomatic tenacity, Washington can rebuild trust and strategic ties with Ankara. But the relationship still has to be managed:

- There is a need to recognize that the U.S. and Turkey have gone from ambivalent allies to antagonists.
- There is a need to develop alternatives to Incirlik Air Base. American officials should never again be forced into a position that leaves U.S. security interests vulnerable to the changing interests of Turkish politicians.
- Turkey's demands that the United States end its military ties with the YPG should be rejected. The YPG has been an effective force fighting the Islamic State and stabilizing northeastern Syria. For the United States to turn its back on the YPG would give Washington a reputation as an unreliable ally.

- There needs to be a stronger public stand on Turkish policies that undermine U.S. policy. Specifically, the United States should end its cooperation with Turkey on the F-35 program. Turkey's open undermining of U.S. interests and policies cannot continue to go unchecked while Turkey enjoys the benefits of America's most advanced military aircraft.

Current Turkey – Russian relations started on 9 August 2016 CE when the countries' leaders held a meeting in St Petersburg, Russia, which was described by a commentator as a 'clear-the-air summit' — the first time the two had met since the dispute over the Russian fighter jet downed by the Turkish air force as well as Erdogan's first trip abroad since the failed coup attempt in Turkey. The BBC commented that the summit, at which Erdogan thanked Putin for his swift support during the coup attempt, *'unnerved the West'*.

Following the assassination of Russian ambassador to Turkey Andrei Karlov on 19 December 2016 CE, the countries' leaders sought to contain any possible damage to relations between the two countries. In December 2016 CE, the two countries initiated the Astana peace talks on Syria peace settlement, subsequently, along with Iran, agreeing to create de-escalation zones in Syria.

On 31 May 2017 CE, Russia lifted most of the sanctions it had imposed on Turkey, which included lifting restrictions on Turkish companies operating in Russia and ended a ban on employing Turkish workers in the country. It also ended an embargo on a range of Turkish imports. President Putin also restored a bilateral agreement on visa-free movement between the two countries.

During Putin's visit to Ankara at the end of September 2017 CE, the Turkish and Russian presidents said they agreed to closely cooperate on ending Syria's civil war. Vladimir Putin's visit to Ankara in December that year was the third face-to-face meeting between the countries' leaders in less than a month and their seventh in a year.

In June 2018, the Russian government-controlled news agency Sputnik, shut down its website in Kurdish language without mentioning any particular reason for the decision. Former employees of Sputnik said that the news agency decided to shut it down at Turkey's request.

In mid-August 2018 CE, Russia and Turkey backed one another in their respective disputes with the United States. Russia condemned U.S. sanctions against Turkey over the detention of Andrew Brunson, while Turkey stated its opposition to U.S.

sanctions on Russia over the annexation of Crimea and interference in the 2016 U.S. elections.

In addition, Turkey and Russia also shared foreign policy on the Venezuelan presidential crisis in January 2019, supporting the regime of Nicolas Maduro as the legitimate government of Venezuela, opposing Western-supported opposition government led by Juan Guaidó.

Turkish foreign minister Mevlut Cavusoglu stated that Turkey was not going to have to choose between Russia and the United States.

On 19 March 2021, Turkish President Erdogan criticized U.S. President Joe Biden for calling Russian President Vladimir Putin a killer. According to Erdogan, Putin gave a very smart and graceful response.

Israel's energy exploration and exportation policies have brought it mostly smooth sailing in the Mediterranean and abroad with stormy politics at home.

The government viewed energy discovery in the Eastern Mediterranean as a source of diplomatic opportunities, a chance for expanded cooperation with other countries. Greece and Cyprus have become closer than ever with Israel, working together on energy projects. The major one is the EastMed gas pipeline, from Israeli waters to the European mainland, via Cyprus and Greece, which is meant to be the longest in the world. Israel's government ratified the plan last month.

But Jerusalem's partners have been eyeing Turkey's actions with concern. Between signing an agreement with the Libyan Government of National Accord, dividing economic rights to the Eastern Mediterranean between Tripoli and Ankara in November, and encroaching on Greece's and Cyprus's exclusive economic zones, conducting a seismic survey near the Greek island of Kastellorizo and putting the Hellenic Navy on alert in recent weeks, Turkey's latest moves in the Eastern Mediterranean could mean difficulties are brewing, with implications for Israel.

Israel and Turkey officially have diplomatic relations, but they have generally been at a very low level since 2010 CE, when IHH, an organization with ties to Turkish President Recep Tayyip Erdogan, sent the Mavi Marmara to challenge the Israely Defnce Force's naval blockade on Gaza, arming some of the people aboard. Israeli Defence Forces naval commandos stopped the ship, killing nine activists.

Still, Israel is not looking for a conflict with Turkey, and believes that Turkey is not trying to escalate things with Israel either. Despite the poor shape of diplomatic ties, Turkey is Israel's 10th-largest trading partner, and there is a huge amount of tourism between the countries, as well as cultural exchanges. Turkish Airlines is the company with the second-highest number of flights departing from Israel.

Publicly, the Foreign Ministry and Energy Ministry have nothing to say on the latest developments with Ankara in the Eastern Mediterranean. But they have been examining the Turkey-Libya agreement, because it could block Israel's ability to export energy to Europe. Turkey essentially gave itself veto rights to the EastMed pipeline.

Israel is obviously frustrated with Turkey's aggressive Eastern Mediterranean approach.... Israel has invested in its partnerships with Greece, Cyprus and Egypt, and does not want to disregard the importance of standing up for its partners."

The Israeli approach has been 'a middle ground', rather than taking major diplomatic steps which reflects a hesitation on both sides, Ankara and Jerusalem, to get into a conflict.

Turkey's calculus... is that the moment Israel gets involved is the moment American engagement and sensitivities will increase in some way, even if only diplomatically. Keeping Israel out of the conversation means the U.S will stay out of the picture they believe.

Israel's challenge, then, is to remain neutral in Turkey's dispute with Greece and Cyprus without hurting its partnership with the latter two countries.

But Israeli interests can still be harmed, even if Jerusalem is not directly involved.

The EastMed project was always a bet, as far as its commercial feasibility was concerned; it is expensive, and energy prices have been low. Now there's a question of the political feasibility. The more the Eastern Mediterranean begins to look like a site for a potential conflict, the less likely energy companies will want to develop serious undertakings like the EastMed pipeline.

Turkey looks at the EastMed project as political. They look at the region and see Greece, Cyprus and Israel are cooperating, and now Egypt, too, but they're not including Turkey. So Turkey will do whatever possible to derail the political feasibility of these kinds of projects, unless they include Turkey.

Prof. Mark Meirowitz, an expert on Turkey at SUNY Maritime College, referred to peace talks between Turkish-speaking northern Cyprus and Greek-speaking Cyprus, most recently in 2015-2017 in Switzerland, in which the sides did not reach an agreement: "*The failure to reach an amicable settlement on resources in the Eastern Mediterranean precipitated the situation.*"

From Turkey's perspective, Meirowitz said, "*Greece and Greek Cyprus gave rights to exploration, so Turkey had to assert its claims or it would have been tremendously disadvantaged.*"

"*The main motivation for Turkey to put forward the claims with Libya is to counterbalance some of the other claims,*" he argued.

Meirowitz viewed the agreement with Libya as a starting point for eventual talks between Turkey and Greece and Cyprus.

Israel, meanwhile, is caught in the middle of that, having

drawn up agreements with Greece and Cyprus on exploration in the Eastern Mediterranean.

"The whole world of maritime delimitation is wide open. There are competing claims that you work out by negotiation. You don't work that out by saying, 'We'll create a coalition and divide it among ourselves and not let Turkey and Turkish Cyprus share.' Turkey and Turkish Cyprus have their own claims based on the Law of the Sea, which should be taken seriously. The imperative would be to work up an amicable discussion and resolution based on the Law of the Sea," he said.

Others warned that Turkey is trying to push the conversation in a particular direction and being very aggressive in doing so, with the many international incidents taking place in the Eastern Mediterranean.

Israel holds a view, both in government and think tanks, that Turkey's behaviour in the Eastern Mediterranean is an extension of Erdogan's neo-Ottoman ambitions and his pursuit of greater influence in the Muslim world. This goes together with his support for Hamas, fiery rhetoric on the Palestinians and funding of organizations hostile to Israel in east Jerusalem.

Some believe that Turkey's *'blue motherland"* policy, strengthening its claim over maritime space in the Eastern Mediterranean, was *'developed by the secular leadership in the Turkish Navy'*, reflecting that *'for decades, Turkish strategists and policymakers have sought to identify opportunities to strengthen Turkey's regional position.'*

At the same time, those policies blended with *'the current flavour of Turkish domestic politics and ideology of Erdogan and his inner circle'*, including creating partnerships with Muslim Brotherhood-affiliated groups across the region

Still, Gabriel Mitchell, a Fellow at Israeli MITVIM, posited that Turkey would *'happily'* be a partner in energy projects with Israel, Greece and Cyprus, if offered to take part.

"Israeli and Turkish officials talked about an Israel-Turkey pipeline as late as 2017," Mitchell said. *"The price was the real sticking point, not political or international legal issues."*

Meirowitz noted the latest concerns about Turkey only highlight *"the necessity to improve Turkish-Israel relations, reinstate the ambassadors and get back to where we were after finally resolving the disagreements following the Mavi Marmara... and in that context of working with one another, try to work out these outstanding issues."*

Turkey's foreign policy is clearly driven by Erdogan. His pursuit of power in the Middle East region has seen him alienate NATO, the USA, occasionally Russia, China and an increasing number of Arab states. The best case is that Turkey becomes a useful regional power, the worst that it sinks into some internal introspection surrounded by wary opponents of the regime. In mid-2021 following a series of missteps by Erdogan it looks likely that the latter scenario will play out; which is surprising.

ISIS

The Islamic State, or ISIS, is a militant organization that emerged as an offshoot of al-Qaeda in 2014 CE. It quickly took control of large parts of Iraq and Syria, raising its black flag in victory and declaring the creation of a caliphate and imposing strict Islamic rule. The group is sometimes also referred to as ISIL — for the Islamic State of Iraq and the Levant — or by its Arabic acronym, 'Daesh'. It is largely made up of Sunni militants from Iraq and Syria but has also drawn thousands of fighters from across the Muslim world and Europe.

Its tactics — including beheadings, the taking of slaves and bans on "un-Islamic" behaviour such as music and smoking — are so brutal that it was even disowned by al-Qaeda. The militants' goal was (and remains) an ultra-conservative caliphate that strictly enforces Shariah, or Islamic, law. ISIS was founded by Abu Bakr al-Baghdadi, and others. He first led al-Qaeda in Iraq, transforming it into an effective and organized fighting force. The group changed its name in April 2013 CE, signaling its broader ambition of establishing a caliphate extending across Iraq and Syria.

In June 2014, ISIS published a manifesto purporting to trace al-Baghdadi's lineage directly back to the Prophet Muhammad.

Russia believes one of its airstrikes may have killed al-Baghdadi in May 2017. However, that has never been confirmed. The group's director of external operations, Abu Muhammad al-Adnani, is on the FBI's Most Wanted List as the man most likely to cause harm in the West. Counterterrorism officials have said that al-Adnani most likely 'greenlighted' the deadly Paris terrorist attacks in November 2015 that killed 130. ISIS doesn't recruit women for battlefield roles, but it still has enlisted women from around the Muslim world and Europe to help build its caliphate.

The group uses social media to get the word out, promising women husbands who are devout jihadis. In its one-time capital, Raqqa, a female brigade enforced their strict interpretation of Shariah by ensuring that women dressed according to their standards of modesty and by punishing them with lashes if they violated the code.

Since 2014 CE, the U.S. has led a coalition of countries carrying out airstrikes against ISIS and in support of Iraqi troops fighting the militants. By the end of 2017 CE, ISIS lost much of its ground in Iraq and Syria, and Iraq declared its war against the militant group over in December. However, while ISIS' self-declared caliphate is in territorial tatters, analysts have warned that the group is retreating into what some call a 'virtual caliphate' from where it will attempt to inspire more lone wolf terror attacks in the West.

ISIS has now focussed its attention of Africa; where great

tracts of the Sahel and Sahara are now under their control occupying many national armies and the French Foreign Legion.

A small but steady flow of money to ISIS from rich individuals in the Gulf continues, say current and former U.S. officials, with Qataris the biggest suppliers. These rich individuals have long served as 'angel investors', as one expert put it, for the most violent militants in the region, providing the "seed money" that helped launch ISIS and other jihadi groups.

No one in the U.S. government is putting a number on the current rate of donations, but former U.S. Navy Admiral and NATO Supreme Commander James Stavridis says the cash flow from private donors is significant now and was even more significant in the early fund-raising done by ISIS and al-Qaeda's affiliate in Syria, the al-Nusrah Front.

"These rich Arabs are like what 'angel investors' are to tech start-ups, except they are interested in starting up groups who want to stir up hatred," said Stavridis, now the dean of the Fletcher School of Diplomacy at Tufts University. *"Groups like al-Nusrah and ISIS are better investments for them. The individuals act as high rollers early, providing seed money. Once the groups are on their feet, they are perfectly capable of raising funds through other means, like kidnapping, oil smuggling, selling women into slavery, etc."*

Stavridis and other current U.S. officials suggest that the biggest share of the individual donations supporting ISIS and the most radical groups comes from Qatar rather than Saudi Arabia, and that the Qatari government has done less to stop the flow than its neighbours in Saudi Arabia and the United Arab Emirates. One U.S. official said the Saudis are "more in line with U.S. foreign policy" than the Qataris. This is not a universally held view; funding is much wider than just Qataris.

Groups like ISIS and al-Nusrah employ fundraisers who meet with wealthy Sunni Arabs. Most of the Arab states have laws prohibiting such fundraising, but U.S. officials say the Qataris do not strictly enforce their laws…but nor do others.

A U.S. intelligence official said the amount provided by wealthy individuals is small relative to the group's other sources, but admitted that the flow continues. *"Although ISIS probably still receives donations from patrons in some of the Gulf countries,"* said the official, *"any outside funding represents a small fraction of ISIS's total annual income."*

The U.S. believes ISIS is taking in about $1 million a day from all sources. The largest source of cash now, say U.S. officials, is oil smuggling along the Turkish border, with ISIS leaders willing to sell oil from conquered Syrian and Iraqi fields for as little as $25 a barrel, a quarter of the going world price. Other previously lucrative sources, like kidnapping for ransom, are not what they once were. As one U.S. official put it, *'there are only so many rich Syrian businessmen'*. Similarly, there are fewer banks to loot.

Admiral. Stavridis, author of the forthcoming book 'Accidental Admiral' suggests that the U.S. must cut off as much funding as it can, calling cash flow the "fourth front" in the war against ISIS, along with helping the Kurdish Peshmerga and the Iraqi military and carrying out a bombing campaign.

As long ago as last March, before ISIS's military advances, a senior Treasury Department official spoke punlically about *"permissive jurisdictions"* that were allowing fundraising on behalf of ISIS and other groups.

"A number of fundraisers operating in more permissive jurisdictions -- particularly in Kuwait and Qatar -- are soliciting donations to fund extremist insurgents, not to meet legitimate humanitarian needs", said David Cohen, undersecretary for terrorism and financial intelligence. *"The recipients of these funds are often terrorist groups, including al-Qaeda's Syrian affiliate, al-Nusrah Front, and the Islamic State of Iraq and the Levant [ISIS]."*

David Phillips, a former senior advisor to the State Department on Iraq and now director of the Program on Peace-building and Human Rights at Columbia University, said the bottom line, financially and politically, is that *"wealthy Arabs are playing a dirty double game"*.

"Their governments claim to oppose ISIS," he said, *"while individuals continue funding terrorist activities"*.

The financial help from *'rich patrons'*, as U.S. intelligence calls them, was also noted this week by Iranian officials, who have been excluded from participating in anti-ISIS discussions. High-ranking officials complained publicly Wednesday about the early role of Arab states in building opposition to the Assad regime to Syria, and blamed them for the consequences.

It is, of course, the height of irony to hear U.S. officials complaining of such tactics.

Recently, Iranian Foreign Minister Mohammed Javad Zarif, in comments to the Council of Foreign Relations, said it was not realistic to expect those who have helped fund ISIS and other groups to now oppose them.

Zarif called the recently convened Paris conference on fighting ISIS a *"coalition of repenters"* who are only now seeing that they have created a monster. The Gulf states were among the countries attending the summit.

"Most participants in that -- in that meeting in one form or another provided support to ISIS in the course of its creation and upbringing and expansion, actually at the end of the day, creating a Frankenstein that came to haunt its creators," Zarif told the CFR. *"So this group has been in existence for a long time. It has been supported, it has been provided for in terms of arms, money, finances by a good number of U.S. allies in the region."*

Iranian President Hassan Rouhani was just as emphatic, asking a string of rhetorical questions.

"Who financed them? Who provided them with money? It's really

clear -- where do the weapons come from?" asked Rouhani. "*The terrorists who have come from all the countries, from which channel [did they enter], where were they trained, in which country were they trained? I don't think it is somehow difficult to identify this information.*"

But U.S. officials suggest that as the group has expanded -- and its range of enemies has broadened – so have its costs, which could make the group vulnerable.

"*Is [the ISIS financial model] sustainable?*" asked Stavridis. "*The bigger they get, is that their downfall?*"

The Qatari Embassy in Washington did not immediately respond to requests for comment. Qatar has previously strongly denied supporting ISIS "*in any way*," including funding.[84] [85]

CHAPTER 15:
ANECDOTAL

General

In a book entitled an 'Introduction to the Middle East' it is important to go beyond the usual descriptive narrative and try and give some insight learnt from knowledge and experience.

The first thing that most westerners, especially, and some others, fail to understand is that the Middle East is not like them, but also very like them. It is not like them in that it is not democratic, it never has been and is unlikely to ever be truly so – barring revolution. The tribal nature of the region remains important and, as in Africa, the clan-based system of a top-down patriarchy still holds true. So politically, economically, socially and culturally it is different. This is something to enjoy and respect in the best sense; but also to be very wary of in the worst.

It is very like other places in that there are those who believe in Islam and religion rules their lives; those that put religion in an important place in their lives; those that pay lip service to religion and its rules; and those who do not pay religion much attention at all. However, still, in the final analysis religion counts in both Sunni and Shia countries. This is important to understand. It is also like other places in that there are country, tribal, family and business rivalries that sometimes go back centuries.

Politically the region is run by 'strongmen' who have a number of key challenges ranging from their support of religion through overpopulation and a very young population in Egypt, Iran, Sudan, and to a lesser extent Iraq and Turkey to the underpopulation in the UAE (where expatriates of various countries outnumber the locals many times). This is a region of history and one where religion and sometimes families have great influence either as rulers, or behind the scenes. This has always to be borne in mind.

Western travellers, in particular, often exhibit a form of unwarranted exceptionalism that is rude, challenging and dangerous. It is rude and challenging in the lack of manners; and dangerous because these are well organised states at national level who have much to fear and react badly to inquisitive foreigners. The case of Mathew Hedges is a salutary one. He was an alleged British spy held for six months by the UAE for being over inquisitive. The world has moved on from the colonial hegemonies in many ways; and, if not, the rulers certainly do not want to be reminded.

Business is certainly done differently than in the West; but more like much of the rest of the world where family contacts (often built over centuries too), position, trust, bribes, 'wasta' in Arabic, are important for oiling the wheels of commerce. 'Wasta' is important. It is described thus:

'Wasta is an Arabic word that loosely translates into nepotism, 'clout' or 'who you know'. It refers to using one's connections and/or influence to get things done, including government transactions such as the quick renewal of a visa or a passport or driving license, waiving of traffic fines, and getting hired for or promoted in a job which usually would take a month. In other words, it amounts to getting something through favouritism rather than merit, or what is informally spoken of in English as "pull" from connections (the opposite of "push"). The English word cronyism overlaps in meaning but is not precisely the same. Roughly equivalent words in other

languages include 'sociolismo' in Cuba; 'blat' in Russia; 'guanxi' in Chinese and 'Vetternwirtschaft' in German, 'protektzia' in Israeli slang, 'un pituto' in Chilean Spanish, In Brazilian-Portuguese it is referred to as 'pistolão', 'QI' (Quem Indica, or Who Indicates), or in the slang 'peixada', 'Pidi Padu' in Malayalam language spoken region of India, 'arka' or 'destek' or 'torpil' in Turkish, 'plecy' in Polish, 'štela' in Bosnian'. Clearly a concept not limited to the Middle East. It is important in the Middle East.

A favourite example of 'wasta' is the expat who, driving lawfully down a road, hit a camel that ventured onto the road in front of him. Clear cut case for the driver one would imagine. Not so, the driver eventually had to pay for both the camel and damages.

On starting my own company in the Middle East I limited my own success by not taking an Arab partner; taking a partner is normal in Arab countries. However, successful companies often get taken over by their Arab partners to the disadvantage of the founder. So, I kept my international business and consulted, traded and coached using a UK company and a Dubai company. This limited some things I could do and not do. To be really successful you need a partner with 'wasta'...but be careful. Having previously been kidnapped in Africa, Russia and the Middle East for NOT taking a bribe I did not want to run into trouble with the authorities for exploiting 'wasta' – it is a double-edged sword.

Just as any international business traveller would expect to have his or her laptop looked at by the intelligence services in most European countries the same can be true in the Middle East. Airports are particularly dangerous areas for remote laptop hacks; as are, obviously, hotels. I stupidly left my laptop in a Middle East airport; sure enough it had been tampered with when I got it back. Fortunately, anything of real interest was round my neck.

In many countries the hospitality and courtesy that is at the core of Islam can be both reassuring and overpowering. This is the other side of life. Beautiful, cultured, welcoming people who will do almost anything to help. When lost I have had people drive miles out of their way to help get me where I want to go.

The key pillars of Islam are: declaration of faith, prayer, giving, fasting during Ramadan, and pilgrimage to Mecca. These are interpreted slightly differently in different sects but the most obvious outcome in the best of people is piety, humility, and concern for those less fortunate.

These traits are most obvious, socially and individually, at Ramadan and can also be seen in the massive financial assistance given by rich Arab countries to the poor; and the amount of humanitarian assistance that is given by many countries, the UAE is a prime example, to the needy of all religions around the world. There are contradictions. The plight of the Palestinians has not, interestingly, been at the forefront of Arabic diplomacy or aid. Individual kidnapping, theft and begging from foreigners is not unknown. Using aid as a cover for arms distribution is not unknown either.

Money is different in the Middle East. It is a financial crossroads, like Hong Kong or Singapore, and mixes a western approach to money with a Sharia/Islamic approach to money with a Hawala system. Sharia banking eschews interest charging, as this is forbidden under Islam in favour of profit sharing. The Hawala system originated in India. It has existed since the 8th century CE between Indian, Arabic, and Muslim traders who operated alongside the Silk Road and beyond, as a protection against theft. It is a popular and informal value transfer system based not on the movement of cash, or on telegraph or computer network wire transfers between banks, but instead on the performance and honour of a huge network of money brokers (known as Hawaladars). Many banks do not comply with the Basel Accords, and many banks are accused of financing terror and money laundering. With Asia and the Middle East outstripping the West in the volume of financial transactions based on cash, rather than derivatives, there is little chance of western banking accords holding sway.

Taxes are relatively new in parts of the Middle East, particularly in the oil rich GCC where VAT has only recently been introduced, most recently in Oman. This raises a conundrum, one of many, as to how populations will eventually react after so many years without having to pay tax. The withdrawal of individual state support, rising prices and taxes (with no representation) is a potentially explosive mix. This has already become a problem in Saudi Arabia.

Until recently gated (2018 CE) you could still go down to the dockside and buy/sell almost anything off the dhows in Dubai. You could transport your car, and much else, quietly, to Saudi Arabia. The father of the current Chairman of one of Dubai's top property groups was a dhow captain; illiterate but fluent in the languages of Swahili to Urdu as he transported goods from as far south as Mozambique to as far east as Mumbai and Goa. Smuggling is still rampant. Counterfeiting is rampant, with fake Rolex watches still widely available; and almost indistinguishable from the real thing.

Drugs are a conundrum in the Middle East. Large quantities of Cannabis and Hemp are grown in the region; mist for 'medical purposes'. Qat is a drug of choice in many countries and the relatively small highs have been a feature of relaxation in the region for centuries. Alcohol is drunk in vast quantitites by nearly 250 000 Saudis visiting Bahrain every weekend except during Ramadan. Drugs are supplied to performers by senior UAE officials at the Abu Dhabi Grand Prix. If you get caigth as a tourist or a working person with drugs you can face the death penalty.

Sanctions have been placed on Lebanon for allegedly trying to supply drugs in fruit and vegetables to Saudi Arabia and others. Members of royal families have killed themselves driving off bridges high on a cocaine mix. The drug trade in various GCC countries is controlled by the governing families. Boat crews caught smuggling drugs, often in fish, are executed.

Much talk in the West has concerned the so-called plight of the foreign workers in Qatar. This has been by people who have been, for some reason, shy to condemn the Uighur issues in China – perhaps linked to the vast numbers of Chinese students these same commentators take money from to teach. As any expatriate taxi driver in the Middle East will tell you he, occasionally she, is better off working in the Middle East than in their own, mostly East and South Asian, countries. Construction workers are often badly treated it is true; and trafficking gangs can run the crews. However, workers need to be constantly watched as they will often evade work and steal. More often than not their pay is better than any equivalent in, say, Bangladesh. For the western liberals it is a difficult 'moral' issue; for many of the workers they are just grateful to have a job. Most of the workers I have met are more interested in feeding and schooling their families.

Over recent years (2015 – 2020 CE) there has been an exodus of foreign workers from the Middle East, especially the GCC, with interesting consequences. One consequence is the employment of nationals to replace the foreign workers. In hotels in Saudi Arabia Saudi women greet you at reception, unheard of five years ago. Saudi men serve food and are restaurant and bar captains, also unheard of five years ago – and anathema to many traditionalists. The foreign worker has to train the national on the job before departure.

Saudis are not used to work, so many hospitality standards have slipped. Saudi camel herders have been turned into taxi drivers with little or no training – so they don't know, for example, the Riyadh roads and don't speak English as the old foreign workers did (who spoke Arabic, English, Hindi etc) and are impolite by nature. In Bahrain, by contrast, every national works – so there is a much more customer centric culture.

The change from foreign to nationals has caused the closure of cold stores in Saudi – this is because the owners can no longer make a profit as their labour costs have increased. They have to pay more to Saudis plus an employment tax. If they want to keep the foreign worker they have to pay a bigger tax, Further Saudis are not as reliable as the foreign worker. So, the upshot is the closure of cold stores with difficult consequences for chilled distribution chains.

Remittances from foreign workers to their home countries (U.S., Europe, Egypt, India, Pakistan, Bangladesh, Philippines, Nepal etc.) have dropped significantly adding further pressure to sometimes stretched economies. As the average British expat would say the Middle East is no longer a place to make and save money.

Disease is rampant in Asian expatriates. It could be stopped before it arrives through appropriate medical checks. This would cost the gangmasters too much money; so exchanges take place to minimise medical checks in host countries. So, diseases are exported to the Middle East. People then become ill, often die or the employers pick up the bill. It is ruthless; but no more ruthless than conditions 'at home',

Tourism can be a bit of a contradiction sometimes. Dubai has exploited its position as an aviation crossroads (at least until the advent of COVID) and turned itself into a multinational tourist centre. 35% of Dubai's economy is directly linked to the airline Emirates. Emirates is one of the most successful airlines in the world. At least until COVID it was responsible for building Dubai into the international travel and tourist hub that it is. As different economies boomed, Russian, Chinese, Indians, other Asians or Americans dominated, supported by a steady flow of Europeans, Africans and some South Americans. Dubai took a more relaxed view than some to the values and standards of visitors; but crossing an Emirati in business or in a bar encourages long prison sentence. That said immigration officials in Dubai are far more accommodating to the careworn traveller than some stories suggest; and certainly more polite than, for example, Heathrow in the UK, by a wide margin.

Saudi Arabia is trying to boost its non-Muslim non-Hajj tourism business. It faces some challenges. Videos of fishing in the Red Sea and catching threatened species don't always go down well in target markets; nor do desert hunting trips for equally rare mammals. Falconry remains a favourite sport – but not, again, favoured by tourists if for threatened species. Many senior Arabs love hunting and will go to Africa, Morocco and Pakistan, in particular, to hunt. They do not subscribe to the western concerns on preservation in quite the same way. In addition, traditionalists do not favour tourism; and Saudi is unlikely to take as relaxed a view as Dubai.

Egypt has the pyramids, Egyptology, the Nile and the Red Sea. It hassles tourists, not always nicely, and has had more than its share of terrorist incidents against tourists. It is trying, and needs, to relaunch its tourist business. As with Saudi it has many, often illiterate, extreme traditionalists who do not like tourists.

Turkey has a relatively successful tourist business built over decades as an attraction for European travellers to the beaches. This is now (at least, again, until COVID) a significant part of Turkey's economy. Relatively quietly Turkish Airlines has built a hub and reputation to match Emirates in many ways.

Overseas assets and dependencies are huge. The Sunni powerhouses of Saudi Arabia, Qatar and the UAE wield enormous financial power, still. Their investments across the world bring them fealty from other Muslim countries such as Egypt, Jordan, Indonesia and Pakistan and income from huge investments in Europe, the U.S. and further afield. An example is the horse racing industry. In both the UK and, probably, the U.S. horse racing would be financially insolvent if it was not for the vast amounts of money ploughed into it through the UAE's Godolphin stable. The UK has huge tracts of land and much of London in the hands of Middle East investors. Sovereign wealth is described elsewhere.

In Denmark, a studied example, Muslim immigrants have put pressure on the health service because of the congenital disorders that accompany them. These issues are generally caused by conditions that affect communities that have been allowed to marry their first cousins over a millennium. This is still permitted in Islam. The consequences are clear in a tour of Saudi Arabia where wheelchairs and hospitals for the congenitally ill are a common sight, if often hidden from general view.

Literacy across the region is relatively low. Egypt probably has the biggest problem with this. Whilst the Quran may be learnt by rote by many, writing and understanding the messages is not so well practised. Therefore, as noted earlier, many of the Imams in Egypt, and elsewhere, are illiterate but feed the populus a radical interpretation of Islam. Relatively few books get translated into Arabic these days...and relatively few Arab books get translated internationally. English is the 'lingua franca' of business and education powered, for many, by the sub-titles on TV news and films.

The role of women in the Middle East is changing. 50 years ago, many Arab women could be seen wearing western clothes and adopting a western culture (much like the men). The conservative forces in Iran and Saudi Arabia, and those that paid fealty to them, have held sway over much of the intervening period except in Libya under Qaddafi and places like Bahrain where much of the local population works for a living. This conservatism got rid of western dress and culture and reconfined women to the household. However, a similar conservatism existed in the iron, steel and coal communities of the UK in the period to the 1980s CE. Here the men held an obvious leading role, but behind the scenes the women had a sisterhood and matriarchy that wielded power behind the scenes. This analogy is appropriate for Saudi Arabia in particular. Experience everywhere shows that when unleashed the development and creative power of women is transformational. This has been understood in many Middle Eastern countries now, including Saudi Arabia. In Saudi women are driving a revolution in business, commerce, public service – but contending with a conservative backlash at the same time. In many other Middle Eastern countries, the process is similar – perhaps not so much in Iran. To cope with the challenges of the region women need to be involved.

The role of non-Arab women ranges from the exotic to the banal. Highly paid western, often trafficked Russian and Ukrainian. prostitutes brought in to serve the top end of Arab society, Bangladeshi girls human trafficked to serve the lower end of Arab society as domestic servants or prostitutes. Filipinos and Indians much the same. The remittances are important if they can get past the madams. Watching a Filipino madame at work is an education. Having trafficked the girls over they then lend them money and they become, indentured would be a nice term, slaves in the worst cases. These madams usually have male criminal partners who are linked back to gangs of the Philippines. Some make it on their own both from the Philippines, India and Africa...many are trafficked and in debt to the gangs. Some are sold by their families. This is an issue with the Indian Dancing Girls for example. Filipino bands: one girl, one gay, a guitarist, bass player and drummer. The format is the same, the entertainment usually pretty good, the pay often poor. Again, organised by criminal 'Simon Cowell' types in the Philippines.

Goats are a menace in the Middle East. They have been, like camels, around for centuries. They are though devastating; they eat everything if uncontrolled. They are responsible for much desertification and soil erosion across the region. The eradication of goats and their replacement with a less damaging herbivore would be hugely beneficial. The challenges of tradition and ranging rights have first to be overcome. Camels, on the other hand, have increasingly become a niche occupation, often focussed on racing.

Many Arabs like hunting and will go to the deserts of Iraq, Morocco, Pakistan and the savannahs of Africa to hunt. They are not, generally, paid up members of the World Wildlife Fund... but rich people looking for a bit of fun. This is 'usual'. The pro – preservation lobbies have a hard time against such thinking both in the Middle East and Asia.

Rulers and Challenges

In the region, despite lip service being paid to democratic institutions, most countries are dictatorships in one way or another.

North West Africa

Libya

The President of Libya is Mohamed Yunus al-Menfi, he was appointed in March 2021 CE, and with colleagues succeeded against the U.S favoured grouping, to guide the country through transition to a new united constitution and country.

Egypt

The President of Egypt is Abdel Fattah el-Sisi. He is a former General and Director of the Intelligence Service. He is effectively a dictator. His biggest challenge is the under-30 population.

Sudan

The President of Sudan is the Sovereignty Council – term due to expire in November 2022 CE. The long-time dictator of Sudan was Omar Al Bashir. The biggest challenges in Sudan are the nearly 50% urban population, the under – 30 population, pressure on farmland, regional conflicts and continuing internal rivalries,

GCC and Yemen

Saudi Arabia

The effective ruler of Saudi Arabia is Crown Prince Mohammed bin Salman, a son of the current King Salman. Known as MBS. His biggest problems are modernisation of the economy to find jobs and purpose for many of the national population under – 30 and to wean the country off oil. He is treading a difficult tightrope. He has lost a lot of credibility through failed foreign policy objectives in Yemen and Qatar, the Khashoggi affair, and the slow tempo of modernisation as well as the problems many changes have created. He has, until recently, taken a tough line with Iran. He has made a number of mistakes diplomatically and fallen out with his old mentor MBZ over regional issues and international agreements.

MBS imprisoned a number of relatives and senior Saudis at the Ritz Carlton in 2017 accusing them of corruption. Some were tortured, others badly treated …many came to deals. It was the revenge, in many ways, of his side of the Royal Family. He will need to take care when the King dies.

Watching MBS in a video taken in a night club surrounded by relatively scantily clad women is a reminder that he likes a hedonistic lifestyle. In 2015 CE he rented Velaa in the Maldives, took a long many beautiful women, had them tested for STDs on arrival. Once word leaked out the 'party' was shut down. Now he has his own mega private yacht, Serene, on which to party.

All this said he has an almost Messianic following amongst many; and certainly most professional Saudi women are great supporters.

Yemen

Yemen is a crisis torn country whose current president is the ex-head of the Armed Forces, Abdrabbuh Mansur Hadi, in power since 2012 CE and leading the Saudi and UAE backed Sunni side of the civil war against the Iranian backed Houthis. The challenges in Yemen are clear; the biggest humanitarian disaster in the world promulgated by Saudi Arabia, UAE and Iran. A young and uneducated population.

Oman

Oman has had a recent peaceful transfer of power from Sultan Qaboos bin Said to his cousin Haitham bin Tariq. The biggest challenge in Oman is debt. The country is weighed down with debt. It also has a large under-30 population. It has often brokered dialogue between Sunni and Shia; and has a long history of maritime contact with Africa and Asia. There have been demonstrations recently regarding lack of jobs.

UAE

The de facto ruler of Abu Dhabi, and the UAE, is Sheikh Mohammed bin Zayed bin Sultan Al Nahyan. Known as MBZ. Another who treads a difficult path. The country has huge wealth and he likes to use it for foreign policy objectives, often linked to promoting Sunni Islam, across the region. Involved in Libya, Sudan, Yemen, Djibouti amongst others. MBZ is a mentor to MBS, and despite their reent differences possibly still is.

MBZ was at the same night club as MBS when videoed with

scantily clad western women. He seemed more at ease than MBS.

The UAE finances political and military parties in a number of countries – linked to the expansion of Sunni Islam in particular.

MBZ views anyone not supportive of the UAE agenda as a 'terrorist organisation'. This is an interesting approach, but by no means unique. It does cause a few issues within the GCC.

Qatar

The ruler of Qatar is Sheikh Tamim bin Hamad al-Thani , The al-Thanis have ruled Qatar since 1880 CE. They, and Yemen, got in the way of the Saudi objective under MBS to unify the Saudi peninsula. They were kicked out of the GCC in 2017 for various reasons and an invasion was only stopped by the U.S. This allowed Turkey to establish an outpost in the peninsula for the first time in a century. It also encouraged dialogue with Iran. Qatar uses its wealth to protect itself and has big allies now in the U.S., Europe, Turkey (so far) and dialogue with Iran. It has been accused of financing terrorism and ISIL. The Al Thanis are respected by many.

Bahrain

The ruler of Bahrain is King Hamad bin Isa Al Khalifa. One way or another this Sunni family and hereditary monarchy has ruled mostly Shia Bahrain since the 18th century CE. The Shia community is its big challenge. Additionally, it is a client state, really, of Saudi Arabia and linked to it by a causeway over which the Saudis invaded during the Arab spring in 2011 to protect the Sunnis and across which over 250 000 Saudi invade at the weekend to 'enjoy' a drink and other more carnal pleasures. Because it is predominantly Shia, Iran takes a close and destabilising interest. The author has witnessed persons emerging from the sea …and Iran has many mini submarines capable of getting close to Bahraini shores. It has an immature 'democratic' body famous for very odd statements and promulgations. There is much respect for the Crown Prince.

Kuwait

Sheikh Nawaf Al-Ahmad Al-Jaber Al-Sabah became Emir of Kuwait on 30 September 2020 CE. Kuwait's biggest challenge, post COVID, is likely to be financial, despite large reserves of cheaply extracted oil. It has a 'democratic' body also famous for some very odd statements.

Iraq

In 1921 CE the author's uncle, same name, was killed at Nasariyah by an IED strapped to his airplane, shortly after he survived an attack on his camp that killed his Indian servant, and in 50 °C heat. In 2021 CE this is written against a personal backdrop of kidnap and personal difficulty in Iraq and elsewhere. In a 100 years not much has changed. The locals are still revolting but, at the moment, against their domestic masters not some colonial power.

The Prime Minister of Iraq is Moustafa Al Kazimi, another former intelligence chief. At one point it looked as though Iraq would split into three with a Kurdish North a Sunni centre and a Shia south. This may still happen. In the meantime, the biggest challenge is responding to the population's demands for a fairer distribution of oil wealth; and the continuing process of recovering politically and economically from the two Gulf Wars in a country riven by corruption.

Iran

Iran has a Supreme leader, the religious leader, and a President, a popularly elected official. The Supreme Leader is Ali

Khamenei, and the President (until autumn 2021 CE) is Hassan Rouhani. The power rests with the Supreme Leader who through a number of powerful councils and committees basically decides who can do and run for what, including the Presidency. Most final decisions can be taken by the Supreme Leader. The Revolutionary National Guard is the key military force and protector of the Supreme Leader. Once confined to domestic issues it is now an expeditionary force. The 2021 Presidential Election was won by Ebrahim Raisi. Formerly a member of the judiciary with a reputation as a 'hard liner'. He will, most likely, take over as the next Supreme Leader. Interestingly his initial public comments have been less hard line than anticipated.

Iran is a very beautiful country with a very intelligent population. It is ruled by a Shia theocracy which has curtailed development in the western sense and promoted conflict in the region through its theocratic competition with Saudi Arabia in particular. This may change.

The Levant

Jordan

The King of the Hashemite Kingdom of Jordan, Abdullah II is Jordan's head of state and monarch. He serves as the head of the Jordanian monarchy—the Hashemite dynasty. His most recent challenge has been his half-brother in a rumoured coup. Aside from that the huge refugee problems, the young population, the neighbours, Israel and Syria, all present challenges to a country not well endowed with natural resources. Comment has been made on the recent coup attempt elsewhere.

Lebanon

The president of Lebanon is Michel Aoun and the Prime Minister designate, as this is written, is Saad Al Hariri (a Saudi). Their biggest challenges are forming a Government, overcoming a ruined economy, and recovering from sanctions imposed by Gulf States for smuggling drugs (possibly a retribution for the rebuttal of MBS's machinations in Lebanon). In addition, coping with Israel and Iranian backed Hezbollah complicates matters in a war-torn country with many refugees.In mid-2021 all the lights went out.

Israel

The last Prime Minister of Israel was Benjamin Netanyahu. He was in power from 2009 CE to 2021 CE, with also a previous term from 1996 CE to 1999 CE.

The new leader of Israel is Naftali Bennet. He has a hard-line reputation; but leads a broad coalition.

Palestine

In 1946 CE two colleagues of the author's father, same name, were murdered by Jews in Palestine during the 1946/47 CE difficulties. The author's father wrote the report on their deaths, the copies taken at the time are in Durham University's Middle East Centre. Not much has changed in the meantime.

In 1983 CE the author and a colleague were arrested in Tunisia for making contact with the PLO. The leader of the PLO at the time was Yasser Arafat. Arafat could have given Palestine statehood.

Today Palestine is split and has many political divisions, especially in Gaza. Any visit is always fraught with understanding which of the many factions control what.

Turkey and Cyprus

Turkey

The President of Turkey is Recep Erdogan. Erdogan is effectively a dictator since the constitutional changes of 2018 CE. Turkey has been increasingly authoritarian since the attempted 'coup' in 2018 CE. Although a well-developed economy, relatively, Turkey still has significant joblessness. It also has key foreign policy objectives in relation to the Kurds, Syria and Iraq. It has had an ambivalent relationship with Israel.

Cyprus

Ersin Tatar is a Turkish Cypriot politician, and the current President of Northern Cyprus. He became the Prime Minister of Northern Cyprus following the collapse of the coalition government of Tufan Erhürman in May 2019 CE and served until his own election as President. He is also the leader of the National Unity Party and served as Leader of the Opposition.

Nicos Anastasiades is a Cypriot politician who has been President of Cyprus since 2013 CE. He was re-elected in 2018 CE. Previously, he was the leader of Democratic Rally between 1997 CE and 2013 CE and served as Member of Parliament from Limassol between 1981 CE and 2013 CE.

Palestine

Despite seeking recognition as a state Palestine is effectively split into two. The West Bank of the Jordan River and Gaza. The West Bank is under Fatah control and the Gaza strip under Hamas control. This split is unhelpful, but plays into he hands of Iran who use Gaza as a proxy state. Simply this annoys both Israel and Sunni Arabs, and contributes to conflict. However, both Turkey and Qatar have assisted Hamas to the annoyance of the UAE and Saudi Arabia in particular. Arms for Hamas have historically been smuggled from Iran via Sudan.

ISIL

Islamic State in the Levant has effectively been defeated. However, the Islamic State and associates such as Al Qaeda and Al Shabab are still active in other parts of the world, notably Africa, and it would be risky to completely rule out any further activity. It is now accepted that money from the Gulf States financed much of ISIL's activity, although this remains a difficult subject of discussion at international level. As recently as June 2021 CE the acting Foreign Minister of Lebanon was rebuked for repeating such.

ISIL fighters came to Dubai for rest and recuperation from time to time. Taking care on a night out took on a new meaning.

For more anecdotes please see Part 1.

CHAPTER 16:
THE FUTURE

The future for the Middle East in general is not looking good. It is in most states overpopulated and relies on food imports. Education remains relatively poor, as do health services. There are relatively few jobs and poorly motivated workforces. The sizeable population under 30 is simply a powder keg waiting to explode. As the world moves to a carbon-free society then the natural resources on which the region has relied for so long to sustain itself will become less valuable. As the COVID crisis of 2020/21 CE has demonstrated even the richest countries become poor in response; and this is true of many Middle Eastern states.

General

The key future issues of fuel, science and innovation, changing workforce, medicine, climate, collision of cultures, China, the decline of the U.S. and democracy will all have their impacts in the region.
Fuel

Fuel will be one of the most interesting continuing developments of the 21st century CE. The Middle East remains awash with oil and gas; and the death knell of oil and gas has been sounded many times. This may work in favour of the Middle East in the short to medium term. In this time scale the money from oil and gas will continue to paper over cracks in Middle Eastern society. In the long-term new fuels will come on stream which will, at the very least, impact, adversely, the price of oil and gas and render, in particular the more populous countries, the Middle East prone to internal and external disruption.

The Innovation Economy

The Middle East is not naturally innovative in the way that the U.S., Europe, Japan and China are. There are pockets of innovation in Israel (a large pocket), the UAE, Turkey and Iran. Elsewhere there is a dependency on foreign innovation. This will place the Middle East firmly in the second tier, at best, of the innovation economy of the 21st century CE.

The Next Workforce

The leading countries' workforces are moving towards a more global, multi-cultural, female, and diverse structure focussed on innovation. This may be modified by COVID. The Middle East still has a very male centric approach to the workforce with, effectively a strong hierarchical and class approach to employment. This will become increasingly irrelevant as general human resource needs increase, expatriates depart and the global economy moves on. This represents a severe challenge for the region.

Longevity Medicine

As the COVID pandemic has highlighted there are winners and losers in medicine. Although there are pockets, again, of medical excellence in the Middle East matching those of the innovation economy, plus Jordan, the rest of the region will be left behind as nanotech, neurotech, and genomics, are developed and lead to longer and healthier lives.

Other Science Developments

The western world and the Asian world are increasingly learning more about quantum physics, multiple universes, teleportation and genomics. Once again, the Middle East is likely to be left behind.

Securing The Future

The threats to our society such as crime, drugs, terrorism already have a stronghold in the Middle East. These are likely to develop as counterpoints to the developments notes above. They will develop in the middle East as the region struggles to be part of a wider global economy and society. The region will turn to crime, drugs and terrorism to balance shortfalls elsewhere in the economies.

The Future of Globalisation

The new realities of global trade are becoming increasingly clear post COVID, China has emerged stronger and more assertive. Its foreign policy is focussed on development and trade in the Middle East. However, this has and will lead to a different sort of dependency than seen during the American hegemony. It will also lead to a more authoritarian world, at least in the Middle East and Asia.

The Future of Climate Change

Climate change whether it be warming or just a change is clearly underway in many different parts of the world. In the Middle East there are two clear trends summer warming and an increase in winter floods. Both of these could be regionally disastrous to a fragile agrarian and more general ecosystem.

The Future of the Individual

The Middle East will be caught in several cleft sticks in regard to the individual. It will need to employ more people and have more jobs. These jobs will not satisfy the population. It needs to bring more women into the workforce, this will challenge men in unforeseeable ways in those countries not used to women in the workforce. Human rights will be challenged, as they are today, by authoritarian regimes, as will liberty and the freedom of the individual. In overpopulated countries with reducing opportunities this will encourage revolution and conflict.

The Future of America and China

The relationship between the U.S. and China will define the 21st century CE. In the Middle East as the U.S security blanket and U.S oil and gas related trade is removed or diminished then China's trade and development diplomacy will be in the ascendant.

The Future of Russia In The Middle East

Russia's future in the Middle East will be defined by its relationships with Iran and Syria. Iran remains a strong partner; and Syria has given, with potentially Jordan, Russia's coveted marine bases in the Eastern Mediterranean and the Red Sea.

The Future of Europe and the UK in the Middle East

Europe does not have a fully cohesive policy for the Middle East. Germany focusses on trade. France focusses, strongly, on its former colonies. Others are also involved in trade. The traders are likely to do better, France is coming under a great deal of external and internal pressure regarding former colonies, including those in the Middle East. This is likely to be a continuing problem.

The UK has re-established a small naval base in Bahrain, and has bult a new one in Duqm, Oman. Despite its military reputation having been severely damaged by the Iraq War and thereafter it still has defence treaties with a number of Middle East countries.

North West Africa

Libya

Libya remains a key hydrocarbon producer with a relatively small population which is unskilled and war weary. The future of Libya will depend on the success, or otherwise, of the 24 December 2021 CE election. As noted elsewhere the division is between the UN recognised Government (GNA) and the rebel army of Khalifa (LNA) backed by Russia, Egypt, Saudi Arabia, France and the UAE.

Libya remains a human trafficking route from Africa to Europe controlled by ISIS and others and represents an existential threat to Europe.

Prognosis: Continued tribal rivalry under a unity government with a potential recovery.

Egypt

Egypt is a Middle Eastern powerhouse. The leading Sunni military power and sustained by huge grants from the U.S. and Saudi Arabia. Despite this it maintains an independent stance on most issues; dealing with Europe, Russia and China in the same way it deals with the U.S. (in many instances). It has a huge and unsustainable population. There is simply no way that it can feed over 100 million people crammed into the urban environs of Cairo, the coast, and the Nile Valley. Autocratic by need and nature (it has a ruling elite) with an under-30 population that continues to grow, jobs continue to relatively diminish. Egypt will one day explode as it did in 2011 CE but probably with greater consequences. The traditional markets for the educated and aggressive Egyptian middle – class such as Saudi Arabia are nationalising expatriate jobs and the consequences in Egypt of the returning expertise and the loss of the remittances are likely to be unhelpful.

Egyptian leaders are keen on huge and expensive landmark

projects. Recent ones have failed spectacularly including a new city and a new irrigation region. These projects drain resources and will be difficult to conclude.

The Suez Canal will possibly become owned, or controlled, by China.

As long as the U.S. and Saudi Arabia pay it will stay out of the Palestinian/Israeli conflict.

Prognosis: A slow descent into chaos.

Sudan

Sudan is a poor country with, again, a large and probably unsustainable population. Its population is already driven to find work overseas and feeds the mercenary army of the UAE amongst others. A prime target for a successful ISIS/Al Shabab take over. Migration North to Europe through the Sahel is an issue.

Prognosis: A failed state.

The GCC and Yemen

Saudi Arabia

Saudi Arabia is the other Sunni powerhouse. Its future depends on the success of MBS, the Crown Prince Mohammed Bin Salman, and his 2030 vision. There have been some missteps along the way. The war in Yemen has not gone well, partly because the Army is not very good. (This may be one underlying reason for the dove-like noises towards Iran recently). The emancipation of women stutters, because of general conservative approaches and religious idealogues. Women could be the saviours of Saudi Arabia; but the men feel very threatened, as they should be. The aggressive pursuit of dissenters, for example Khashoggi, does not play well to target markets. The wholesale round up of the other half of the royal family did not play well either. So, some subtlety is required to succeed internationally; and some radical changes in culture to succeed internally with the 2030 plans. The grand plans have to be met with good social change, practical planning, and good project delivery. It is not clear that Saudi Arabia has a resilient national infrastructure. Without oil Saudi Arabia is currently unsustainable.

MBS' has bet the bank on inward investment and large scale infrastructure projects. They are not looking good at the moment.

Prognosis: A Palace coup on the death of the King and a difficult future.

Yemen

The Yemeni war, part of a plan by MBS to unite the Saudi peninsula, has not gone well and tuned into a great humanitarian disaster. The Saudi Army has not performed well and nor has the UAE mercenary army, with exceptions. Once again strategy has failed to be supported by operational performance. Yemen is another relatively huge population and is a failed state. It is difficult to see it recovering in the short term whilst one part of the population is a proxy for Saudi Arabia and the other for Iran. Yemen will continue to be a Northern Ireland type problem for Saudi Arabia. Yemen is not a sustainable state and peace is on hold for now.

Prognosis: A failed state.

Oman

Oman has a big debt problem. Solving the debt problem is the number one issue. It is and will continue to be a huge Chinese creditor. Other than that, it is a more sustainable state than some because the population as a whole is used to working, unlike those that have depended on expatriates.

Prognosis: Survival with difficulty.

UAE

The UAE could be described as a disruptive and Machiavellian state. Although this may well be true it is often described as such by larger equally disruptive and Machiavellian states. The effective ruler MBZ is certainly a player. He has participated in Yemen with Saudi, withdrawn but left mercenaries there. He has interfered in Sudan and used Sudanese mercenaries in Yemen. He has covered military supplies to East Libya as humanitarian aid. He has been both a mentor and competitor to MBS in Saudi Arabia. He led the denouncement of Qatar as a terrorist supporter. Note: the term terrorist supporter in this context means someone who does not agree with the MBZ foreign policy. The UAE has a relatively small national population and great wealth, so it will be interesting and uncertain how the future plays out especially as the foreign policy pursued is not mainstream except in terms of an unclear UAE national interest other than the expansion of Sunni Islam. Others may categorise MBZ as heading a terrorist organisation if the definitions are reversed.

Dubai will survive as long as aviation survives. In 2020 -21 Emirates declared an 88% fall in traffic and lost over $5bn. The state continues to support the airline. 35% of the economy depends on Emirates. It has paid for most of its infrastructure so will relatively flourish if aviation returns post-COVID. It remains in debt to its richer Emirate, Abu Dhabi, and has been bailed out by them on more than one occasion.

The other Emirates are not rich and depend on their richer siblings for survival.

Prognosis: A retrenched survival.

Qatar

Qatar has a very small indigenous population and great wealth. The wealth is a weapon it has used to survive and deny both Saudi Arabia and the UAE their controlling aspirations of some five years ago. It is diplomatically astute and has, since the GCC embargo, built a greater wall of influence than it has before, straddling many different countries and philosophies. It is, despite a recent issue with the finance minister, less corrupt than some of its neighbours. Water is scarce and basic water rights an issue.

Prognosis: A positive future.

Bahrain

Bahrain's position as a Saudi client state with a large Shia population places it in a cleft stick. It must pay attention to its large neighbour, from whence much cash flow is derived. It must also contain an unruly and Iran backed Shia population. Its ruling family has tried a benign approach, which has failed on more than one occasion. It has required hard measures to maintain social order. It has slick PR campaign, which is not backed by reality...this is unfortunate as if operational effectiveness was better it would rival Dubai.

China has an interest in Bahrain evidenced by the disproportionate size of its Huawei office.

Prognosis; If Saudi fails it may fall to Iran (a previous occupier).

Kuwait

Kuwait has large and very cheaply extracted oil reserves. As long as oil is needed Kuwait will survive as long as it keeps its foreign debt under control. The tense relationships with its neighbours, Saudi Arabia, Iraq and Iran are likely to continue. The ruler is at risk because although experienced in other roles he is new and untested in the role.

Prognosis: Survival.

Iran

Iran remains a conundrum. It has a clear religious philosophy, Islam as practiced by Shias. It is a theocracy where the Supreme Leader, in practice, has absolute power. Like Russia it has an intelligentsia that has been weakened and cowed by the State. However, it is still a technical leader in the region. Iran builds most of its own military hardware. It has strong armed forces, and the National Revolutionary Guard is probably second to Turkey in military effectiveness. Despite its relatively high technical ability Iran is now challenged by some low levels of literacy and joblessness.

Its new President, Ebrahim Raisi, is likely to be the next Supreme Leader – so there is a fundamental shift in the leadership profile of Iran towards the hardliners. That said there are already overtures to a more positive diplomacy; and secret talks have recently been held with Saudi Arabia.

Iran has good relations with Russia and increasingly good relations with China.

Russia was the first country to recognise Iran after the 1979 CE revolution. They are neighbours and belong to the same counter NATO military organisation. Iran buys Russian military hardware.

China has recently signed a 25-year cooperation agreement with Iran. Iran sits astride the old silk road; which is the historical basis for the Chinese belt and road initiative. China is a near neighbour. China has an eye on Chababahar port in the southeast as part of the recent Iranian deal. This will annoy

India who sees the port as its access route to Afghanistan and Central Asia. The agreement is said to have been in the works since Chinese President Xi Jinping visited Iran in 2016, also agreeing to increase bilateral trade more than 10-fold to $600bn in the next decade.

No details of the agreement have yet to be officially published, but it is expected to be a sweeping "strategic accord" that includes significant Chinese investments in Iran's key sectors such as energy and infrastructure, in addition to military cooperation.

It comes as both Iran and China are under different levels of sanctions imposed by the U.S.

After unilaterally abandoning Iran's 2015 CE nuclear deal with world powers – that also included China – former U.S President Donald Trump imposed harsh sanctions on Iran that have blacklisted its entire financial system.

While saying he wants to restore the deal, President Joe Biden has so far refused to lift any sanctions, saying Iran must first act to fulfil commitments it scaled back in response to U.S sanctions.

China and Russia have called on the U.S to restore the deal by lifting sanctions, while traders and analysts say Iran's oil exports to China have significantly increased in March despite U.S warnings...

Prognosis: Despite its large population Iran probably has the resources and structure to survive over the long term. The new President will be a long-term fixture.

Iraq

Iraq is unlikely to remain as a unitary state. It may become some sort of Federation but with Iran supporting a Shia south, Saudi supporting a Sunni centre and the Kurds independently trying to form their own state (with Turkey vehemently opposing such) unity is an unlikely scenario. The best alternative will be a three state federation.

The internal position will remain difficult with growing numbers wanting to see a fairer distribution of oil revenue, faster reconstruction and a stable currency. Insurgency will remain a problem.

Prognosis: Survival as a federation or Iran takes over the south.

The Levant

Jordan

Jordan is weighed down by large debts and a refugee population that consumes time, effort and money at the expense of the indigenous population. Jordan is home to nearly 5 million refugees from Palestine, Iraq and Syria. It is viewed as stable although recently there have been fractures in the ruling monarchy. It is a popular tourist destination and health tourist destination. It is unlikely to prosper, despite a relatively high-income society, because of the political difficulties it will encounter in due course and its refugee problem. It has few natural resources.

Its recent attempted palace coup is symptomatic of two very different approaches within the royal family. The internationally comfortable King; and the tribally well-connected Crown Prince. The King remains in the ascendant for now.

Prognosis: A difficult future.

Syria

Syria is currently a failed state trying to recover from the civil war. 50% of its pre civil war population is displaced.

In this recovery, and in the war, it has been supported by Russia. Russia has received in return a foothold in the Mediterranean. There are over 5 million Syrian refugees in neighbouring and other countries. It will take at least ten years, if things go well to rebuild Syria. It is, at least, a country that can feed itself. There is an issue in the North East to settle between Syria, Turkey and the Kurds.

A Presidential election is due. Assad will win it as the only other permitted candidate is an Assad supporter and largely unknown.

Prognosis: Survival with Russia's help.

Lebanon

Lebanon is another current failed state. It has recovered from such a position before and has a very resourceful population. However, this time the depth of the financial crisis it faces may not be sufficient to see a recovery. It is difficult to see a quick way out.

Prognosis: A failed state.

Israel

The dynamics of East Mediterranean politics are changing because of the energy resources in the East Mediterranean. This forcing some overdue co-operation. It also creates tensions and brings both the U.S. and Russia into the mix.

The Abraham Accords have changed the overall face of Middle East politics with wholesale alignment, almost, of Sunni and Israel against Shia Iran. 'My enemy's enemy is my friend'. As long as it holds it will be a good step forward, particularly as the U.S. withdraws security cover.

The new Government is being tested, wants to

go in a different direction to Netanyahu but is
a mixture of very hard right and left.

Prognosis: Survival, possibly flourishing.

Palestine

Palestine's fractured internal politics and lack of support from
many Arab nations make its efforts for statehood difficult
to succeed. Neither Egypt nor Jordan are sympathetic and
both address alleged terrorism and smuggling harshly,
Along with the large numbers of refugees in Jordan and
elsewhere the overall impact of Palestine in the Arab world
is negative. It does not further help its cause by being
seen as dishonourable at a state level and dishonest at a
personal level. Palestinians are not always welcome in
Arab nations as refugees or visitors. It served the purpose
of Iran and other anti-Israeli countries, particularly the
USSR for a while, but now with a new landscape developing
in the Middle East it is becoming an anachronism.

Prognosis: Survival through some sort of
Middle East brokered deal.

Turkey and Cyprus

Turkey

Turkey is one of the most interesting countries to watch in
the future. It is now energy self-sufficient, has a proven armed
forces which seem recovered from the 2016 coup. It can feed
itself, if necessary, it has a relatively healthy industrial and
service sector. It has a hard-line dictator with a strategy.

Prognosis: A growing power and influence
at risk of internal collapse.

Cyprus

Northern Cyprus is a bargaining chip for Turkey in regard to discussions with the European Union and, now, the Eastern Mediterranean energy giants.

Prognosis: Turkey will keep its illegitimate occupation going.

ISIS

It would be foolish to underrate ISIS. Although seemingly defeated in the Levant many of its leaders are still abroad and can rely on substantial funds from, particularly, Gulf Sunni sympathisers. The focus of its attention has now moved to Africa where it will create havoc in the near – failed states of the Sahel, Central Africa and southern East Africa. This will continue to bring it into conflcit with Europe as it manages the illegal human trafficking from Africa to Europe. It will tie down French forces, in particular. It will create sleeper cells in Europe. It could rebuild sufficient resources to reactivate in the Middle East.

Prognosis: Will remain active.

CHAPTER 17:
CONCLUSION

Leadership in the Middle East is authoritarian and likely to remain so. All the States discussed in this book are authoritarian regimes of one sort or another. Most have their intelligence chiefs either running the country or close to the top of power. This reinforces the control and surveillance of all populaces. Some say this is necessary to keep countries safe from external and internal trouble; it is certainly the case that iot fits a historical model of clan or tribe leadership. Elites run all these countries; sometimes these are military (Egypt) sometimes families (Saudi Arabia). Most populations are repressed except when it is the rulers' interest not be repressive:

The semi- emancipation of women in Saudi Arabia is driven by a need to employ more nationals. The national workforces in Oman and Bahrain reflect a lack of national resources. The Emiratis control their own tightly but enrich them in a country where they are very much the minority. The same pertains in Qatar. Iran is a hard-line theocracy rules by theocrats and the National Guard at the expense of the people who are nowhere near as religious as their leaders. This is unlikely to change anytime soon.

This not an era of absolute authoritarian stability. The region is a miserable collection of failed states and stagnant states, made worse by COVID. Young people have not seen any benefits since 2011 and have grown larger in absolute numbers since. The material benefits once provided, especially in the Gulf, by oil revenues in exchange for political quiescence is a contract that is falling apart.

Tribe

This book looked at Tribe early on. Tribe remains important in the Middle East despite some claims, particularly in Saudi Arabia, to the contrary. As the challenges take hold internally expect tribe to be as relevant to the outcome as it ahs been over the past three millennia.

Religion

The contest between Sunni and Shia will continue. How violent this contest remains, and it is very violent at the moment (ISIS Yemen, Iraq, Bahrain, Saudi Arabia, Lebanon, Palestine), depends on Saudi Arabi and Iran. A number of recent secret meetings offers some hope.

Population

Population in the region is out of control. Over and above any other factor apart from perhaps water this will jeopardise the Middle East.

Oil and Gas/Fuel

The death of the hydrocarbon economy has been proclaimed ebery year of my lifetime. It has not happened. Today though there are other drivers, real or perceived, in climate change, the hydrogen economy, the solar poweed economy, other and continuing hydrocarbon discoveries. The latetr may prolong any Middle East demise, but the other factors will hasten the waning of Middle East influence in the world.

Water

The overall lack of water in the Middle east is a critical and imminent disruptive factor. In addition, the cost of manufacturing fresh water from the sea is likely to become unaffordable over time. These factors will create conflict.

Climate Change

Climate change has hit the Middle East. Rainfall, flooding, temperatures are all changing. The overall effects are negative and expensive. Early invasions of the Middle East were caused by climate change elsewhere; expect no less in the future, internally or externally driven conflict

Women

The record of men's treatment of women in the middle East, in a modern context, is not good. Elsewhere in the world bringing women into the management and development of economies has usually resulted in very positive outcomes. Middle East men, however, feel threatened; so expect a patchy outcome.

Health

There are some important health issues which will have important ramification sin the future. The first of these is anti - biotic resistant diseases and infections, these will rise exponentially. The second if the increasing financial burden, already huge in Saudi Arabia, of genetic disorders. The third is the rise in TB. The fourth is the impact of Coronaviruses, and similar pandemics. These will represent a continuing challenge.

Science

With the exception of Israel, Turkey and Iran scientific development will be patchy in the Middle East. The UAE and Egypt have pockets of scientific excellence.

External State Forces

The external state forces discussed in this book have been centred on China, the USA and Russia. Each has its own approach.

For now, at least, China's Belt and Road initiative, and the general assistance and development programmes that go with it, have the ascendancy in Chinese diplomacy. Some countries, e.g. Oman, will have to be careful not to fall into a Chinese debt trap. Others such as the UAE, a country which has global ambitions that match China's in the development of logistics hiubs, must be careful not to cause a rift in relations. As Stalin said quantity ahs a quality all of its own – and although rich the Middle East is probably no match for China in terms of finance or manpower.

The U.S., a few months into Biden's administration as this is written is continuing to redefine its role in the Middle East. It appears that the Abraham Accords will continue, not least because the UAE and Israel are getting close. At the same time the security blanket that was the American half of the oil compact that existed over the last 80 years or so has been replaced by encouragement to rely on regional organisations to improve security and stability in the region. It looks as though there are signs that this may work.

Russia has won some friends and scored some diplomatic victories over the last decade in the Middle East. It is certainly in a better position than it was. It has a friend in Iran; it has secured Syria and found a naval base for itself on the Mediterranean coast. It has another potential base in Jordan. It remains to be seen of it can partially fill the security and financial gap left by a departing U.S, This is unlikely because it probably does not have enough money. That said it is going to be around, renewed, for some time.

Europe has maintained a solid interest in the Iran nuclear deal but elsewhere its policy is all over the place with France and Germany often taking opposite positions, Greece and Italy in the debate over the Mediterranean hydrocarbon resources. NATO is split, clearly, between Greece and Turkey; and many other issues regarding the Middle East.

Internal Forces

Some potential internal forces have already been mentioned. In general internal forces are likely to frame how things turn out for the Middle East as much as external forces.

Libya: The key to success is making the united Government work; otherwise it will fall into civil war again.

Egypt: Sisi needs to hold onto power and give the younger generation something to do; otherwise, Egypt may slip into chaos.

Sudan: Sudan has always needed a strong leader; and probably need sone again to prevent the state breaking apart.

Saudi Arabia: MBS will be defined by the success or otherwise of his 2030 Vision. There could well be a internal royal family conflict on the death of King Salman.

Yemen: the humanitarian disaster will get worse before it gets better. Its only real hope is a deal between Saudi and Iran.

UAE: the UAE will keep its own people under control, there are relatively few of them. How this plays out in a wider Middle East is unclear.

Oman: Oman has to manage its finances to succeed long term. Otherwise, the new Sultan is likely to have a short reign.

Qatar

Qatar will liley thrive with few challenges internally. It will need to keep its small population on side. If it does this it will manage the future.

Bahrain

Bahrain will remain something of a powder keg. Its saving grace, like Yemen, will be if Saudi and Iran can come to a deal. Otherwise, it will stay as a thorn in Saudi's side and may even be taken over by Iran.

Kuwait

Kuwait's internal challenge will be finance.

Iran

Iran's internal challenge will be keeping an increasingly restive population under control. It may shout loud on the international stage, but all is not well on the home front.

Iraq

Iraq has an internal problem managing its populace, two thirds at least want to be in a different country. There is regular protest regarding unfair distribution of oil revenues.

Jordan

Jordan's king is well liked internationally. Nationally his half-bother is more liked. Expect trouble; especially when the money runs out from the U.S. and Russia does not replace it.

Syria

Syria will rebuild around its current rump with Russian help.

Lebanon

Lebanon will become a failed state; it is already in reality. To become reborn it needs massive help; and it is not clear where that will come from.

Israel

The internal developments in Israel depend on whether or not the new Prime Minister, Bennett, can hold a coalition together and deal with the growing disenchantment of a growing number of Arabs and some Israelis. Overall it should be a positive future unless there is a civil war. Again if things settle between Saudi and Iran then the future looks bright.

Palestine

Palestine, for many reasons and for many agendas, keeps missing opportunities to create a formal state. It probably ahs one more chance if Saudi and Iran can agree a resolution. If not it is doomed to failure from its own hubris.

Turkey

Turkey is safe internally for a while. However, Erdogan's opposition is growing and will become better organised. Then it will be in trouble again. Meantime it is the growing power in the Middle East.

Cyprus

Northern Cyprus will follow Turkey's instructions. How severe the internal division remains partly depends on the outcome of the energy diplomacy around the Eastern Mediterranean.

ISIS

ISIS will remain a factor as longas there is a will by Sunnis to extend Sunni Islam – whether this be in the Middle East or Africa.

Overall

Turkey, Iran and probably Saudi can survive as integral states. Egypt may join them. Neither Saudi nor Egypt can feed themselves. All other states described and discussed in this book are at risk in a post -oil world, in a world dominated by China and in a world recovering from COVID. They are particularly at risk from overpopulation, lack of water, and a restless young.

All in all, the Middle East will remain a challenging region; but perhaps less internationally relevant than over the last 80 years.

As an individual courtesy and good manners go a long way.[86]

[1] Hyslop, M.P. (2021) *On The Middle East Part 1: An Expatriate Journal 2014 – 2019*, Reiver, UK.

[2] Fisher, W.B. (1971) *The Middle East*, Methuen, London.

[3] Anderson, B. R. O. (1991) *Imagined Communities: Reflections on the Origin and Spread of Nationalism*, Verso, New York.

[4] Payind, A. & McClimans, M. (2010) *Keys to Understanding The Middle East*, Ohio State University, Columbus.

[5] Breasted, J.H., Henry, J. & Beard, C.A. (Eds) (1914) *Outlines of European History*, Vol. 1 pp 56-57. Ginn, Boston.

[6] Perez, D. (1978) *The Middle East Today* Holt, Rinehart and Winston New York.

[7] Embeling, G. (2010) *The Geography of the Middle East* The Oriental Institute, University of Chicago,

[8] Fisher, W.B. (1971) *The Middle East*, Methuen, London.

[9] National Geographic Quaternary Period, Available at: www.nationalgeographic/science/quaternary period.com Accessed 8 March 2021

[10] Fisher, W.B. (1971) *The Middle East*, Methuen, London,

[11] Perez, D. (1978) *The Middle East Today*, Holt, Rinehart and Winston New York.

[12] Hyslop, M.P. (1983) *Fresh Water Conflict in the Middle East* PhD Thesis University of Durham, UK. And ff.

[13] The theory of government in Islam, by The Internet Islamic University

[14] The History of Al-Khilafah Ar-Rashidah (The Rightly Guided Caliphates) School Textbook, By Dr. 'Abdullah al-Ahsan, `Abdullah Ahsan

[15] The Crisis of the Early Caliphate By Richard Stephen Humphreys, Ste-

phen (EDT) Humphreys from The History of al-Tabari

[16] The Reunification of the Abbasid Caliphate By Clifford Edmund (TRN) Bosworth, from The History of al-Tabari

[17] Return of the Caliphate to Baghdad By Franz Rosenthal from The History of al-Tabari

[18] Pan-Islamism: Indian Muslims, the Ottomans and Britain (1877–1924) By Azmi Özcan

[19] Baghdad during the Abbasid Caliphate from Contemporary Arabic and Persian Sources By Guy Le Strange

[20] The Fall of the Caliphate of Cordoba: Berbers and Andalusis in conflict By Peter C. Scales

[21] Khilafat and Caliphate, By Mubasher Ahmad

[22] The abolition of the Caliphate, From The Economist 8 March 1924

[23] The Clash of the Caliphates: Understanding the real war of ideas, By Tony Corn, Small Wars Journal, March 2011

[24] Hüseyin Yılmaz. *Caliphate Redefined: The Mystical Turn in Ottoman Political Thought*. Princeton University Press, 2018. ISBN 978-1-4008-8804-7.

[25] *Abulafia, David. The New Cambridge Medieval History. Cambridge University Press. ISBN 0-521-36291-1.*

[26] *Amitai, Reuven (1987). "Mongol Raids into Palestine (AD 1260 and 1300)". Journal of the Royal Asiatic Society: 236–255.*

[27] *Grousset, René (1935). Histoire des Croisades III, 1188-1291 (in French). Editions Perrin. ISBN 2-262-02569-X.*

[28] *Demurger, Alain (2007). Jacques de Molay (in French). Editions Payot & Rivages. ISBN 978-2-228-90235-9.*

[29] *Jackson, Peter (2005). The Mongols and the West: 1221-1410. Longman. ISBN 978-0-582-36896-5.*

[30] *Lebédel, Claude (2006). Les Croisades, origines et conséquences (in French). Editions Ouest-France. ISBN 2-7373-4136-1.*

[31] *Luisetto, Frédéric (2007). Arméniens & autres Chrétiens d'Orient sous la domination Mongole (in French). Librairie Orientaliste Paul Geuthner S.A. ISBN 9782705337919.*

[32] *Maalouf, Amin (1984). The Crusades Through Arab Eyes. New York: Schocken Books. ISBN 0-8052-0898-4.*

[33] *Maalouf, Amin (1983). Les croisades vues par les Arabes. JC Lattes.*

[34] *Michaud, Yahia (Oxford Centre for Islamic Studies) (2002). Ibn Taymiyya, Textes Spirituels I-XVI (PDF) (in French). "Le Musulman", Oxford-Le Chebec.*

[35] *Morgan, David (2007). The Mongols (2nd ed.). Blackwell Publishing. ISBN 978-1-4051-3539-9.*

[36] *Richard, Jean (1996). Histoire des Croisades. Fayard. ISBN 2-213-59787-1.*

[37] *Runciman, Steven (1987) [1952-1954]. A history of the Crusades 3. Penguin Books. ISBN 978-0-14-013705-7.*

[38]*Schein, Sylvia (October 1979). "Gesta Dei per Mongolos 1300. The Genesis of a Non-Event". The English Historical Review. **94** (373): 805–819. doi:10.1093/ehr/XCIV.CCCLXXIII.805. ISSN 0013-8266. JSTOR 565554.*

[39] Agoston, Gabor and Bruce Masters, eds. *Encyclopedia of the Ottoman Empire* (2008)

[40] Faroqhi, Suraiya. *The Ottoman Empire: A Short History* (2009) 196pp

[41] *Finkel, Caroline (2005). Osman's Dream: The Story of the Ottoman Empire, 1300–1923. Basic Books. ISBN 978-0-465-02396-7.*

[42] *Hathaway, Jane (2008). The Arab Lands under Ottoman Rule, 1516–1800. Pearson Education Ltd. ISBN 978-0-582-41899-8.*

[43] *Howard, Douglas A. (2017). A History of the Ottoman Empire. Cambridge: Cambridge University Press. ISBN 978-0-521-72730-3.*

[44] *Imber, Colin (2009). The Ottoman Empire, 1300–1650: The Structure of Power (2 ed.). New York: Palgrave Macmillan. ISBN 978-0-230-57451-9.*

[45] *İnalcık, Halil; Donald Quataert, eds. (1994). An Economic and Social History of the Ottoman Empire, 1300–1914. Cambridge University Press. ISBN 978-0-521-57456-3.* Two volumes.

[46] Kia, Mehrdad, ed. *The Ottoman Empire: A Historical Encyclopedia* (2 vol 2017)

[47] Lord Kinross. *The Ottoman centuries: the rise and fall of the Turkish empire* (1979) online popular history espouses old "decline" thesis

[48] McCarthy, Justin. *The Ottoman Turks: An Introductory History to 1923.* (1997) Questia.com, online edition.

[49] Mikaberidze, Alexander. *Conflict and Conquest in the Islamic World: A Historical Encyclopedia* (2 vol 2011)'

[50] Miller, William. *The Ottoman Empire and its successors, 1801–1922* (2nd ed 1927) online, strong on foreign policy.

[51] Quataert, Donald. *The Ottoman Empire, 1700–1922.* 2005. ISBN 0-521-54782-2.

[52] Şahin, Kaya. "The Ottoman Empire in the Long Sixteenth Century." *Renaissance Quarterly* (2017) 70#1: 220–234 online

[53] Somel, Selcuk Aksin. *Historical Dictionary of the Ottoman Empire* (2003). pp. 399 excerpt

[54] Stavrianos, L. S. *The Balkans since 1453* (1968; new preface 1999) online

[55]Tabak, Faruk. *The Waning of the Mediterranean, 1550–1870: A Geohistorical Approach* (2008)

[56] Antonius,G. (1938) *The Arab Awakening.* London: H. Hamilton.

[57] Busch, Briton C. (1971) *Britain, India, and the Arabs, 1914–1921.* Berke-

ley: University of California Press, 1971.

[58] Darwin, J. (1981) *Britain, Egypt, and the Middle East.* New York: St. Martin's, 1981

[59] Freedman, Lawrence, and Karsh, Efraim. *The Gulf Conflict, 1990–1991.* Princeton, NJ: Princeton University Press, 1993.

[60] Hopwood, Derek. *Tales of Empire.* London: I. B. Tauris, 1989.

[61] Hurewitz, J. C. *The Middle East and North Africa in World Politics,* 2d edition. New Haven, CT: Yale University Press, 1975).

[62] Kedourie, Elie. *The Chatham House Version, and Other Middle Eastern Essays.* London: Weidenfeld & Nicolson, 1970.

[63] Kedourie, Elie. *In the Anglo–Arab Labyrinth.* Cambridge, U.K., and New York: Cambridge University Press, 1976.

[64] Kyle, Keith. *Suez.* New York: St. Martin's, 1991.

[65] Lawrence, T. E. *Seven Pillars of Wisdom.* London: J. Cape, 1935.

[66] Louis, William Roger. *The British Empire in the Middle East, 1945–1951.* Oxford: Clarendon Press, 1984.

[67] Monroe, Elizabeth. *Britain's Moment in the Middle East,* 2d edition. Baltimore, MD: Johns Hopkins University Press, 1981.

[68] Monroe, Elizabeth. *Philby of Arabia.* London: Faber and Faber, 1973.

[69] Porath, Yehoshua. *In Search of Arab Unity.* London: Cass, 1986.

[70] Searight, Sarah. *The British in the Middle East.* New York: Atheneum, 1970.

[71] Storrs, Ronald. *Orientations.* London: I. Nicholson & Watson, 1937.

[72] Tidrick, Kathryn. *Heart-Beguiling Araby.* Cambridge, U.K., and New York: Cambridge University Press, 1981.

[73] Wilson, Mary. *King Abdullah, Britain, and the Making of Jordan.* Cambridge, and New York: Cambridge University Press, 1987.

[74] **Bernard Wasserstein** Encyclopedia of the Modern Middle East and North Africa

[75] In regard to the Six Days War this is a comprehensive bibliography:

    1. al-Qusi, Abdallah Ahmad Hamid. (1999). *Al-Wisam fi at-Ta'rikh.* Cairo: Al-Mu'asasa al-'Arabiya al-Haditha. No ISBN available.

    2. Aloni, Shlomo (2001). *Arab–Israeli Air Wars 1947–1982.* Osprey Aviation. ISBN 978-1-84176-294-4

    3. Alteras, Isaac. (1993). *Eisenhower and Israel: U.S.–Israeli Relations, 1953–1960*, University Press of Florida. ISBN 978-0-8130-1205-6.

    4. Bailey, Sydney (1990). *Four Arab–Israeli Wars and the Peace Process.* London: The MacMillan Press. ISBN 978-0-312-04649-1.

    5. Bar-On, M. (2006). Never-Ending Conflict: Israeli Military History,

6. Bard, M. G. (2002, 2008). The Complete Idiot's Guide to Middle East Conflict. NY: Alpha books

7. Bar-On, Mordechai; Morris, Benny & Golani, Motti (2002). "Reassessing Israel's Road to Sinai/Suez, 1956: A "Trialogue"". In Gary A. Olson (ed.), *Traditions and Transitions in Israel Studies: Books on Israel, Volume VI*(pp. 3–42). SUNY Press. ISBN 978-0-7914-5585-2

8. Bar-On, Mordechai (2006). *Never-Ending Conflict: Israeli Military History*, ISBN 978-0-275-98158-7

9. Bard, Mitchell G. (2002, 2008). *The Complete Idiot's Guide to Middle East Conflict*. NY: Alpha Books. ISBN 978-0-02-864410-3. 4th Edition ISBN 978-1-59257-791-0. Chapter 14, "Six Days to Victory" is reproduced online as *The 1967 Six-Day War*. at the Jewish Virtual Library of the American-Israeli Cooperative Enterprise.

10. Ben-Gurion, David. (1999). Ben-Gurion diary: May–June 1967. *Israel Studies*4(2), 199–220.

11. Black, Ian (1992). *Israel's Secret Wars: A History of Israel's Intelligence Services*. Grove Press. ISBN 978-0-8021-3286-4

12. Bober, Arie (ed.) (1972). *The other Israel*. Doubleday Anchor. ISBN 978-0-385-01467-0.

13. Boczek, Boleslaw Adam (2005). *International Law: A Dictionary*. Scarecrow Press. ISBN 978-0-8108-5078-1

14. Borowiec, Andrew. (1998). *Modern Tunisia: A Democratic Apprenticeship*. Greenwood Publishing Group. ISBN 978-0-275-96136-7.

15. Bowen, Jeremy (2003). *Six Days: How the 1967 War Shaped the Middle East*. London: Simon & Schuster. ISBN 978-0-7432-3095-7

16. Brams, Steven J. & Jeffrey M. Togman. (1998). *Camp David: Was the agreement fair?* In Paul F. Diehl (Ed.), *A Road Map to War: Territorial Dimensions of International Conflict*. Nashville: Vanderbilt University Press. ISBN 978-0-8265-1329-8.

17. Brecher, Michael. (1996). Eban and Israeli foreign policy: Diplomacy, war and disengagement. In *A Restless Mind: Essays in Honor of Amos Perlmutter*, Benjamin Frankel (ed.), pp. 104–117. Routledge. ISBN 978-0-7146-4607-7

18. Bregman, Ahron. (2000). *Israel's Wars, 1947–1993*. Routledge. ISBN 978-0-415-21468-1.

19. Bregman, Ahron (2002). *Israel's Wars: A History Since 1947*. London: Routledge. ISBN 978-0-415-28716-6

20. Burrowes, Robert & Muzzio, Douglas. (1972). The Road to the Six Day War: Towards an Enumerative History of Four Arab States and Israel, 1965–67. *The Journal of Conflict Resolution*, Vol. 16, No. 2, Research Perspectives on the Arab–Israeli Conflict: A Sym-

posium, pp. 211–26.
21. Cohen, Raymond. (1988) Intercultural Communication between Israel and Egypt: Deterrence Failure before the Six-Day war. *Review of International Studies*, Vol. 14, No. 1, pp. 1–16
22. Christie, Hazel (1999). *Law of the Sea*. Manchester: Manchester University Press. ISBN 978-0-7190-4382-6
23. Churchill, Randolph & Churchill, Winston. (1967). *The Six Day War*. Houghton Mifflin Company. ISBN 978-0-395-07532-6
24. Colaresi, Michael P. (2005). *Scare Tactics: The politics of international rivalry*. Syracuse University Press. ISBN 978-0-8156-3066-1
25. Cuau, Y. (1971). Israël attaque, éditions Robert Laffont, Collection J'ai lu.
26. Eban, Abba (1977). *Abba Eban: An Autobiography*. Random House. ISBN 978-0-394-49302-2
27. Ehteshami, Anoushiravan and Hinnebusch, Raymond A. (1997). *Syria & Iran: Middle Powers in a Penetrated Regional System*. London: Routledge. ISBN 978-0-415-15675-2
28. *Eshkol, Levi (1967). Prime-Minister Levi Eshkol – His words and his writings*. ISA-PMO-PrimeMinisterBureau-000d0t9. *Israel Government Archives. Retrieved 6 June 2018.*
29. *Feron, James (13 May 1967). "Israelis Ponder Blow at Syrians; Some Leaders Decide That Force is the Only Way to Curtail Terrorism Some Israeli Leaders See Need for Force to Curb Syrians". The New York Times.*
30. El-Gamasy, Mohamed Abdel Ghani. (1993). *The October War*. The American University in Cairo Press. ISBN 978-977-424-316-5.
31. Gawrych, George W. (2000). *The Albatross of Decisive Victory: War and Policy Between Egypt and Israel in the 1967 and 1973 Arab-Israeli Wars*. Greenwood Press. ISBN 978-0-313-31302-8. Available in multiple PDF files from the Combat Studies Institute and the Combined Arms Research Library, CSI Publications in parts.
32. Gelpi, Christopher (2002). *Power of Legitimacy: Assessing the Role of Norms in Crisis Bargaining*. Princeton University Press. ISBN 978-0-691-09248-5
33. Gerner, Deborah J. (1994). *One Land, Two Peoples*. Westview Press. ISBN 978-0-8133-2180-6, p. 112
34. Gerteiny, Alfred G. & Ziegler, Jean (2007). *The Terrorist Conjunction: The United States, the Israeli-Palestinian Conflict, and Al-Qā'ida*. Greenwood Publishing Group. ISBN 978-0-275-99643-7, p. 142
35. Gilbert, Martin. (2008). *Israel – A History*. McNally & Loftin Publishers. ISBN 978-0-688-12363-5. Chapter available online:

Chapter 21: Nasser's Challenge.

36. Goldstein, Erik (1992). *Wars and Peace Treaties, 1816–1991.* Routledge. ISBN 978-0-415-07822-1

37. Green, Stephen J. (1984). *Taking Sides: America's Secret Relations With Militant Israel.* William Morrow & Co. ISBN 978-0-688-02643-1.

38. Haddad, Yvonne. (1992). Islamists and the "Problem of Israel": The 1967 Awakening. *Middle East Journal,* Vol. 46, No. 2, pp. 266–85.

39. Hajjar, Sami G. The Israel-Syria Track, *Middle East Policy,* Volume VI, February 1999, Number 3. Retrieved 30 September 2006.

40. Hammel, Eric (1992). *Six Days in June: How Israel Won the 1967 Arab–Israeli War.* Simon & Schuster. ISBN 978-0-7434-7535-8

41. Hattendorf, John B. (2000). *Naval Strategy and Power in the Mediterranean: Past, Present and Future.* Taylor & Francis. ISBN 978-0-7146-8054-5.

42. Handel, Michael I. (1973). *Israel's political-military doctrine.* Center for International Affairs, Harvard University. ISBN 978-0-87674-025-5

43. Hart, Alan (1989) *Arafat, A political biography.* Indiana University Press ISBN 978-0-253-32711-6.

44. Herzog, Chaim (1982). *The Arab-Israeli Wars.* Arms & Armour Press. ISBN 978-0-85368-367-4

45. Herbert, Nicholas (17 May 1967). *Egyptian Forces On Full Alert: Ready to fight for Syria.* The Times, p. 1; Issue 56943; col E.

46. Herzog, Chaim (1989). *Heroes of Israel: Profiles of Jewish Courage.* Little Brown and Company. ISBN 978-0-316-35901-6.

47. Higham, Robin. (2003). *100 Years of Air Power and Aviation.* TAMU Press. ISBN 978-1-58544-241-6.

48. Hinnebusch, Raymond A. (2003). *The international politics of the Middle East.* Manchester University Press. ISBN 978-0-7190-5346-7

49. Israel Ministry of Foreign Affairs (2004). *Background on Israeli POWs and MIAs.*

50. Israel Ministry of Foreign Affairs (2008). *The Six-Day War (June 1967).*

51. "Israel Reportedly Killed POWs in '67 War; Historians Say Deaths of Hundreds of Egyptians Was Covered Up Israel Reportedly Killed POWs in '67 War; Historians Say Deaths of Hundreds of Egyptians Was Covered Up", *The Washington Post,* 17 August 1995, p. A.30 (fee required).

52. James, Laura (2005). The Nassar And His Enemies: Foreign Policy Decision Making In Egypt On The Eve Of The Six Day War. *The Middle East Review of International Affairs.* Volume 9, No. 2, Article 2.

53. *"Israelis Say Tape Shows Nasser Fabricated 'Plot'; Recording Said to Be of Phone Call to Hussein Gives Plan to Accuse U.S. and Britain". The New York Times. 9 June 1967. p. 17. Retrieved 28 June 2007.*

54. Jia, Bing Bing. (1998). *The Regime of Straits in International Law* (Oxford Monographs in International Law). Oxford University Press, U.SA. ISBN 978-0-19-826556-6.

55. Koboril, Iwao and Glantz, Michael H. (1998). *Central Eurasian Water Crisis.* United Nations University Press. ISBN 978-92-808-0925-1

56. *Krauthammer, Charles (18 May 2007). "Prelude to the Six Days". The Washington Post. pp. A23. ISSN 0740-5421. Retrieved 20 June 2008.*

57. *Laron, Guy (21 February 2017). The Six Day War: The Breaking of the Middle East. Yale University Press. ISBN 978-0-300-22632-4.*

58. Laurens, H. (2011). *La Question de Palestine*, tome 4 (Le rameau d'olivier et le fusil du combattant), Fayard.

59. Lavoy, Peter R.; Sagan, Scott Douglas & Wirtz, James J. (Eds.) (2000). *Planning the Unthinkable: How New Powers Will Use Nuclear, Biological, and Chemical Weapons.* Cornell University Press. ISBN 978-0-8014-8704-0.

60. Leibler, Isi (1972). *The Case For Israel.* Australia: The Executive Council of Australian Jewry. ISBN 978-0-9598984-0-8.

61. Lenczowski, George. (1990). *American Presidents and the Middle East.* Duke University Press. ISBN 978-0-8223-0972-7.

62. Lyndon Baines Johnson Library. (1994). [*permanent dead link*] Transcript, Robert S. McNamara Oral History[*permanent dead link*], Special Interview I, 26 March 1993, by Robert Dallek, Internet Copy, LBJ Library. Retrieved 20 July 2010.

63. *"McNamara: U.S Near War in '67". The Boston Globe. 16 September 1983. p. 1.*

64. Mansour, Camille. (1994). *Beyond Alliance: Israel and U.S Foreign Policy.* Columbia University Press. ISBN 978-0-231-08492-5.

65. Maoz, Zeev (2006). *Defending the Holy Land: A Critical Analysis of Israel's Security & Foreign Policy.* The University of Michigan Press. ISBN 978-0-472-03341-6

66. Morris, Benny (2001) *Righteous Victims* New York, Vintage Books. ISBN 978-0-679-74475-7

67. Miller, Benjamin. (2007). *States, Nations, and the Great Powers: The Sources of Regional War and Peace.* Cambridge University Press. ISBN 978-0-521-69161-1

68. Murakami, Masahiro. (1995). *Managing Water for Peace in the Middle East: Alternative Strategies.* United Nations University Press. ISBN 978-92-808-0858-2.

69. *Mutawi, Samir A. (18 July 2002). Jordan in the 1967 War. Cam-*

bridge University Press. ISBN 978-0-521-52858-0.

70. Nordeen, Lon & Nicole, David. (1996). *Phoenix over the Nile: A history of Egyptian Air Power 1932–1994. Washington DC: Smithsonian Institution. ISBN 978-1-56098-626-3.*

71. "Mediterranean Eskadra". (2000). Federation of American Scientists.

72. Oren, Michael (2002). *Six Days of War.* Oxford University Press. ISBN 978-0-19-515174-9

73. Oren, Michael. (2005). The Revelations of 1967: New Research on the Six Day War and Its Lessons for the Contemporary Middle East, *Israel Studies,* volume 10, number 2. (Subscription required).

74. Oren, Michael. (2006). "The Six-Day War", in Bar-On, Mordechai (ed.), *Never-Ending Conflict: Israeli Military History.* Greenwood Publishing Group. ISBN 978-0-275-98158-7.

75. Parker, Richard B. (1996). *The Six-day War: A Retrospective.* University Press of Florida. ISBN 978-0-8130-1383-1.

76. *Parker, Richard B. (August 1997). "U.SAF in the Sinai in the 1967 War: Fact or Fiction" (PDF). Journal of Palestine Studies. **XXVII** (1): 67–75. doi:10.1525/jps.1997.27.1.00p0164l.*

77. Phythian, Mark (2001). *The Politics of British Arms Sales Since 1964.* Manchester: Manchester University Press. ISBN 978-0-7190-5907-0

78. Pimlott, John. (1983). Middle East Conflicts: From 1945 to the Present. Orbis. ISBN 978-0-85613-547-7.

79. *Pollack, Kenneth Michael (2004). Arabs at War: Military Effectiveness, 1948–1991. U of Nebraska Press. ISBN 978-0-8032-0686-1.*

80. *Pollack, Kenneth Michael (2005). "Air Power in the Six-Day War". The Journal of Strategic Studies. **28** (3): 471–503. doi:10.1080/01402390500137382. S2CID 216090004.*

81. Prior, Michael (1999). *Zionism and the State of Israel: A Moral Inquiry.* London: Routledge. ISBN 978-0-415-20462-0

82. Quandt, William B. (2005). *Peace Process: American Diplomacy and the Arab–Israeli Conflict Since 1967.* Brookings Institution Press and the University of California Press; 3 edition. ISBN 978-0-520-24631-7

83. Quigley, John B. (2005). *Case for Palestine: An International Law Perspective.* Duke University Press. ISBN 978-0-8223-3539-9

84. Quigley, John B. (1990). *Palestine and Israel: A Challenge to Justice.* Duke University Press. ISBN 978-0-8223-1023-5

85. Rabil, Robert G. (2003). *Embattled Neighbors: Syria, Israel, and Lebanon.* Lynne Rienner Publishers. ISBN 978-1-58826-149-6

86. Rabin, Yitzhak (1996). *The Rabin Memoirs.* University of California Press. ISBN 978-0-520-20766-0.

87. Rauschning, Dietrich; Wiesbrock, Katja & Lailach, Martin (eds.) (1997). Key Resolutions of the United Nations General Assembly 1946–1996. Cambridge University Press. ISBN 978-0-521-59704-3.

88. Rikhye, Indar Jit (1980). *The Sinai Blunder*. London: Routledge. ISBN 978-0-7146-3136-3

89. Robarge, David S. (2007). *Getting It Right: CIA Analysis of the 1967 Arab-Israeli War*, Center for the Study of Intelligence, Vol. 49 No. 1

90. Rubenberg, Cheryl A. (1989). *Israel and the American National Interest*. University of Illinois Press. ISBN 978-0-252-06074-8

91. Sachar, Howard M. (1976, 2007) *A History of Israel from the Rise of Zionism to Our Time*. New York: Alfred A. Knopf. ISBN 978-0-394-48564-5; ISBN 978-0-375-71132-9.

92. Sadeh, Eligar (1997). *Militarization and State Power in the Arab–Israeli Conflict: Case Study of Israel, 1948–1982*. Universal Publishers. ISBN 978-0-9658564-6-1

93. Sandler, Deborah; Aldy, Emad & Al-Khoshman Mahmoud A. (1993). *Protecting the Gulf of Aqaba. – A regional environmental challenge*. Environmental Law Institute. 0911937463.

94. Seale, Patrick (1988). *Asad: The Struggle for Peace in the Middle East*. University of California Press. ISBN 978-0-520-06976-3

95. Segev, Samuel (1967). A Red Sheet: the Six Day War.

96. *Segev, Tom (2005). Israel in 1967. Keter. ISBN 978-965-07-1370-6.*

97. Segev, Tom (2007). *1967: Israel, the War, and the Year that Transformed the Middle East* Metropolitan Books. ISBN 978-0-8050-7057-6

98. Sela, Avraham (1997). *The Decline of the Arab-Israeli Conflict: Middle East Politics and the Quest for Regional Order*. SUNY Press. ISBN 978-0-7914-3537-3

99. Shafqat, Saeed (2004). *Islamic world and South Asia: Rise of Islamism and Terror, Causes and Consequences?*. In Kaniz F. Yusuf (Ed.) *Unipolar World & The Muslim States*. Islamabad: Pakistan Forum, pp 217–246.

100. Shemesh, Moshe (2008). *Arab Politics, Palestinian Nationalism and the Six Day War*. Sussex Academic Press. ISBN 978-1-84519-188-7.

101. *Shlaim, Avi (2000). The Iron Wall: Israel and the Arab World. W. W. Norton & Company. ISBN 978-0-393-32112-8.* ISBN 978-0-393-04816-2

102. Shlaim, Avi (2007) *Lion of Jordan: The Life of King Hussein in War and Peace*Vintage Books ISBN 978-1-4000-7828-8

103. Shlaim, Avi; Louis, William Roger (13 February 2012), *The 1967 Arab–Israeli War: Origins and Consequences*, Cambridge Univer-

sity Press ISBN 978-1-107-00236-4

104. Smith, Hedrick (15 June 1967). "As the Shock Wears Off; Arab World, Appraising Its Defeat, Is Split as It Gropes for Strategy". The New York Times. p. 16. Retrieved 28 June 2006.

105. Smith, Hedrick (15 September 1967). "Envoys Say Nasser Now Concedes U.S. Didn't Help Israel". The New York Times. pp. Page 1, Col. 5, Page 3, Col. 1.

106. Stein, Janice Gross. (1991). The Arab-Israeli War of 1967: Inadvertent War Through Miscalculated Escalation, in Avoiding War: Problems of Crisis Management, Alexander L. George, ed. Boulder: Westview Press.

107. Stephens, Robert H. (1971). Nasser: A Political Biography. London: Allen Lane/The Penguin Press. ISBN 978-0-7139-0181-8

108. Stone, David (2004). Wars of the Cold War. Brassey's. ISBN 978-1-85753-342-2

109. Tolan, Sandy (4 June 2007). "Rethinking Israel's David-and-Goliath past". Salon.com. Retrieved 29 April 2010.

110. Tucker, Spencer (2004). Tanks: An Illustrated History of Their Impact. ABC-CLIO. ISBN 978-1-57607-995-9

111. United Nations (967, 5 June). 1347 Security Council MEETING : June 5, 1967. Provisional agenda (S/PV.1347/Rev.1). On a subpage of the website of The United Nations Information System on the Question of Palestine (UNISPAL).

112. van Creveld, Martin (2004). Defending Israel: A Controversial Plan Toward Peace. Thomas Dunne Books. ISBN 978-0-312-32866-5

113. Youngs, Tim. (2001). Developments in the Middle East Peace Process 1991–2000 London: International Affairs and Defence Section, House of Commons Library. ISSN 1368-8456.

114. Finkelstein, Norman (2003). Image and Reality of the Israel–Palestine Conflict. Verso. ISBN 978-1-85984-442-7.

115. Barzilai, Gad (1996). Wars, Internal Conflicts, and Political Order: A Jewish Democracy in the Middle East. New York University Press. ISBN 978-0-7914-2944-0

116. Cristol, A Jay (2002). Liberty Incident: The 1967 Israeli Attack on the U.S. Navy Spy Ship. Brassey's. ISBN 978-1-57488-536-1

117. Finkelstein, Norman (June 2017). Analysis of the war and its aftermath, on the 50th anniversary of the June 1967 war (3 parts, each about 30 min)

118. Gat, Moshe (2003). Britain and the Conflict in the Middle East, 1964–1967: The Coming of the Six-Day War. Praeger/Greenwood. ISBN 978-0-275-97514-2

119. Hammel, Eric (October 2002). "Sinai air strike: June 5, 1967". Military Heritage. 4 (2): 68–73.

120. Hopwood, Derek (1991). Egypt: Politics and Society. London:

Routledge. ISBN 978-0-415-09432-0

121. Hussein of Jordan (1969). *My "War" with Israel*. London: Peter Owen. ISBN 978-0-7206-0310-1

122. Katz, Samuel M. (1991) *Israel's Air Force*; The Power Series. Motorbooks International Publishers & Wholesalers, Osceola, WI.

123. Makiya, Kanan (1998). *Republic of Fear: The Politics of Modern Iraq*. University of California Press. ISBN 978-0-520-21439-2

124. Morris, Benny (1997). *Israel's Border Wars, 1949–1956*. Oxford: Oxford University Press. ISBN 978-0-19-829262-3

125. Pressfield, Steven (2014). *The Lion's Gate: On the Front Lines of the Six Day War*. Sentinel HC, 2014. ISBN 978-1-59523-091-1

126. Rezun, Miron (1990). "Iran and Afghanistan." In A. Kapur (Ed.). *Diplomatic Ideas and Practices of Asian States* (pp. 9–25). Brill Academic Publishers. ISBN 978-90-04-09289-1

127. Smith, Grant (2006). *Deadly Dogma*. Institute for Research: Middle Eastern Policy. ISBN 978-0-9764437-4-2

128. Oren, Michael (April 2002). *Six Days of War: June 1967 and the Making of the Modern Middle East*. Oxford University Press. ISBN 978-0-19-515174-9

129. *Bowker, Robert (2003). Palestinian Refugees: Mythology, Identity, and the Search for Peace. Lynne Rienner Publishers. ISBN 978-1-58826-202-8.*

130. *McDowall, David (1 July 1991). Palestine and Israel: The Uprising and Beyond. University of California Press. ISBN 978-0-520-07653-2.*

131. *Oren, Michael B. (2002). Six Days of War: June 1967 and the Making of the Modern Middle East. Oxford University Press. p. 171. ISBN 978-0-19-515174-9.*

132. How The U.SSR Planned To Destroy Israel in 1967 by Isabella Ginor. Published by *Middle East Review of International Affairs* (MERIA) Journal Volume 7, Number 3 (September 2003).

133. [Zaloga, S. (1981). Armour of the Middle East Wars 1948-78 (Vanguard). Osprey Publishing

[76] Sergei Boeke, *Transitioning from Military Interventions to a Long-Term Counter-Terrorism Policy* (International Centre for Counter-Terrorism – The Hague, 2014)

[77] *Coughlin, Stephen (2015). Catastrophic Failure: Blindfolding America in the Face of Jihad. CreateSpace Independent Publishing Platform. ISBN 978-1511617505.*

[78] Jackson, Richard. *Writing the War on Terrorism: Language, Politics and Counter-Terrorism*. Manchester & New York: Manchester University Press, 2005. ISBN 0719071216.

[79] Al Qaeda: Facts About the Terrorist Network and Its History of Attacks - HISTORY

[80] A bibliography of the Arab Spring is as follows:

1. Aa. Vv. (2011), The New Arab Revolt: What Happened, What It Means, and What Comes Next, Council on Foreign Relations, Foreign Affairs, Maggio-Giugno.

2. Abaza, M. (2011), Revolutionary Moments in Tahrir Square, American University of Cairo, 7 May 2011, www.isa-sociology.org.

3. Abdih, Y. (2011), Arab Spring: Closing the Jobs Gap. High youth unemployment contributes to widespread unrest in the Middle East Finance & Development, in Finance & Development (International Monetary Fund), Giugno.

4. Alfadhel, Khalifa. The Failure of the Arab Spring (Cambridge Scholars Publishing, 2016). ISBN 978-1-4438-9789-1

5. *Anderson, L (May–June 2011). "Demystifying the Arab Spring: Parsing the Differences between Tunisia, Egypt, and Libya". Foreign Affairs. **90**(3).*

6. Beinin, J. – Vairel, F. (2011), (a cura di), Social Movements, Mobilization, and Contestation in the Middle East and North Africa, Stanford, CA, Stanford University press.

7. *Brownlee, Jason; Masoud, Tarek; Reynolds, Andrew (2013). The Arab Spring: the politics of transformation in North Africa and the Middle East. Oxford: Oxford University Press.*

8. *Browers, Michaelle (2009). Political Ideology in the Arab World: Accommodation and Transformation. New York: Cambridge University Press. ISBN 978-0-521-76532-9.*

9. Cohen, R. (2011), A Republic Called Tahrir, in New York Times.

10. Dabashi, Hamid. *The Arab Spring: The End of Postcolonialism*(Palgrave Macmillan; 2012) 182 pages

11. *Darwish, Nonie (28 February 2012). The demon We Don't Know: The Dark Side of Revolutions in the Middle East. John Wiley & Sons.*

12. *Davies, Thomas Richard (2014). "The failure of strategic nonviolent action in Bahrain, Egypt, Libya and Syria: 'political ju-jitsu' in reverse"(PDF). Global Change, Peace & Security. **26** (3): 299–313. doi:10.1080/14781158.2014.924916. S2CID 145013824.*

13. *Gardner, David (2009). Last Chance: The Middle East in the Balance. London: I.B. Tauris. ISBN 978-1-84885-041-5.*

14. Gause, F. G. (2011), Why Middle East Studies Missed the Arab Spring: The Myth of Authoritarian Stability, in Foreign Affairs, July/August.

15. *Goldstone, Jack A.; Hazel, John T., Jr. (14 April 2011). "Understanding the Revolutions of 2011: Weakness and Resilience in Middle Eastern Autocracies". Foreign Affairs (May/June 2011).*

16. *Haddad, Bassam; Bsheer, Rosie; Abu-Rish, Ziad, eds. (2012). The*

Dawn of the Arab Uprisings: End of an Old Order?. London: Pluto Press. ISBN 978-0-7453-3325-0.

17. Kaye, Dalia Dassa *(2008)*. *More Freedom, Less Terror? Liberalization and Political Violence in the Arab World*. Santa Monica, CA: RAND Corporation. ISBN 978-0-8330-4508-9.

18. Krüger, Laura-Theresa, and Bernhard Stahl. "The French foreign policy U-turn in the Arab Spring–the case of Tunisia." *Mediterranean Politics*23.2 (2018): 197-222 online.

19. Lutterbeck, Derek. (2013). Arab Uprisings, Armed Forces, and Civil-Military Relations. Armed Forces & Society, Vol. 39, No. 1 (pp. 28–52)

20. Ottaway, Marina; Choucair-Vizoso, Julia, eds. *(2008)*. *Beyond the Façade: Political Reform in the Arab World*. Washington, DC: Carnegie Endowment for International Peace. ISBN 978-0-87003-239-4.

21. Pelletreau, Robert H. *(24 February 2011)*. *"Transformation in the Middle East: Comparing the Uprisings in Tunisia, Egypt and Bahrain"*. Foreign Affairs.

22. Phares, Walid *(2010)*. *Coming Revolution: Struggle for Freedom in the Middle East*. New York: Simon & Schuster. ISBN 978-1-4391-7837-9.

23. Posusney, Marsha Pripstein; Angrist, Michele Penner, eds. *(2005)*. *Authoritarianism in the Middle East: Regimes and Resistance*. Boulder: Lynne Rienner. ISBN 978-1-58826-317-9.

24. Roberts, Adam, Michael J. Willis, Rory McCarthy and Timothy Garton Ash (eds.), *Civil Resistance in the Arab Spring: Triumphs and Disasters*, Oxford University Press, Oxford, 2016. ISBN 978-0-19-874902-8. Arabic language edition published by All Prints Publishers, Beirut, 2017. ISBN 978-9953-88-970-2.

25. Rosiny, S. and Richter, T. (2016). "The Arab Spring: Misconceptions and Prospects". *GIGA Focus Middle East No. 4/2016*

26. Steinitz, Chris and McCants, William (2014). Reaping the Whirlwind: Gulf State Competition after the Arab Uprisings. Arlington, VA: CNA Corporation.

27. Struble Jr., Robert *(22 August 2011)*. *"Libya and the Doctrine of Justifiable Rebellion"*. Catholic Lane.

28. Tausch, Arno *(2015)*. *Globalization, the environment and the future "greening" of Arab politics*. Connecticut: REPEC.

29. Tausch, Arno *(Fall 2013)*. *"A Look at International Survey Data About Arab Opinion"*. Middle East Review of International Affairs. **17** *(3): 57–74*. SSRN 2388627.

30. Tausch, Arno *(Spring 2016)*. *"The Civic Culture of the Arab World: A Comparative Analysis Based on World Values Survey Data"*. Middle East Review of International Affairs. **20** *(1): 35–*

        59.   *doi:10.2139/*
ssrn.2827232. S2CID 157863317. SSRN 2827232.

31. Tausch, Arno (2015). *The political algebra of global value change.*
    General models and implications for the Muslim world. With Almas
    Heshmati and Hichem Karoui (1st ed.). Nova Science Publishers,
    New York. ISBN 978-1-62948-899-8.
32. United States. Congress. Senate. Committee on Foreign Re-
    lations. Subcommittee on International Operations and Or-
    ganizations, Human Rights, Democracy, and Global Women's
    Issues. (2012). *Women and the Arab Spring: Joint Hearing before*
    the Subcommittee on International Operations and Organizations,
    Human Rights, Democracy, and Global Women's Issues and the
    Subcommittee on Near Eastern and South and Central Asian
    Affairs of the Committee on Foreign Relations, United States
    Senate, One Hundred Twelfth Congress, First Session, November 2,
    2011. Washington, D.C.: U.S. G.P.O.
33. *Amanda Jacoby, Tamil (2013). "Israel's relations with Egypt and*
    Turkey during the Arab Spring: Weathering the Storm". Israel Jour-
    *nal   of   Foreign   Affairs.   **VII**   (2):   29–*
    42. doi:10.1080/23739770.2013.11446550. S2CID 148402328.

[81] ISIL Bibliography

1. *Abass, Ademola (2014). Complete International Law: Text, Cases*
   and Materials (2nd ed.). Oxford: Oxford University Press.
2. *Al-Yaqoubi, Muhammad (2015). Refuting ISIS: A Rebuttal*
   Of Its Religious And Ideological Foundations. Sacred Know-
   ledge. ISBN 978-1-908224-12-5.
3. *Boffey, Daniel. "'Islamic State' is a slur on our faith, say leading*
   Muslims". The Guardian.
4. *Gerhard Böwering, ed. (2013). The Princeton Encyclopedia*
   of   Islamic   Political   Thought.   Princeton   University
   Press. ISBN 978-0-691-13484-0.
5. *Chulov, Martin (11 December 2014). "Isis: the inside story". The*
   Guardian.
6. *Fishman,   Brian   (2008).   "Using   the   Mistakes   of   al-*
   Qaeda's Franchises to Undermine Its Strategies". Annals of
   the American Academy of Political and Social Science. **618**:
   46–54. doi:10.1177/0002716208316650. JSTOR 40375774. S2
   CID 146236345.
7. *Fraile Ordonez, Siobhan (28 September 2015). "The Non-Islamic*
   Non-State". St Andrews Foreign Affairs Review. Archived from the
   original on 14 February 2019. Retrieved 27 January 2020.
8. *Simon, Steven (2008). "The Price of the Surge: How U.S. Strategy Is*
   Hastening Iraq's Demise". Foreign Affairs. Vol. 87 no. 3. pp. 57–72,
   74–76. JSTOR 20032651.
9. *Tausch, Arno (Spring 2015). "Estimates on the Global Threat*

of Islamic State Terrorism in the Face of the 2015 Paris and Copenhagen Attacks" (PDF). *Middle East Review of International Affairs. Rubin Center, Research in International Affairs, Idc Herzliya, Israel.* **19** *(1). SSRN 2702356. Archived from the original (PDF) on 13 April 2018. Retrieved 22 November 2019*

[82] Based on some work by Ziva Dahl. Ziva Dahl is a senior fellow with the news and public policy group Haym Salomon Center. Ziva writes and lectures about U.S.-Israel relations, U.S. foreign policy, Israel, Zionism, anti-Semitism, and BDS on college campuses. Her articles have appeared in such publications as The Hill, New York Daily News, New York Observer, the Washington Times, American Spectator, American Thinker and Jerusalem Post.

[83] As quoted in Hyslop, M.P. (2014) *Obstructive Marketing* London, Routledge. Jonsson, D.J. (2007) 'Sovereign Wealth Funds: A Potential Tool of Asymmetric Warfare' Available at: www.newmediajournal.us/guest/jonsson/08112007,htm (Accessed: 16 June 2021).

[84] Harkove, L (2020) 'Turkey Is Testing The limits of the Middle East' Available at: Turkey is testing the limits in the Middle East - The Jerusalem Post (jpost.com) (Accessed: 30 June 2021)

[85] Windren, R. (2014) 'Who's Funding ISIS?. Available at: Who's Funding ISIS? Wealthy Gulf 'Angel Investors,' Officials Say (nbcnews.com) (Accessed: 30 June 2021).

[86] The following are general references used in the production of this book which will continue to be excellent reference points for those interested in the Middle East:

1. Al Jazeera, Qatari News Agency, www.aljazeera.com
2. Azo Mining www.azomining.com
3. Chatham House www.chathamhouse.org
4. Christian Science Monitor www.csmonitor.com
5. CIA Factbook www.ciafactbook.com
6. Encyclopedia Britannica www.britannica.com
7. Expatriate Life www.easyexpat.com
8. General Geography www.countryaah.com
9. Heritage www.heritage.com
10. IISS/Bahrain Dialogue www.iiss.org/contact-us/bahrain
11. Information www.infoplease.com
12. ResearchGate www.researchgate.com
13. Sudan www.ugfacts.net
14. The Economist www.theeconomist.com
15. Wikipedia www.wikpedia.com
16. World Atlas www.worldatlas.com

End.

BOOKS BY THIS AUTHOR

On The Middle East: Part 1 An Expatriate Journal 2014 -2019

A light hearted diary of the author's time in the Middle East, and elsewhere, 2014 - 2019.

On War

This book looks at the changing nature of warfare and the threat to Britain. It includes comments on the origin of COVID - 19 and the UK Refrendum to leave the EU.

Obstructive Marketing

The casual, criminal, capital, competition, cultural and critical infrastrucure barriers to marketing in a global trading environment, with case studies and comments on China in particualr.

Critical Information Infrastructures: Resilience And Protection

An early view on protecting international and national critical information infrastructures.